Foreign Exchange and Money Markets

Butterworth-Heinemann –
The Securities Institute
A publishing partnership

About The Securities Institute

Formed in 1992 with the support of the Bank of England, the London Stock Exchange, the Financial Services Authority, LIFFE and other leading financial organizations, the Securities Institute is the professional body for practitioners working in securities, investment management, corporate finance, derivatives and related businesses. Their purpose is to set and maintain professional standards through membership, qualifications, training and continuing learning and publications. The Institute promotes excellence in matters of integrity, ethics and competence.

About the series

Butterworth-Heinemann is pleased to be the official **Publishing Partner** of the Securities Institute with the development of professional level books for: Brokers/Traders; Actuaries; Consultants; Asset Managers; Regulators; Central Bankers; Treasury Officials; Compliance Officers; Legal Departments; Corporate Treasurers; Operations Managers; Portfolio Managers; Investment Bankers; Hedge Fund Managers; Investment Managers; Analysts and Internal Auditors, in the areas of: Portfolio Management; Advanced Investment Management; Investment Management Models; Financial Analysis; Risk Analysis and Management; Capital Markets; Bonds; Gilts; Swaps; Repos; Futures; Options; Foreign Exchange; Treasury Operations.

Series titles

- **Professional Reference Series**
    The Bond and Money Markets: *Strategy, Trading, Analysis*
- **Global Capital Markets Series**
    The REPO Handbook
    The Gilt-Edged Market
    Foreign Exchange and Money Markets: *theory, practice and risk management*
    IPO and Equity Offerings

For more information

For more information on **The Securities Institute** please visit:
    www.securities-institute.org.uk

and for details of all **Butterworth-Heinemann Finance** titles please visit:
    www.bh.com/finance

Foreign Exchange and Money Markets

Theory, Practice and Risk Management

Bob Steiner

OXFORD   AMSTERDAM   BOSTON   LONDON   NEW YORK
SAN DIEGO   SAN FRANCISCO   SINGAPORE   SYDNEY

Butterworth-Heinemann
An imprint of Elsevier Science Linacre House, Jordan Hill, Oxford OX2 8DP
225 Wildwood Avenue, Woburn, MA 01801-2041
A division of Reed Educational and Professional Publishing Ltd

First published 2002

British Library Cataloguing in Publication Data
Steiner, Bob
   Foreign exchange and money markets : theory, practice and
   risk management. – (Global aid capital market series)
   1. Foreign exchange   2. Money market
   I. Title
   332.4'5

Library of Congress Cataloguing in Publication Data
A catalogue record for this book is available from the Library of Congress

ISBN 0 7506 5025 7

For information on all Butterworth-Heinemann finance publications
visit our website at www.bh.com/finance

Transferred to digital printing in 2007.

Contents

To my wife Barbara,
as always

About the Author

Bob Steiner is Managing Director of Markets International Ltd, an independent company specializing in training in a range of areas related to the international financial markets, treasury and banking.

He has also written the best-selling *Mastering Financial Calculations*, and *Mastering Repo Markets* (both published by Financial Times Prentice-Hall) and *Key Market Concepts* (published by Reuters and Pearson Education).

Bob was previously senior consultant with HSBC, where he worked in London and New York in the dealing area as consultant to major US and European companies on treasury management. He has also been treasurer and fund manager of H P Bulmer Holdings PLC and English and American Insurance Group PLC, both active in currency and interest rate management. He has also worked in the Overseas Department of the Bank of England, and with the European Commission in Brussels.

His academic background is an honours degree in mathematics from Cambridge University, followed by further studies in economics with London University. He is a member of ACI – The Financial Markets Association, and the Association of Corporate Treasurers.

Bob himself spends a considerable amount of time training bankers, systems staff, corporate staff and others involved in the financial markets. In addition to general and in-house courses, he personally runs courses for all the ACI's professional exams for dealers – the ACI Diploma, the Dealing Certificate and the Settlements Certificate – on behalf of various national ACI associations across Europe.

Note from the author

Although this book is called *Foreign Exchange and Money Markets*, the chapters on the money markets come first. This is because there are some money market ideas which it might be useful to have covered before some of the material on foreign exchange.

I would be very grateful for any comments on the book, or ideas on any additional areas which readers feel could be usefully included.

Bob Steiner

Markets International Ltd
Aylworth
Naunton
Cheltenham
Gloucestershire GL54 3AH

Markets International Ltd

Training and consultancy for the international financial markets

Markets International Ltd is an independent company providing training to banks and companies on financial markets and mathematics, risk management techniques, analysis and management policy, credit analysis, technical analysis and other financial subjects.

The company also provides advice to finance directors and treasurers of international companies on foreign exchange, money markets and other treasury matters. This ranges from written studies reviewing existing management policies and procedures to the development of appropriate hedging strategies.

Among the subjects covered in Markets International Ltd's workshops on financial markets and banking, are:

- Foreign Exchange and Interest Rate Risk Management
- Financial Mathematics
- Repos
- Corporate Exposure Management
- Technical Analysis
- Accounting for Derivatives
- Credit Analysis

The company also runs workshops aimed specifically at the following exams of ACI – The Financial Markets Association:

- ACI Diploma
- ACI Dealing Certificate
- ACI Settlements Certificate

For further information on in-house training opportunities, or public courses, please contact:

Bob Steiner
Managing Director
Markets International Ltd
Aylworth, Naunton, Cheltenham, Glos GL54 3AH, UK
Telephone: +44(0)1451-850055
Fax: +44(0)1451-850367
E-mail: Markets@FSBdial.co.uk

Part 1
Introduction

Some basic concepts

Currency codes

Throughout the book, we have generally used ISO codes (also used by the SWIFT system) to abbreviate currency names – for example, GBP for sterling, USD for US dollars and EUR for euros. You can find a list of codes in Appendix C.

Hedging, speculation and arbitrage

Some activity in the financial markets is driven by underlying commercial needs. Companies, banks and individuals borrow money because they need to finance their activities. Conversely, investors with surplus funds need to keep their money somewhere and wish to earn a return on it because otherwise it will dwindle in real value because of inflation. Through the mechanisms of the financial markets, the investors effectively lend, directly or indirectly to the borrowers. Also, organizations involved internationally need at some point to convert cashflows from one currency to another. Other organizations need to buy or sell commodities because that is an essential part of their business.

Beyond these activities, however, there are at least three distinct motivations for dealing: speculation, hedging and arbitrage – although deals often contain elements of more than one category:

- **Speculation** A trader in a bank or elsewhere will often deliberately establish a risky position where there was no risk in the first place, because he believes he can make a profit by doing so. This is *speculation*. For example, a trader who believes that the price of gold is going up might buy gold, without any commercial need to do so. If the price of gold does rise as he expects, he will make a profit. If it falls, he will make a loss.

- **Hedging** In the opposite way to this, to *hedge* (or to *cover*) means to protect against the risks arising from potential market movements in exchange rates, interest rates or other variables. This could be a company protecting against the risk that the value of its future income in a foreign currency is vulnerable because that currency might weaken soon, or a company protecting against the possible future increase of interest rates, which would increase the company's borrowing costs. Alternatively, it might be a bank dealer deciding that a speculative position he has already taken has now become too risky and choosing to insulate the position against any further market movements.

- **Arbitrage** The third broad category involves packages of more than one deal in different but related markets. If a dealer sees that the prices of two financial instruments which should be in line are in fact not in line, he can deal in both instruments simultaneously in such a way as to lock in a profit but take no, or little, risk. This is *arbitrage*.

Spot, forward, value dates and short dates

In general, each type of financial transaction has a normal time-cycle for settlement. For example, if a dealer does a straightforward foreign exchange deal today to buy US dollars and sells euros then, under normal circumstances, he expects that he will receive the dollars and pay the euros not today, but in two business days' time. This delay is essentially to allow enough time for the mechanics of the cash transfers involved. In foreign exchange, this is referred to as trading for value *spot*. Each market has its own normal convention, sometimes for settlement after a delay like this, and sometimes for settlement on the same day as the transaction. In both the foreign exchange and international money markets, for example, the usual convention is spot, as just described. Money market deals in a domestic market, however – i.e. in the same currency as the market in which they take place (for example, a US dollar deposit in the USA) – are generally settled on the same day as they are transacted.

In many markets, it is also possible to undertake a transaction where the two parties agree that the settlement will be on a later date than normal. This is called a *forward* deal. Similarly, with a transaction such as a foreign exchange spot deal or an international money market deal, it is possible to agree on settlement earlier than normal.

A futures contract is very similar in concept to a forward, but is traded on a recognized exchange, rather than between any two parties. This gives rise to certain important mechanical differences.

Both money market deposits and foreign exchange forwards are normally quoted for certain regular dates – for example, 1, 2, 3, 6 and 12 months forward. These dates are quoted over the spot date. This means that the 1-month forward rates are calculated for one calendar month after the present spot value date. For example, if today is 19 April and the spot value date is 21 April, then the 1-month forward value date will be 21 May. No adjustment in the forward value date is made for any weekends or public holidays between the spot date and the forward delivery date. However, if the forward delivery date falls on a weekend or holiday, the value date becomes the next business day.

One exception to this last rule is when the spot value date is at or close to the end of the month. Suppose that the spot value date is earlier than the last business day of the month, but the forward value date would fall on a non-business day. If moving the forward value date to the next business day would result in it falling in the next month, it is instead brought back to the previous business day in order to stay in the same calendar month. This is called the *modified following* convention.

Another exception arises if the spot value date is exactly the last business day of a month. In this case, the forward value date is the last business day of the corresponding forward month. This is referred to as dealing *end-end*.

Any month that is not a regularly quoted date, for example for 4 or 5 months' maturity, is called an *in-between* month because it is between the regular dates. A forward deal may in fact be arranged for value on any business day (or any day which is a business day in both currencies for foreign exchange). Dates which do not fit in with calendar month dates are called *broken dates* or *odd dates*.

Example

Today is Monday 27 October 2003.

The spot value date is Wednesday 29 October 2003.

The 1-month value date is Friday 28 November 2003 (modified following convention because 29 November is a Saturday and

...ess day – Monday 1 December – is in the next

value date is Monday 29 December.

...nesday 25 February 2004.

The spot value date is Friday 27 February 2004 (which is the last business day of February because 29 February is a Sunday).

The 1-month value date is Wednesday 31 March 2004 (end-end convention).

The 2-month value date is Friday 30 April 2004 (end-end convention).

Short dates

Value dates earlier than 1 month are referred to as *short dates*. There are certain regular dates usually quoted, and the terminology used is the same in the deposit market and the foreign exchange market, as follows:

Overnight: a deposit or foreign exchange swap from today until tomorrow

Tom-next: a deposit or foreign exchange swap from tomorrow until the next day (spot)

Spot-next: a deposit or foreign exchange swap from spot until the next day

Spot-a-week: a deposit or foreign exchange swap from spot until a week later

Tomorrow means the next working day after today and next means the next working day following (i.e. spot).

Some basic terminology

- **The cash market** *Cash market* is an expression sometimes used for the spot market in something as opposed to the forward market. It is also used, quite separately, for transactions where, on the settlement date, the whole value of something will potentially be settled in the normal way. This is distinct from *contracts for differences*, where the cash amount to be settled is never intended to be the full principal amount underlying the transaction; instead settlement is made of only the difference between two prices or rates.

- **Bid, offer and spread** In general, dealers who make a market in anything (i.e. dealers whose business is to quote prices to any creditworthy counterparty who asks) quote a *two-way* price. This means that the dealer quotes two prices simultaneously – one at which he buys something or borrows money, and the other at which he sells something or lends money.

  The *bid* price or rate is the price at which the dealer quoting the price is prepared to buy or borrow. The *offer* (or *ask*) price is the price at which he is prepared to sell or lend. The difference between them, representing a profit to the dealer, is called the *spread.*

- **Long, short and square** A *long* position is a surplus of purchases over sales of a given currency or asset, or a situation which naturally gives rise to an organization benefiting from a strengthening of that currency or asset. To a money market dealer, however, a long position is a surplus of borrowings taken in over money lent out (which gives rise to a benefit if that currency weakens rather than strengthens).

  A *short* position is a surplus of sales over purchases of a given currency or asset, or a situation which naturally gives rise to an organization benefiting from a weakening of that currency or asset. To a money market dealer, however, a short position is a surplus of money lent out over borrowings taken in (which gives rise to a benefit if that currency strengthens rather than weakens).

  A *square* position is one in which sales exactly match purchases, or in which assets exactly match liabilities.

- **Eurocurrency** Historically, the terms Euro and *Eurocurrency* have been used to describe any instrument which is owned outside the country whose currency is involved. The term does not imply 'European'. For example, a US dollar deposit made by a US resident in New York is in domestic dollars, but a dollar deposit made in Tokyo is in Eurodollars. Similarly, US dollar commercial paper issued outside the USA is Eurocommercial paper while US dollar commercial paper issued inside the USA is domestic US commercial paper. Confusingly, this term has nothing whatever to do with the European Monetary Union currency also called the 'euro'.

Essential financial arithmetic

Percentages

When using interest rates, '4.7%', '4.7/100' and '0.047' all mean exactly the same. Throughout the book, when we have used an interest rate in a calculation, we have not multiplied it by 100. For example, if we do a calculation involving an interest rate of 4.7%, we generally write this in the calculation as '0.047' and **not** '4.7'. Similarly, whenever we speak of 'an interest rate', we always mean a number like 0.047, not a number like 4.7.

When referring to interest rates, a *basis point* always means 0.01% (which is the same as 0.01/100 or 0.0001). Note that this is not necessarily the same as a foreign exchange *point*.

Simple interest calculations

On short-term financial instruments, interest calculations are usually *simple* rather than *compound*. This means that no account is taken of interest on interest – i.e. how much interest is earned when reinvesting an interim interest payment. This is generally appropriate in the money markets because there is usually, although not always, only one single interest payment, at maturity.

Suppose that I place GBP 1 million on deposit at 5.3% for 92 days. As the 8% is generally quoted as if for a whole year rather than for only 92 days, the interest I expect to receive is the appropriate proportion of 5.3%:

$$\text{GBP } 1{,}000{,}000 \times 0.053 \times \frac{92}{365} = \text{GBP } 13{,}358.90$$

The total proceeds after 92 days are therefore the return of the principal, plus the interest:

$$\text{GBP } 1{,}000{,}000 + \text{GBP } 13{,}358.90 = \text{GBP } 1{,}013{,}358.90$$

Note that it is possible to write this last calculation in a slightly neater way:

$$\text{GBP } 1{,}000{,}000 \times \left(1 + \left(0.053 \times \frac{92}{365}\right)\right) = \text{GBP } 1{,}013{,}358.90$$

Simple interest earned = principal amount

$$\times \text{ interest rate} \times \frac{\text{days}}{\text{year}}$$

Maturity proceeds = principal amount

$$\times \left(1 + \left(\text{interest rate} \times \frac{\text{days}}{\text{year}}\right)\right)$$

'Days' means the number of calendar days in the period, in the usual way, including the first date but not the last date. 'Year' means the number of days in a conventional year – see the next section.

The different day/year conventions

ACT/360 and ACT/365

As a general rule in the money markets, the calculation of interest takes account of the exact number of calendar days in the period in question, as a proportion of a year.

However, the number of days in a 'year' is often not the usual 365. Instead, it is more often 360. This is simply a convention used in many financial markets around the world. For example, if a bank quotes an interest rate of 5.3% per year on a deposit of USD 1 million, it does not really mean that it pays exactly 5.3% over a full calendar year of 365 days. In fact, it pays slightly more than that, since it

$$\text{USD } 1,000,000 \times 0.053 \times \frac{365}{360} = \text{USD } 53,736.11$$

Sterling deposits, on the other hand, assume that there are 365 days in a year. In both cases, the year base remains the same – 360 or 365 – regardless of whether or not a leap year is involved. Thus a deposit of GBP 1 million at 5.3% which lasts exactly one year, but includes 29 February in its period (a total of 366 days), will actually pay interest of slightly more than 5.3% – in fact:

$$\text{GBP } 1,000,000 \times 0.053 \times \frac{366}{365} = \text{GBP } 53,145.21$$

There is thus a variation between different money markets in the conventions used for the number of days assumed to be in the year base. The convention used for all sterling money market transactions is usually referred to as *ACT/365* – i.e. the actual number of calendar days in the period, divided by 365. The convention used for all transactions in US dollars and euros is usually referred to as *ACT/360* – the actual number of calendar days in the period, divided by 360.

Most money markets use the ACT/360 convention. The exceptions which use ACT/365 include the international markets and the domestic markets in the following currencies:

Sterling
Hong Kong dollar
Singapore dollar
Malaysian ringgit
Taiwan dollar
Thai baht
South African rand

and the domestic (but not international) markets in the following:

Japanese yen
Canadian dollar
Australian dollar
New Zealand dollar

Example 1

Interest is quoted on a GBP 1 million deposit at 5.3%. The deposit runs from 31 October 2003 to 5 March 2004. What is the amount of interest paid?

There are 126 days from 31 October to 5 March (including 29 February 2004). The interest amount is therefore:

$$\text{GBP } 1,000,000 \times 0.053 \times \frac{126}{365} = \text{GBP } 18,295.89$$

Example 2

Interest is quoted on a USD 1 million deposit at 5.3%. The deposit runs from 31 October 2003 to 5 March 2004. What is the amount of interest paid?

The interest amount is:

$$\text{USD } 1,000,000 \times 0.053 \times \frac{126}{360} = \text{USD } 18,550.00$$

30/360

There are some exceptions to the two conventions above. For example, Swedish Treasury bills and some other markets use a convention called *30/360* (also known as 30(E)/360 or 360/360), which is also used in some European bond markets. In this convention, the 'year' has 360 days and the number of days in the period is calculated differently from the calendar.

Each month is assumed to have 30 days, regardless of what the calendar says, so that the 31st day of any month is treated as if it were the 30th day of that month. To calculate the number of days in any period therefore, use the following rules:

- First, change any date which is 31st to 30th.
- Second, multiply the difference between the months by 30.
- Third, add the difference between the days.

Example 3

Interest is quoted on a EUR 1 million deposit at 5.3% on a 30/360 basis (unusually!). The deposit runs from 31 October 2003 to 5 March 2004. What is the amount of interest paid?

First, change 31 October to 30 October. Second, there are 5 months from October to March and $5 \times 30 = 150$. Third, there are -25 days from 30th to 5th. There are therefore 125 days from 31 October to 5 March on a 30/360 basis.

$$\text{EUR } 1,000,000 \times 0.053 \times \frac{125}{360} = \text{EUR } 18,402.78$$

The ACT/365 and 30/360 conventions are sometimes referred to as *bond basis* (because bond markets use similar conventions). The ACT/360 convention is sometimes referred to as *money market basis*.

In Appendix A we have given a list of the conventions used in some markets.

Converting between the different conventions

It is possible to convert an interest rate quoted on one basis to what it would be if it were quoted on another basis. For example:

Interest rate on ACT/360 basis

$$= \text{interest rate on ACT/365 basis} \times \frac{360}{365}$$

Interest rate on ACT/365 basis

$$= \text{interest rate on ACT/360 basis} \times \frac{365}{360}$$

Interest rate on ACT/360 basis = interest rate on 30/360 basis

$$\times \frac{\text{days in period measured on 30/360 basis}}{\text{days in period measured on ACT/360 basis}}$$

Interest rate on 30/360 basis = interest rate on ACT/360 basis

$$\times \frac{\text{days in period measured on ACT/360 basis}}{\text{days in period measured on 30/360 basis}}$$

Example 4

A dealer quotes for a EUR 1 million deposit from 5 May to 31 August, at 4.7% on an ACT/360 basis in the usual way. What would the quote be if the customer wanted it converted to an ACT/365 basis or a 30/360 basis?

There are 118 actual calendar days from 5 May to 31 August.

There are 115 days on a 30/360 basis.

$$\text{Interest rate on ACT/365 basis} = 4.7\% \times \frac{365}{360} = 4.7653\%$$

$$\text{Interest rate on 30/360 basis} = 4.7\% \times \frac{118}{115} = 4.8226\%$$

Present value

As in Example 2, if I deposit USD 1 million for 126 days at 5.3%, I receive interest of USD 18,550.00:

$$\text{USD } 1,000,000 \times 0.053 \times \frac{126}{360} = \text{USD } 18,550.00$$

The total proceeds including principal at the end of 126 days are therefore USD 1,018,550.00. This could be written as:

$$\text{USD } 1,000,000 \times \left(1 + \left(0.053 \times \frac{126}{360}\right)\right) = \text{USD } 1,018,550.00$$

Suppose that I ask the question: "How much do I need to put on deposit now so that, after 126 days, I will receive back USD 1,018,550.00?" Clearly, the answer is USD 1,000,000. However, how would we have calculated the answer if we did not already know? The answer is the reverse of how we calculated the end proceeds above:

$$\frac{\text{USD } 1,018,550.00}{\left(1 + \left(0.053 \times \frac{126}{360}\right)\right)} = \text{USD } 1,000,000$$

The amount we have calculated is known as the *present value* of USD 1,018,550.00 because it is the value now of that cashflow in the future. Given a choice between receiving USD 1,018,550.00 after 126 days, or USD 1,000,000 now, I would be equally happy with either, because if I start with the USD 1,000,000 now and put it on deposit, I can accumulate USD 1,018,550.00 by the end of 126 days. The present value so calculated depends on the interest rate used and the time until the future cashflow.

We can do the same thing for any amount, any period, any interest rate and any day/year convention. For example, if we need to know how much we need to put on deposit now so that, after 57 days at 6.1%, we will receive back GBP 2,483,892.71, the answer is:

$$\frac{\text{GBP } 2,483,892.71}{\left(1 + \left(0.061 \times \frac{57}{365}\right)\right)} = \text{GBP } 2,460,454.36$$

$$\text{Present value} = \frac{\text{amount of future cashflow}}{\left(1 + \left(\text{interest rate} \times \frac{\text{days}}{\text{year}}\right)\right)}$$

in general, this ~~~~~~~ ~~~~~~
behind market calculations – the *time value of money*. As long as interest rates are not negative, it is better to have any given amount of money sooner rather than later because, if you have it sooner, you can place it on deposit to earn interest on it. The extent to which it is worthwhile having the money sooner depends on the interest rate and the time period involved.

Present values are fundamental to pricing money market instruments, because the present value of a future cashflow is its value, or worth, now. It is therefore the amount of money which one is prepared to pay now for any instrument which generates that cashflow in the future.

The calculation of a present value is sometimes known as *discounting* a future value to a present value and the interest rate used is sometimes known as the *rate of discount*.

Example 5

What is the present value at 6.5% of a cashflow of USD 1 million which will arise after 90 days?

$$\text{Present value} = \frac{\text{amount of future cashflow}}{\left(1 + \left(\text{interest rate} \times \frac{\text{days}}{\text{year}}\right)\right)}$$

$$= \frac{\text{USD } 1,000,000}{\left(1 + \left(0.065 \times \frac{90}{360}\right)\right)} = \text{USD } 984,009.84$$

Calculating the yield on an investment or the cost of a borrowing

Another useful related calculation is the answer to the question: "If we know how much money we invest at the beginning of an investment and we know the total amount achieved at the end, including any interest, what is our rate of return, or yield, on the investment over the period we have held it?" The same question can be asked about the cost of a borrowing, if we know the amount borrowed at the start and the total amount repaid at the end, including interest. The answer is found by turning round the formula above, to give:

$$\text{Yield} = \left(\frac{\text{cashflow at the end}}{\text{cashflow at the start}} - 1 \right) \times \frac{\text{year}}{\text{days}}$$

Note that this formula is correct only where there are no cashflows in the middle of the investment – only at the start and the end. If there were more cashflows, we would need to compound, because we would be able to earn interest on interest.

Exactly the same idea works for the cost of a borrowing.

Example 6

I buy a painting for EUR 24,890. I keep the painting for 198 days. I then sell it for EUR 26,525. What yield have I made on this investment?

$$\text{Yield} = \left(\frac{\text{cashflow at the end}}{\text{cashflow at the start}} - 1 \right) \times \frac{\text{year}}{\text{days}}$$

$$= \left(\frac{26,525}{24,890} - 1 \right) \times \frac{360}{198} = 0.1194 = 11.94\%$$

Example 7

I buy a painting for GBP 24,890. I keep the painting for 198 days. I then sell it for GBP 23,000. What yield have I made on this investment?

$$\text{Yield} = \left(\frac{\text{cashflow at the end}}{\text{cashflow at the start}} - 1 \right) \times \frac{\text{year}}{\text{days}}$$

$$= \left(\frac{23,000}{24,890} - 1 \right) \times \frac{365}{198} = -0.1400 = -14.00\%$$

In this case, I have a negative yield – i.e., I have made a loss.

Example 8

I borrow USD 356,897.21 for 213 days. At the end, I repay a total of USD 368,363.43. What is the total cost of this borrowing?

$$\text{Rate} = \left(\frac{\text{cashflow at the end}}{\text{cashflow at the start}} - 1 \right) \times \frac{\text{year}}{\text{days}}$$

$$= \left(\frac{368,363.43}{356,897.21} - 1 \right) \times \frac{360}{213} = 0.0543 = 5.43\%$$

Compounding two or more interest rates together (a strip)

Suppose that I borrow EUR 1 million for 73 days at 4.7%. At maturity, I borrow the whole amount again – principal and the interest – for another 124 days at 4.9%. What is my simple interest rate over the combined period of 197 days?

At the end of 73 days, the interest cost is EUR 9,530.56:

$$\text{EUR } 1,000,000 \times 0.047 \times \frac{73}{360} = \text{EUR } 9,530.56$$

The whole amount to be refinanced is therefore EUR 1,009,530.56. The interest cost on this at 4.9% for a further 124 days is EUR 17,038.63:

$$\text{EUR } 1,009,530.56 \times 0.049 \times \frac{124}{360} = \text{EUR } 17,038.63$$

The total repayment of principal plus interest after 197 days is therefore EUR 1,026,569.19 (=EUR 1,009,530.56 + EUR 17,038.63). The interest cost is therefore 4.855%:

$$\text{Interest rate} = \left(\frac{\text{cashflow at the end}}{\text{cashflow at the start}} - 1 \right) \times \frac{\text{year}}{\text{days}}$$

$$= \left(\frac{1,026,569.19}{1,000,000} - 1 \right) \times \frac{360}{197} = 0.04855 = 4.855\%$$

The same idea can be used if the borrowing is rolled over more than once, as long as the total length of time is not longer than a year. This process of compounding together more than one rate is called *stripping*. The overall result can be expressed as a formula:

Creating a strip

The simple interest rate for a period up to one year

$$
= \left(
\begin{array}{l}
\left(1 + \left(\text{first interest rate} \times \dfrac{\text{days in first period}}{\text{year}} \right) \right) \\[2mm]
\times \left(1 + \left(\text{second interest rate} \times \dfrac{\text{days in second period}}{\text{year}} \right) \right) \\[2mm]
\times \cdots\cdots\cdots\cdots \\[2mm]
\times \left(1 + \left(\text{last interest rate} \ \times \dfrac{\text{days in last period}}{\text{year}} \right) \right) - 1
\end{array}
\right)
$$
$$
\times \frac{\text{year}}{\text{total days}}
$$

This can be applied to the example above, to give 4.855% as expected:

$$\left(\left(1+\left(0.047 \times \frac{73}{360}\right)\right) \times \left(1+\left(0.049 \times \frac{124}{360}\right)\right) - 1\right) \times \frac{360}{197}$$

$$= 0.04855 = 4.855\%$$

This idea works in exactly the same way for rolling over an investment as for rolling over a borrowing, as in the following example.

Example 9

An investor deposits USD 3 million at 5.3% for 92 days. At maturity, he rolls over the whole principal and interest at 5.4% for 30 days. At maturity, he again rolls over the accumulated principal and interest at 5.6% for 62 days. What is his overall simple rate of interest earned over the whole six months?

$$\left(\begin{array}{c}\left(1+\left(0.053 \times \frac{92}{360}\right)\right) \times \left(1+\left(0.054 \times \frac{30}{360}\right)\right) \\ \times \left(1+\left(0.056 \times \frac{62}{360}\right)\right) - 1\end{array}\right) \times \frac{360}{184}$$

$$= 0.05463 = 5.463\%$$

Interpolation

In the money market and foreign exchange market, prices are generally quoted for standard periods such as 1 month, 2 months etc. If a dealer needs to quote a price for an *odd date* (or *broken date*) between these periods, he needs to *interpolate*. In the money markets, straight-line interpolation is generally used, as follows.

Suppose, for example, that the 1-month rate (30 days) is 8.0% and that the 2-month rate (61 days) is 8.5%. The rate for 39 days assumes that interest rates increase steadily (i.e. in a straight line) from the 1-month rate to the 2-month rate. The increase from 30 days to 39 days will therefore be a 9/31 proportion of the increase from 30 days to 61 days. The 39-day rate is therefore:

$$8.0\% + \left((8.5\% - 8.0\%) \times \frac{9}{31}\right) = 8.1452\%$$

The same process can be used for interpolating exchange rates.

Example 10

The interest rate for 3 months (92 days) is 15.2%. The interest rate for 4 months (123 days) is 15.0%. What is the rate for 104 days, using straight-line interpolation?

$$15.0\% + \left((15.0\% - 15.2\%) \times \frac{(104 - 92)}{(123 - 92)} \right) = 14.9226\%$$

Paying interest with different frequencies

If a dealer lends GBP 1 million to a customer at 5.3% for 182 days, he will normally receive total proceeds at the end of GBP 1,013,427.40:

$$\text{GBP } 1,000,000 \times 0.053 \times \frac{182}{365} = \text{GBP } 26,427.40$$

$$\text{GBP } 1,000,000 + \text{GBP } 26,427.40 = \text{GBP } 1,026,427.40$$

If, however, the customer agrees to pay the same interest rate but to pay the interest in two instalments – after 91 days and 182 days – the dealer will be better off. This is because, when he receives the first interest instalment after 91 days, he can reinvest it until the end of 182 days. This will earn him extra money, as interest on interest. How much extra will depend on the interest rate at which he can reinvest the instalment. If we assume that the rate is still 5.3%, the total proceeds achieved by the end of 182 days will be GBP 1,026,602.00:

- After 91 days, receive first interest instalment of GBP 13,213.70:

$$\text{GBP } 1,000,000 \times 0.053 \times \frac{91}{365} = \text{GBP } 13,213.70$$

- Reinvest this amount at 5.3% for the next 91 days, to earn an extra GBP 170.79:

$$\text{GBP } 13{,}213.70 \times 0.053 \times \frac{91}{365} = \text{GBP } 174.60$$

- At the end of 182 days, receive the second interest instalment of GBP 13,213.70 plus the principal back of GBP 1,000,000.
- The total proceeds are GBP 1,026,306.99:

$$\text{GBP } 13{,}213.70 + \text{GBP } 174.60 + \text{GBP } 1{,}013{,}213.70$$

$$= \text{GBP } 1{,}026{,}602.00$$

The total interest which the dealer has achieved is therefore GBP 26,602.00, on a principal of GBP 1 million. This is the same result the dealer would have achieved if he had quoted a rate of 5.335% with all the interest paid at the end (the difference of GBP 0.08 is due to rounding):

$$\text{GBP } 1{,}000{,}000 \times 0.05335 \times \frac{182}{365} = \text{GBP } 26{,}601.92$$

5.3% is said to be the *nominal rate* quoted to the customer with 3-monthly or quarterly interest payments and 5.335% is said to be the 6-monthly or semi-annual *equivalent rate*.

These calculations assume that all interim cashflows can be reinvested at the same original interest rate. Although this is unrealistic, it is a useful simplifying assumption to make, in order to be able to compare interest rates with different interest payment frequencies. It is possible to use a formula to convert the 5.3% quoted with quarterly interest payments to the semi-annual equivalent rate of 5.335%:

Equivalent rate with interest paid M times per year

$$= \left(\left(1 + \left(\frac{\text{rate with interest paid } N \text{ times per year}}{N} \right) \right)^{\left(\frac{N}{M} \right)} - 1 \right) \times M$$

In the example we have been considering, the customer has agreed to pay the 5.3% in quarterly instalments – that is, effectively four times per year (even though the loan only lasts for 6 months). We want to calculate what this is worth to the dealer if interest were paid 6-monthly – that is, effectively twice per year (again, even though the loan only lasts for 6 months). Using the formula above agrees with our answer:

Equivalent rate with interest paid twice per year

$$= \left(\left(1 + \left(\frac{\text{rate with interest paid four times per year}}{4}\right)\right)^{\left(\frac{4}{2}\right)} - 1\right) \times 2$$

$$= \left(\left(1 + \left(\frac{0.053}{4}\right)\right)^{\left(\frac{4}{2}\right)} - 1\right) \times 2 = 0.05335 = 5.335\%$$

Note that the calculation method we have given here is almost always satisfactory but is not quite correct mathematically. This is because the 6-month period of 182 days used in our example is not exactly half a year (that would be $182\frac{1}{2}$ days, which is not realistic). Similarly, if interest were paid quarterly, the payment periods would not be exactly equal periods of $91\frac{1}{4}$ days but slightly different periods, depending on weekends etc.

Example 11

A dealer quotes 5.3% for a 5-year deposit with interest paid once per year. What equivalent rate should he quote if the customer prefers to receive the interest quarterly?

Equivalent rate with interest paid four times per year

$$= \left(\left(1 + \left(\frac{\text{rate with interest paid once per year}}{1}\right)\right)^{\left(\frac{1}{4}\right)} - 1\right) \times 4$$

$$= \left(\left(1 + \left(\frac{0.053}{1}\right)\right)^{\left(\frac{1}{4}\right)} - 1\right) \times 4 = 0.05198 = 5.198\%$$

Effective rates

The equivalent yield with interest paid only once per year is known as the annual equivalent rate, or the *effective rate*. Consider, for example, a deposit for 3 months. The effective yield is the interest which would be accumulated by the end of the year if the deposit were rolled over three times – i.e. the principal and interest at the end of 3 months were all reinvested at the same rate, and then all again at the end of 6 months and all again at the end of 9 months.

The same idea can be extended to a deposit for an odd period, such as, say, 59 days. If the deposit is rolled over repeatedly, its maturity will never quite coincide with exactly one year, because 365 is not an exact multiple of 59. Nevertheless, it is still possible to consider the effective rate as the annual rate which achieves the same compound result, as follows:

$$\text{Effective rate} = \left(1 + \left(\text{nominal rate quoted} \times \frac{\text{days}}{\text{year}}\right)\right)^{\left(\frac{365}{\text{days}}\right)} - 1$$

Example 12

A dealer is trying to compare two different US dollar investments. The first is for 153 days at a yield of 9.1% and the second is for 87 days at a yield of 9.05%. Assuming that there are no other significant differences between the two investments, which is better? It may be, for example, that the dealer believes that interest rates will be higher after 87 days than now – in which case he would probably prefer the 87-day investment because then he could roll it over at a higher yield when it matures. Ignoring any such expectations, however, it is useful to be able to compare the two investments on a like-for-like basis.

One approach therefore is to compare the effective rate of each investment. The first has an effective rate of 9.475% and the second 9.501%, so on this basis, the shorter investment has a lower nominal rate but a higher effective rate:

$$\left(1 + \left(0.091 \times \frac{153}{360}\right)\right)^{\left(\frac{365}{153}\right)} - 1 = 0.09475 = 9.475\%$$

$$\left(1 + \left(0.0905 \times \frac{87}{360}\right)\right)^{\left(\frac{365}{87}\right)} - 1 = 0.09501 = 9.501\%$$

Exercises

1 An amount of 5 million is placed on deposit from 17 August to 31 December at 6.7%. What would be the interest earned if the rate had been quoted on an ACT/365, ACT/360 or 30/360 basis?

2 A dealer quotes a rate of 6.7% on a 30/360 basis for an investment from 17 August to 31 December. What would be the equivalent rate if the customer asked him to quote it instead on an ACT/365 basis?

3 What is the present value of a cashflow of EUR 5,327.21 arising in 276 days, using 4.2% as the rate of discount?

4 I buy an investment for GBP 2,345,678.91 and sell it one week later for GBP 2,350,000.00. What is my yield?

5 The interest rate for 6 months (183 days) is 9.00% and the rate for 7 months (214 days) is 9.15%. What is the rate for 193 days?

6 A dealer quotes a customer 7.35% to borrow for one year with interest paid monthly. The customer prefers to pay interest quarterly. What rate should the dealer quote instead?

7 Which of the following is the cheapest for a borrower?

- 6.7% annual money market basis
- 6.7% semi-annual money market basis
- 6.7% annual bond basis
- 6.7% semi-annual bond basis.

8 What is the effective yield of a 45-day deposit in euros, with a nominal rate quoted of 4.6%?

9 A company borrows US dollars at 5.1% for 183 days and then at maturity refinances the principal and interest at 5.3% for a further 92 days. What is the simple cost of borrowing over the 9 months?

Part 2
Money Markets

3

Overview of money market instruments

Introduction

The term *money market* is used to include all short-term financial instruments which are based on an interest rate, whether the interest rate is actually paid (as in a cash deposit) or only implied in the way the instrument is priced and settled (as in an FRA). Longer-term instruments are covered by the term *capital market*.

The underlying instruments are essentially those used by one party (the borrower, seller or issuer) to borrow money and by the other party (the lender, buyer or investor) to lend money. The main such instruments are:

Fixed deposit	} borrowing
Certificate of deposit (CD)	} by banks
Commercial paper (CP)	borrowing by companies
	(or in some cases, banks)
Bill of exchange	borrowing by companies
Treasury bill	borrowing by a government

These instruments have different names in different markets – for example, each country's government issues something equivalent to a Treasury bill in its own market – but the characteristics are essentially the same as described here.

Each of the above instruments represents an obligation on the borrower to repay the amount borrowed at maturity, plus interest if appropriate. As well as these underlying borrowing instruments, there are other money market instruments which are linked to these, or at least to the same interest rate structure, but which are not direct obligations on the issuer in the same way:

Repurchase agreement	effectively cash borrowing using another instrument (such as a bond) as collateral
Forward-forward borrowing Futures contract Forward rate agreement	used to trade or hedge short-term interest rates for future periods

The money market is linked to other markets though arbitrage mechanisms. Arbitrage occurs when it is possible to achieve the same result in terms of position and risk though two alternative mechanisms which have a slightly different price. The arbitrage involves achieving the result via the cheaper method and simultaneously reversing the position via the more expensive method – thereby locking in a profit which is free from market risk (although still probably subject to credit risk). For example, if I can buy one instrument cheaply and simultaneously sell at a higher price another instrument or combination of instruments which has identical characteristics, I am arbitraging. In a completely free market with no other price considerations involved, the supply and demand effect of arbitrage tends to drive the two prices together until the arbitrage opportunity ceases to exist.

For example, the money market is linked in this way to the forward foreign exchange market, through the ability to create synthetic deposits in one currency, by using foreign exchange deals combined with money market instruments. Similarly it is linked to the capital markets (long-term financial instruments) through the ability to create longer-term instruments from a series of short-term instruments (such as a 2-year interest rate swap from a series of 3-month FRAs).

The yield curve

If I wish to borrow money for 3 months, the interest rate is likely to be different – possibly higher and possibly lower – from what the rate would be if I wished instead to borrow for 6 months. The *yield curve* shows how interest rates vary with term to maturity. For example, a Reuters screen might show the following rates:

1 month	9.5%
2 months	9.7%
3 months	10.0%
6 months	10.0%
12 months	10.2%
2 years	10.5%

In a free market, these rates show where the market on average believes rates 'should' be, as supply and demand would otherwise tend to move the rates up or down. A yield curve where longer-term rates are higher than shorter-term rates is known as a *normal* or *positive* yield curve; a curve where longer-term rates are lower than shorter-term rates is known as *negative* or *inverted*; a curve where rates are approximately the same across the range of maturities is known as *flat*.

There are in fact an infinite number of yield curves, because yield depends on credit risk as well as maturity. For example, if I am choosing between investing for 6 months in a security issued by the government of a particular country, and a security issued by a medium-risk company in that same country, I would expect the latter to have a significantly higher yield to compensate for the higher risk. A security issued by a government in its own currency is generally considered to represent virtually zero credit risk, because the government can always print its own money to redeem the security if necessary, regardless of the state of the economy. This does not apply to a security issued by a government in a foreign currency.

There are therefore as many different yield curves as there are levels of creditworthiness. In practice, one generally considers a yield curve as referring to either government risk or first-class bank risk.

The yield on any security also depends on liquidity – how easy it is to liquidate a position in that security by selling it if necessary. If there are two securities issued by exactly the same organization but one is more liquid than the other, it should be traded at a slightly lower yield because investors will be more willing to own it.

Liquidity in turn depends partly on creditworthiness. In any domestic money market, a Treasury bill (see below) should be the most liquid instrument, since, even in dire circumstances, the government can in theory always print money to redeem its own securities. In the UK market, eligible bills (see below) are also very liquid, as they can be sold to the Bank of England.

There are various factors which influence the shape of the yield curve:

- **Economic performance**   Expectations of future rates, and hence current longer-term rates also, are affected by market expectations of future inflation.
- **Central bank operations**   Intervention in the market by the central bank, involving buying and selling securities, can change the availability of securities of different maturities. If this causes a shortage of supply for investors at a particular maturity, yields will rise at that maturity. If the market believes that the central bank is about to change official 3-month rates, for example, this expectation will already have been factored into the market 3-month rate.
- **Borrowing demand**   An increase or decrease in borrowing in any particular maturity will tend to increase or decrease yields at that maturity. For example, if the government either increases or decreases its borrowing requirement, this will affect the yield curve at the maturities sought by the government. Similarly if the government shortens or lengthens the maturity of its debt when it rolls over maturing debt, this tends to make longer-term yields lower than shorter-term yields or vice versa.
- **Liquidity preference**   The typical shape for the yield curve, in the absence of other factors, is positive because, if there is no advantage in investing for a longer term, investors would prefer to invest short-term since their investments are then more liquid. Also, the risk of losing money is greater with a longer-term security than with a shorter-term security, because its price is more sensitive to yield changes. Therefore, an incentive is necessary to attract longer-term investors. This is a supply and demand effect: borrowers prefer long-term and investors prefer short-term, so the price of money is driven up for the long term.
- **Market segmentation**   Bank investors tend to invest short-term and institutional investors like pension funds tend to invest long-term, with fewer investors in the medium-term. In the absence of any other factors, this would tend to encourage a humped yield curve shape.

Some more terminology

- **Negotiable security**   A *security* is a financial asset sold initially for cash by a borrowing organization (the issuer). A security which can be sold and bought again subsequently – i.e. transferred from one party to another – is referred to as *negotiable.*

- **Primary market and secondary market** When a security is issued, the original purchaser is said to be buying it in the primary market. All subsequent transactions – whether they are on the same day or much later during the life of the security – are said to be secondary market transactions.

- **Face value/notional principal** For securities, the principal amount is generally known as the *face value* (which can be thought of as the principal amount written on the face of the instrument). It is also sometimes called the *nominal amount.* With some instruments such as an FRA (see Chapter 6), the principal amount is never actually transferred to either party, but is used as a reference amount for calculation purposes. In this case, it is referred to as a *notional* principal.

- **Coupon/yield** A certificate of deposit pays interest at maturity – sometimes only at maturity but sometimes also during the CD's life – as well as repaying the principal. For example, a CD might be issued with a face value of £1 million, which is repaid on maturity together with interest of say 10% calculated on the number of days between issue and maturity. The 10% interest rate is called the *coupon.* The coupon is fixed once the CD is issued. This should not be confused with the *yield,* which is the current rate of return available in the market when investing, or buying and selling an instrument, and varies continually.

- **Discount**

  1 An instrument which does not carry a coupon is a *discount instrument.* Because there is no interest paid on the principal, a buyer will only ever buy it for less than its face value (unless yields are negative!) – i.e. at a discount. For example, Treasury bills are almost always discount instruments.

  2 The word discount is also used in the very specialized context of a *discount rate* quoted in the US and UK markets on certain instruments. This is explained in detail below.

  3 To *discount* a cashflow means to calculate its present value, as discussed in Chapter 2.

- **Bearer/registered** A *bearer security* is one where the issuer pays the principal (and coupon if there is one) to whoever is holding the security at maturity. This enables the security to be held anonymously. A *registered security* by contrast is one where the owner is considered to be whoever is registered centrally as the owner; this registration is changed each time the security changes hands.

- **LIBOR** *LIBOR* means London interbank offered rate – the interest rate at which one London bank offers money as a cash deposit to another London bank of top creditworthiness. *LIBID* means London interbank bid rate – the interest rate at which one London bank of top creditworthiness bids for money as a cash deposit from another bank. LIBOR is therefore always the higher side of a two-sided interest rate quotation (which is quoted high–low in some markets and low–high in others). *LIMEAN* is the average between the two sides. In practice, the offered rate for a particular currency at any moment is generally no different in London from any other major center, although it is possible for reserve costs, credit considerations etc. to make a slight difference. LIBOR is therefore often just shorthand for offered interest rate.

  Specifically, however, LIBOR for a particular currency also means the average offered rate for that currency quoted by a group of banks in London at 11:00 a.m. This is a reference rate, calculated by the BBA (British Bankers' Association) each day, which is used as a benchmark for agreeing rates between two parties for loans, FRAs and other instruments. Similarly, *EURIBOR* refers specifically to the interbank offered rate for euros reported as a reference rate by the ACI and the EBF. There is therefore both a euro LIBOR (for euros at 11:00 a.m. in London) and EURIBOR (for euros at 11:00 a.m. in Europe). *STIBOR* is the reference rate in Stockholm for Swedish kronor, *BUBOR* for forints in Budapest etc.

- **Fixed rate or floating rate** Many instruments pay a *fixed* rate – that is, an interest rate or coupon which is determined when the instrument is issued and remains fixed throughout its life, regardless of whether the interest is paid only at maturity or on several occasions. Others pay a *floating* rate. This means that the interest rate is changed in line with market conditions at certain predetermined times (for example, refixed each 6 months to the current LIBOR).

- **Bid and offer** The offered rate, at which a bank wishes to lend funds to another bank of top credit quality, is higher than the bid rate, at which it wishes to take funds. In most markets, the bid rate is quoted first in a two-way price and the offerred rate second – for example, '5.17/5.27%'. In the London market, however, the quote is traditionally reversed from bid/offer to offer/bid – for example, '5.27/5.17%'. There is no ambiguity in this, since the lower number is always the bid for cash and the higher number is always the offer for cash, regardless of which comes first.

- **Basis point** When discussing interest rates, a *basis point* is always 0.01% (which is the same as 0.0001). Note that this is not necessarily the same as a *point* in foreign exchange, which can vary according to the size of the exchange rate.

Money market instruments

Fixed deposit/loan

A *fixed deposit* is a deposit placed with a bank for an agreed length of time. It is not negotiable, and it is expected therefore to be held to maturity. It is generally possible for the depositor to *break* the deposit – that is, terminate it early – but effectively at a penalty cost. Conceptually, a fixed deposit is exactly the same as a loan or borrowing – the terminology varies only according to circumstance and whether you are borrowing or lending: a company lending money to the bank is making a deposit but a company borrowing money from the bank is taking a loan. A fixed deposit is also known as a *term deposit, time deposit* or *clean deposit.*

Term:	from 1 day to several years, but usually less than 1 year
Interest:	usually all paid on maturity, but deposits of over a year (and sometimes those of less than a year) pay interest more frequently – commonly each year or each 6 months. A 19-month deposit, for example, would generally pay interest at the end of one year and then at maturity.
Quotation:	as an interest rate
Currency:	any domestic or international currency
Settlement:	generally same day for a domestic deposit, 2 working days for Eurocurrency
Registration:	there is no registration
Negotiable:	not negotiable

Certificate of deposit (CD)

A certificate of deposit is a security issued to a depositor by a bank or building society, to raise money in the same way as a time deposit. A CD is, however, negotiable. This gives the investor flexibility in two ways. Firstly, he can liquidate the CD if he needs the cash back sooner than anticipated. Secondly, it allows him to take a view on how interest rates will move, which is linked to the price at which the CD can be bought and sold. For example, if he buys a 6-month CD at 5% and one week later interest rates have fallen to 4.5%, he can then sell the CD and make a capital profit. Because of this flexibility, the yield on a CD (which, when it is first issued, is the same as the coupon) should be slightly lower than the yield on a deposit for the same term with the same bank.

Term:	generally up to 1 year, although CDs can be issued for up to 5 years in the London market.
Interest:	usually pays a coupon, although occasionally not. Interest is usually all paid on maturity, but CDs of over a year (and sometimes those of less than a year) pay interest more frequently – commonly each year or each 6 months. Some CDs pay a floating rate (FRCD), which is paid and refixed at regular intervals.
Quotation:	as a yield
Currency:	any domestic or international currency
Settlement:	generally same day for a domestic deposit, 2 working days for Eurocurrency
Registration:	usually in bearer form
Negotiable:	yes

Treasury bill (T-bill)

Treasury bills are domestic instruments issued by governments to raise short-term finance. The exact name of the instrument varies from country to country.

Term:	generally 13, 26 or 52 weeks; in France also 4 to 7 weeks, for example; in the UK generally 13 weeks
Interest:	generally non-interest bearing, issued at a discount
Quotation:	Sterling T-bills in the UK and T-bills in the USA are quoted as a discount rate. Euro T-bills in the UK and T-bills in other countries are quoted as a yield

Currency:	usually the currency of the country; however, the UK government, for example, also issues T-bills in euros
Registration:	sometimes a bearer security, sometimes registered
Negotiable:	yes

Commercial paper (CP)

Commercial paper is an unsecured promissory note. It is issued usually by a company (although some banks also issue CP) in the same way that a CD is issued by a bank. CP is, however, usually not interest-bearing. A company generally needs to have a rating from a credit agency for its CP to be widely acceptable. Details vary between markets. For example:

Domestic US CP

Term:	from 1 day to 270 days; usually very short term
Interest:	non-interest bearing
Quotation:	as a discount rate
Currency:	domestic US dollars
Settlement:	same day
Registration:	in bearer form
Negotiable:	yes

Eurocommercial paper (ECP)

Term:	from 1 to 365 days; usually between 30 and 180 days
Interest:	usually non-interest bearing
Quotation:	as a yield, calculated on the same year basis as other money market instruments in that Eurocurrency
Currency:	any Eurocurrency but largely US dollars
Settlement:	2 working days
Registration:	in bearer form
Negotiable:	yes

Bill of exchange

A bill of exchange is used by a company essentially for trade purposes. It is an unconditional order in writing from one party to another, requiring the second party to pay an amount on a future date. The party originating the bill (this is the party to whom the money is owed) is called the *drawer* of the bill. The party to whom the bill requires the money to be paid (usually the same as the drawer) is the *payee*. The party owing the money is the *drawee* of the bill. When the drawee accepts liability to pay the amount, it becomes the *acceptor*. If a bank stands as guarantor to the drawer, it is also said to accept the bill by endorsing it appropriately. A bill accepted in this way is a *bankers' acceptance (BA)*.

A commercial or finance company can also address a bill directly to a bank, rather than to a trading partner, and discount it immediately at the bank, in order to raise funds for general purposes rather then to finance a specific sale of goods.

In the UK, if the bank accepting a bill is one on a specific list of banks published by the Bank of England, the bill becomes an *eligible bill* which means it is eligible for discounting by the Bank of England (i.e. the Bank of England is willing to buy it), and it will therefore command a slightly lower yield than an ineligible bill.

Term:	from 1 week to one year but usually less than 6 months
Interest:	non-interest bearing
Quotation:	in the USA and UK, quoted as a discount rate, but elsewhere as a yield
Currency:	mostly domestic, although it is possible to draw foreign currency bills
Settlement:	available for discount the same day it is drawn
Registration:	in bearer form
Negotiable:	yes, although in practice banks often tend to hold until maturity the bills they have discounted

Repo

A *repo* is an arrangement whereby one party sells a security such as a bond to another party and simultaneously agrees to repurchase the same security at a subsequent date at an agreed price. This is equivalent to the first party borrowing cash from the second party against collateral, and the interest rate reflects this – i.e. it is slightly lower than an unsecured cash borrowing because it is collateralized. The security involved will often be of high credit quality, such as a government bond. A reverse repurchase agreement (*reverse repo*) is the same arrangement viewed from the other party's perspective. The deal is generally a repo if it is initiated by the party borrowing money and lending the security and a reverse repo if it is initiated by the party borrowing the security and lending the money.

A repo is also known as a *repurchase agreement, RP, classic repo* or *US-style repo*. A variation on the structure which achieves essentially the same result is a sell/buy-back.

As the second leg of a repo reverses the first leg, it can be seen as one party lending the security and the other party borrowing the security. Because of this, the *borrower* in a repo is generally the party borrowing the security and lending the cash, whereas the *lender* is the party lending the security and borrowing the cash.

Term:	usually very short term, although in principle a repo can be for any term
Interest:	implied in the difference between the purchase and repurchase prices
Quotation:	as a yield
Currency:	any currency
Settlement:	generally cash against delivery of the security (DVP)
Registration:	N/A
Negotiable:	no

Deposits and coupon-bearing instruments

Fixed deposits

As discussed in Chapter 2, interest on a fixed deposit is normally paid in one single amount at maturity:

$$\text{Interest earned} = \text{principal} \times \text{interest rate} \times \frac{\text{days}}{\text{year}}$$

The total repayment at maturity, including principal and interest, is then given by either:

$$\text{Maturity proceeds} = \text{principal amount}$$
$$+ \left(\text{principal amount} \times \text{interest rate} \times \frac{\text{days}}{\text{year}}\right)$$

or:

$$\text{Maturity proceeds} = \text{principal amount}$$
$$\times \left(1 + \left(\text{interest rate} \times \frac{\text{days}}{\text{year}}\right)\right)$$

Throughout the book, 'days' means the number of days in the period, including the first date but not the last date; in the money markets, this generally means the number of actual calendar days in the normal way. 'Year' means the number of days in a conventional year, which in the money markets is generally 360 or 365.

Example 1

A dealer takes a fixed deposit of EUR 5 million from a customer for 73 days at 4.63%. At maturity, he repays EUR 5,046,943.06:

$$\text{EUR } 5{,}000{,}000 + \left(\text{EUR } 5{,}000{,}000 \times 0.0463 \times \frac{73}{360} \right)$$

$$= \text{EUR } 5{,}046{,}943.06$$

or:

$$\text{EUR } 5{,}000{,}000 \times \left(1 + \left(0.0463 \times \frac{73}{360} \right) \right) = \text{EUR } 5{,}046{,}943.06$$

Quoting for fixed deposits with delayed interest settlement

A fixed deposit for longer than 1 year conventionally pays interest at the end of each year and then at maturity. Sometimes a customer asks for all the interest to be paid at maturity instead but for the interest rate to be quoted on a simple basis. Effectively in this case, the bank is keeping the interim interest payments, reinvesting them until maturity, and then giving them to the customer. In quoting to the customer in such a case, account must therefore be taken of the rate at which it is possible to reinvest the interim cashflows. The calculation for the interest rate to be quoted to the customer in this case is considered in Chapter 6.

Taking a position

A company borrows money because it needs to finance its operations. An investor deposits money in a bank because he wishes to earn interest on it. To some extent, a bank will also have similar underlying requirements – funding its operations and investing surpluses. To a large extent, however, a money market trader borrows and lends money as an activity in itself, in order to make a profit from doing so. This can be through fixed deposits and repos, or through negotiable securities.

To earn profit from dealing, the dealer's objective is to borrow (i.e. take in deposits, issue securities or sell securities) at a lower interest rate and lend (i.e. make deposits, lend money or buy securities) at a higher interest rate.

A dealer who has been borrowing and lending in one particular maturity needs to know his net position, average interest rate and profit or loss in that maturity.

Example 2

You borrow USD 5 million for 1 month (31 days) at 4.75%, you lend USD 4 million for 1 month at 4.77%, you borrow USD 8 million for 1 month at 4.72% and you lend USD 6 million for 1 month at 4.79%. The current 1-month rate is 4.71/4.82%. What is your net position, your average rate and your profit or loss?

$$+5,000,000 \times 0.0475 = +237,500$$
$$-4,000,000 \times 0.0477 = -190,800$$
$$+8,000,000 \times 0.0472 = +377,600$$
$$-6,000,000 \times 0.0479 = -287,400$$

$$+3,000,000 \qquad\qquad +136,900$$

$$\frac{136,900}{3,000,000} = 0.04563 = 4.563\%$$

The net position is therefore long of USD 3 million at an average rate of 4.563%. The dealer can compare this average rate with the current market rate to determine whether he is running a profit or a loss; in this example, he is running a profit.

To calculate the profit, assume that he closes out his position by lending USD 3 million at the current rate of 4.71% (the bid side because he will be hitting someone else's bid rate). This would give a profit of 0.147% (=4.71% − 4.563%) for 31 days on USD 3 million:

$$\text{USD } 3,000,000 \times 0.00147 \times \frac{31}{360} = \text{USD } 380$$

Typically, the present value of this amount would then be calculated (see Chapter 2) to give the dealer's profit:

$$\frac{\text{USD } 380}{\left(1 + \left(0.0471 \times \dfrac{31}{360}\right)\right)} = \text{USD } 378$$

The exact average rate and profit or loss will depend on whether the transactions are all for exactly the same maturity. It may be that the dealer has grouped together on his book various deals which have slightly different maturities, but are all within 1 month.

For someone trading in repos rather than deposits, the calculation is the same since repos can be seen as secured deposits.

As discussed below, when a dealer is trading in negotiable securities, a change in interest rates appears as a change in the value of the security. When interest rates rise, the value of a security falls and vice versa. Therefore a dealer hoping that interest rates will rise is the same as a dealer hoping that prices will fall.

Suppose that a dealer effectively borrows by selling security A at a lower interest rate and effectively lends by buying security B (with the same term and coupon as security A) at a higher interest rate. This means that when he sells security A, he receives a higher price for it than he pays when he buys security B. His profit therefore appears as a capital gain.

The price of a CD

When a CD is issued, the original purchaser in the primary market pays the face value for it. In this way, if the original purchaser holds it until maturity, it is the same as a fixed deposit – he pays the principal amount at the start and receives back the principal amount plus coupon at the end.

If the CD is sold again to someone else during its life, however, the amount paid will depend on its value at that time. For an instrument such as a CD which pays a coupon, that value in the market depends on both the coupon rate, because the coupon rate affects the size of the cashflow received at maturity, and the current yield which varies from time to time.

For any security, the price an investor is prepared to pay is essentially the present value of the future cashflow which he will receive at maturity because he owns it. This is the same as the cash investment needed now, at the current market yield, to achieve this amount at maturity. This present value depends, as explained in Chapter 2, on the yield he expects to earn, the time to the cashflow and the size of the cashflow.

> Price = present value

The coupon paid at maturity of a CD is calculated at the coupon rate, for the term of the CD, based on the CD's face value:

Coupon amount = face value

$$\times \text{ coupon rate } \times \frac{\text{days from issue to maturity}}{\text{year}}$$

The total maturity proceeds of a CD are the face value plus the coupon:

Maturity proceeds = face value

$$+ \left(\text{face value} \times \text{coupon rate} \times \frac{\text{days from issue to maturity}}{\text{year}} \right)$$

Exactly as with the maturity proceeds of a fixed deposit, this can be rewritten slightly more neatly as follows:

Maturity proceeds = face value

$$\times \left(1 + \left(\text{coupon rate} \times \frac{\text{days from issue to maturity}}{\text{year}} \right) \right)$$

The value of this CD now – the amount which must be paid to buy it – is the present value now of the maturity proceeds:

Amount paid

$$= \frac{\text{face value} \times \left(1 + \left(\text{coupon rate} \times \dfrac{\text{days from issue to maturity}}{\text{year}} \right) \right)}{\left(1 + \left(\text{yield} \times \dfrac{\text{days from settlement to maturity}}{\text{year}} \right) \right)}$$

The price is normally quoted based on a face value amount of 100.

For a CD

Maturity proceeds = face value

$$\times \left(1 + \left(\text{coupon rate} \times \frac{\text{days from issue to maturity}}{\text{year}} \right) \right)$$

Amount paid

$$= \frac{\text{face value} \times \left(1 + \left(\text{coupon rate} \times \dfrac{\text{days from issue to maturity}}{\text{year}} \right) \right)}{\left(1 + \left(\text{yield} \times \dfrac{\text{days from settlement to maturity}}{\text{year}} \right) \right)}$$

Example 3

A CD is issued with face value USD 3 million, a coupon of 5.25% and a term of 91 days. A dealer buys this CD in the secondary market, when it has only 30 days left to maturity and the yield is quoted as 5.17/5.27%. How much does he pay for it?

On the two-sided quote he receives, he will have the worse side because he is the price-taker. As the purchaser of the CD, he would prefer to invest at 5.27%, so in fact he can only deal at 5.17%.

$$\frac{\text{USD } 3,000,000 \times \left(1 + \left(0.0525 \times \frac{91}{360}\right)\right)}{\left(1 + \left(0.0517 \times \frac{30}{360}\right)\right)} = \text{USD } 3,026,772.16$$

Note that because the price of a CD is the present value of its cashflow at maturity, the price goes up as the yield down and vice versa. The holder of a CD therefore wants interest rates to fall, so that he can sell the CD at a profit. This is in fact true of any security, including those which do not pay a coupon:

At any given time:

A higher yield means a lower price
A lower yield means a higher price

Example 4

In Example 3, if the yield at which the dealer purchased the CD were 5.08% instead of 5.17%, the amount he would pay for it would be more:

$$\frac{\text{USD } 3,000,000 \times \left(1 + \left(0.0525 \times \frac{91}{360}\right)\right)}{\left(1 + \left(0.0508 \times \frac{30}{360}\right)\right)} = \text{USD } 3,026,998.21$$

The time left to maturity also affects the value of CD. As the time to maturity shortens, the value increases. Therefore if the time to maturity shortens (so that the value rises) and at the same time the yield rises (so that the value falls), there is no obvious answer – without calculating using the formula – to the question: "Has the value risen or fallen?" However, if the time to maturity shortens and the yield falls, the value of the CD will always rise because both effects are in the same direction.

In Chapter 2 we saw that the yield earned on any investment can be calculated as:

$$\text{Yield} = \left(\frac{\text{cashflow at the end}}{\text{cashflow at the start}} - 1 \right) \times \frac{\text{year}}{\text{days}}$$

Suppose that I buy a CD and then sell it again later. The yield that I have earned over this period of holding the CD can be calculated in this way. The cashflow at the start is the amount I pay for the CD when I buy it. The cashflow at the end is the amount I receive for the CD when I sell it.

It is in fact possible to combine this formula with the one given earlier for the price of a CD, to give the following:

For a CD

Yield over holding period

$$= \left(\frac{\left(1 + \left(\text{purchase yield} \times \dfrac{\text{days from purchase to maturity}}{\text{year}}\right)\right)}{\left(1 + \left(\text{sale yield} \times \dfrac{\text{days from sale to maturity}}{\text{year}}\right)\right)} - 1 \right)$$

$$\times \frac{\text{year}}{\text{days held}}$$

Example 5

The dealer in Example 3, having purchased the CD as described in that example, then sells it again a week later, when it has only 23 days left to maturity, when yields are quoted as 5.07/5.17%.

This time, assuming that he is again the price-taker, he will deal on the other side of the price at 5.17% (the same rate at which he purchased the CD originally) – as a price-taker, he deals at the higher yield, which implies the lower price.

The amount he receives on the sale is:

$$\frac{\text{USD } 3,000,000 \times \left(1 + \left(0.0525 \times \frac{91}{360}\right)\right)}{\left(1 + \left(0.0517 \times \frac{23}{360}\right)\right)} = \text{USD } 3,029,804.88$$

The return he has made on his investment over the 7 days is as follows:

$$\frac{\text{Yield over the}}{\text{holding period}} = \left(\frac{\text{cashflow at the end}}{\text{cashflow at the start}} - 1\right) \times \frac{\text{year}}{\text{days held}}$$

$$= \left(\frac{3,029,804.88}{3,026,772.16} - 1\right) \times \frac{360}{7}$$

$$= 0.0515 = 5.15\%$$

Alternatively, using the formula given above:

$$\text{yield on holding a CD} = \left[\frac{\left(1 + \left(0.0517 \times \frac{30}{360}\right)\right)}{\left(1 + \left(0.0517 \times \frac{23}{360}\right)\right)} - 1\right] \times \frac{360}{7}$$

$$= 0.0515 = 5.15\%$$

Note that in Example 5, the dealer purchased the CD at a yield of 5.17% and sold it again later at the same yield of 5.17%, but that the yield he has earned by doing so is less than 5.17%. This will always be the case if he buys and sells at the same yield.

Money market yield of a bond in its last coupon period

The same idea we have used to value a CD can be used to value any security where there is only one cashflow left. Suppose, for example, that a dealer wishes to invest for 5 months in a security issued by Bank A. This could be because he considers that Bank A represents both a good yield and an acceptable credit risk.

Suppose that the dealer is able to choose between a CD previously issued by that bank which now has 5 months left to maturity and a bond issued by that bank several years ago, but which also now has

5 months left to maturity. From the investor's point of view, assuming that the two securities are equally liquid, he might be indifferent to whether he buys the first or the second. They both represent a single cashflow in 5 months' time. Therefore in valuing the bond, he could value it in exactly the same way as the CD, on the basis of a money market yield. There is more than one way of doing this. Our approach here is to calculate a money market yield which is exactly comparable with the yield on a money market instrument.

The bond market is outside the scope of this book. It is worth noting, however, that the normal convention for expressing the yield of a bond is slightly different from this. A bond price is also normally quoted excluding *accrued coupon* (a *clean price*), unlike a CD price which includes everything (a *dirty price*).

Example 6

An investor purchases a bond, face value EUR 10 million, which pays an annual coupon of 7%. The price he pays, including accrued coupon, is 104.98326 per 100 face value. There are 158 days left until maturity of the bond.

Almost all fixed-rate bonds pay a coupon which is calculated as a round amount, rather than on the basis of the exact number of calendar days in the coupon period. Therefore the coupon paid by the issuer of this bond at maturity will be exactly EUR 700,000 (=EUR 10 million × 7%), regardless of exactly how many days there have been since the last coupon was paid, or the effect of any non-business days at either end of the coupon period.

The cashflow which the investor is purchasing – face value plus coupon – is therefore EUR 10,700,000 in 158 days' time. The amount he is paying is EUR 10,498,326. Therefore the money market yield is:

$$\left(\frac{\text{cashflow at the end}}{\text{cashflow at the start}} - 1\right) \times \frac{\text{year}}{\text{days}} = \left(\frac{10,700,000}{10,498,326} - 1\right) \times \frac{360}{158}$$

$$= 0.04377 = 4.377\%$$

Breaking a fixed deposit

A fixed deposit is expected to be held to maturity. It is generally possible, however, for the depositor to break the deposit – that is, terminate it early – although the bank will usually charge the customer a penalty for this.

The bank wishes to make sure that it is not losing by repaying the deposit early. This can be achieved as follows:

- First, calculate the amount (principal plus interest) which it would have expected to repay on the normal maturity date of the deposit.
- Second, calculate how much the bank will need to borrow at current market rates, from now until that original maturity date, in order to repay that same amount as originally expected.

If the bank repays this amount to the depositor, it will be neither losing nor gaining. This amount is in fact the present value of the original maturing principal and interest. The rate of discount to be used is the rate at which the bank believes it could borrow new money, taking into account any spread over LIBOR which it typically pays.

Example 7

A customer places a deposit of GBP 1 million with you at 5.12% for 183 days. After 30 days, the customer asks to break the deposit. The interest rate at that time is 5.92/6.04% for 153 days. Your bank normally funds itself at around LIBOR plus 10 basis points. If you agree to break the deposit, how much cash might you agree to return to your customer?

The maturing proceeds of the deposit, if it is not broken, would be:

$$\text{GBP } 1,000,000 \times \left(1 + \left(0.0512 \times \frac{183}{365}\right)\right) = \text{GBP } 1,025,670.14$$

If you repay the cash early, you would need to refinance at around 6.14% (=6.04% + 0.10%). The present value of the maturing deposit at this rate of discount is:

$$\frac{\text{GBP } 1,025,670.14}{\left(1 + \left(0.0614 \times \frac{153}{365}\right)\right)} = \text{GBP } 999,934.30$$

You would therefore repay a total (including interest) of GBP 999,934.30 because, if you borrow this amount from a different source now at current rates, you will need to repay GBP 1,025,670.14 – i.e. the same amount that you originally expected to repay. You are therefore left in the same position as if the deposit had not been broken.

In practice, you might wish to protect yourself by taking a more pessimistic view on the rate at which you can refund yourself in the market, and therefore use an interest rate higher than 6.14% to discount to a present value.

The customer in this example receives back a total of less than he deposited. If interest rates had fallen rather than risen since the deposit had been made, the repayment amount calculated in this way would be rather higher, to the customer's advantage. However, in order to discourage customers from breaking deposits, the bank might agree to do so only on condition that the interest rate used for the calculation is unrealistically high.

The calculation used here is in fact the same as calculating the price of a CD – it is the present value of the maturing amount.

To calculate the total amount repayable when a fixed deposit is broken

First, calculate the principal plus interest due on the normal maturity date.

Second, calculate the present value of this, using the bank's funding rate.

CDs paying more than one coupon

Most CDs are short-term instruments paying interest only at maturity. Some CDs, however, are issued with a maturity of several years. In this case, interest is paid periodically – generally every 6 months or every year. The price for a CD paying more than one coupon will therefore depend on all the intervening coupons before maturity, valued at the current yield.

Suppose that a CD has several more coupons yet to be paid, the last of which will be paid on maturity together with the face value of the CD.

The pricing method is first to discount the final cashflow – the final coupon payment plus the face value of the CD – back to the previous coupon payment date, using the current yield as the rate of discount.

The result is then added to the coupon payment actually made on that date and the combined total is then discounted back again to the previous coupon payment date, also using the current yield as the rate of discount.

This new result is then again added to the coupon payment actually made on that date and the combined total again discounted back.

This process continues until the nearest coupon payment outstanding. The value thus reached is finally discounted back to the transaction settlement date.

Throughout the process, both the calculation of each coupon payment and each discounting are performed using the exact number of days in the relevant coupon period.

To value a CD with more than one coupon payment outstanding:

- Calculate each future cashflow
- Discount the final cashflow back to the previous coupon date, using the current yield as the rate of discount
- Add the coupon on that date and repeat the process until the nearest outstanding coupon
- Add that coupon and discount back to the settlement date

Example 8

A CD with face value USD 10 million and semi-annual coupons of 5.5% per annum is issued on 16 May 2000 with a maturity of 5 years. You purchase the CD on 20 August 2003 at a yield of 4.5%. What amount do you pay?

The previous coupon date was 16 May 2003. As 16 November 2003 and 16 May 2004 are both Sundays, the remaining coupon dates, lengths of coupon period and coupon amounts are as follows:

Coupon date	Days since previous coupon	Coupon payment
17 November 2003	185	USD 10 million $\times$ 0.056 $\times \dfrac{185}{360}$ = USD 287,777.78
17 May 2004	182	USD 10 million $\times$ 0.056 $\times \dfrac{182}{360}$ = USD 283,111.11
16 November 2004	183	USD 10 million $\times$ 0.056 $\times \dfrac{183}{360}$ = USD 284,666.67
16 May 2005	181	USD 10 million $\times$ 0.056 $\times \dfrac{181}{360}$ = USD 281,555.56

The final cashflow is therefore USD 10,281,555.56. Discounting this back 6 months at 4.5% gives a value of:

$$\frac{\text{USD } 10,281,555.56}{\left(1 + \left(0.045 \times \frac{181}{360}\right)\right)} = \text{USD } 10,054,081.96$$

Adding this to the 16 November 2004 coupon of USD 284,666.67 gives a total of USD 10,338,748.63. Discounting this back 6 months at 4.5% gives a value of:

$$\frac{\text{USD } 10,338,748.63}{\left(1 + \left(0.045 \times \frac{183}{360}\right)\right)} = \text{USD } 10,107,538.68$$

Adding this to the 17 May 2004 coupon of USD 283,111.11 gives a total of USD 10,390,649.79. Discounting this back 6 months at 4.5% gives a value of:

$$\frac{\text{USD } 10,390,649.79}{\left(1 + \left(0.045 \times \frac{182}{360}\right)\right)} = \text{USD } 10,159,520.69$$

Adding this to the 17 November 2003 coupon of USD 287,777.78 gives a total of USD 10,447,298.47. Discounting this back a further 89 days from 17 November 2003 to 20 August 2003 at 4.5% gives a value of:

$$\frac{\text{USD } 10,447,298.47}{\left(1 + \left(0.045 \times \frac{89}{360}\right)\right)} = \text{USD } 10,332,351.06$$

This is therefore the amount for which the CD can be purchased.

Exercises

1 You are quoted 4.50% for a 273-day deposit of GBP 2 million. What amount do you expect to receive back at the end of 9 months?

2 You lend EUR 10 million for 3 months at 4.28%, you lend EUR 3 million for 3 months at 4.23% and you borrow EUR 9 million for 3 months at 4.25%. What is your net position and your average rate?

3 A bank issues a CD with a face value of USD 5 million, a term of 181 days and a coupon of 4.7%.

(a) What are the total maturity proceeds of the CD?

(b) You buy this CD when it has only 129 days left until maturity, on a quote of 4.80%/4.85%. What amount do you pay for it?

(c) You then sell this same CD when it has only 122 days left until maturity, on a quote of 5.05/5.10%. What amount do you receive for it?

(d) Over the 7 days that you have held the CD, what yield have you earned on your investment?

(e) At what different yield would you need to have sold in (c) in order to have achieved an overall yield on the investment to you of 4.80%?

4 You are a dealer. A customer places a deposit of EUR 5 million with you at 4.64% for 92 days. After 61 days, the customer asks to break the deposit. Interest rates at the time are as follows. Your bank normally funds itself at around LIBOR plus 5 basis points. If you agree to break the deposit, how much cash might you return to your customer?

1 month	4.70/4.80%
2 months	4.65/4.75%
3 months	4.60/4.70%

Discount instruments

Discount instruments

Instruments which pay no coupon are known as discount instruments, because the amount paid for them is always less than the face value. This is so because, otherwise, the investor would earn a negative return. Commercial paper, for example, is a discount instrument.

Consider, for example, commercial paper issued for 91 days with a face value of EUR 10 million. On maturity, the investor receives only the face value of EUR 10 million. If the yield on the paper is 4.7%, the amount the investor will be willing to pay now for the paper is its present value calculated at 4.7%:

$$\text{Price paid} = \frac{\text{EUR } 10{,}000{,}000}{\left(1 + \left(0.047 \times \dfrac{91}{360}\right)\right)} = \text{EUR } 9{,}882{,}589.34$$

The idea that the amount paid is the present value is exactly the same here as in the previous chapter for coupon-bearing instruments. The difference in calculation arises only in that the coupon is zero here.

For a discount instrument

Maturity proceeds = face value

Amount paid

$$= \frac{\text{face value}}{\left(1 + \left(\text{yield} \times \dfrac{\text{days from settlement to maturity}}{\text{year}}\right)\right)}$$

Example 1

A dealer buys US dollar Euro-CP with face value USD 3 million, at a yield of 5.17%, when it is issued with 30 days' maturity. The amount he pays for it is:

$$\frac{\text{USD } 3,000,000}{\left(1 + \left(0.0517 \times \frac{30}{360}\right)\right)} = \text{USD } 2,987,130.45$$

7 days later, he sells it at a yield of 5.17%. It now has only 23 days to maturity, so the price he sells it for is:

$$\frac{\text{USD } 3,000,000}{\left(1 + \left(0.0517 \times \frac{23}{360}\right)\right)} = \text{USD } 2,990,123.46$$

The return he has made on his investment over the 7 days is given by the same formula as before:

Yield over the holding period

$$= \left(\frac{\text{cashflow at the end}}{\text{cashflow at the start}} - 1\right) \times \frac{\text{year}}{\text{days held}}$$

$$= \left(\frac{2,990,123.46}{2,987,130.45} - 1\right) \times \frac{360}{7} = 0.0515 = 5.15\%$$

In the last example, the yield earned over the holding period of 7 days was calculated as shown in the section on 'Calculating the yield on an investment or the cost of a borrowing' in Chapter 2. An alternative, as in the previous chapter, is to use the following formula:

For instruments quoted on a yield

Yield over holding period

$$= \left(\left(\frac{\left(1 + \left(\text{purchase yield} \times \dfrac{\text{days from purchase to maturity}}{\text{year}}\right)\right)}{\left(1 + \left(\text{sale yield} \times \dfrac{\text{days from sale to maturity}}{\text{year}}\right)\right)}\right) - 1\right)$$

$$\times \frac{\text{year}}{\text{days held}}$$

In the previous example, this gives as before:

$$\text{Yield over holding period} = \left(\frac{\left(1 + \left(0.0517 \times \frac{30}{360}\right)\right)}{\left(1 + \left(0.0517 \times \frac{23}{360}\right)\right)} - 1 \right) \times \frac{360}{7}$$

$$= 0.0515 = 5.15\%$$

Discount/true yield

For certain discount instruments in the USA and the UK, a further complication arises in the way the interest rate is generally quoted – as a *discount rate* instead of a yield.

With a yield, the investor in a security asks the question: "If I invest a certain amount at the beginning, how much extra will I receive by the end?" The answer is his yield on the investment, expressed as a proportion of the amount invested. For example, if he invests GBP 100 for one year and receives back a total of GBP 110 at the end of a year, he has earned GBP 10 extra. This represents 10% of the GBP 100 originally invested.

With a discount rate, however, the investor asks instead: "If I receive a certain amount back at the end, how much less will I need to invest at the beginning?" The answer is the discount amount on the investment. With the same investment as above, if he will receive back GBP 110 at the end of the year but only invests GBP 100 at the beginning, there is a discount amount of GBP 10. This represents 9.091% of the GBP 110 received at the end.

In this example, therefore, the yield is 10% but the discount rate is 9.091%. In general, the discount rate is the amount of discount expressed as a percentage per year of the face value, rather than as a percentage per year of the original amount paid.

The discount rate is always less than the corresponding yield. Any investment could be expressed either in terms of yield or in terms of discount rate. In practice, however, the market convention is to use yield in almost all financial markets worldwide, but to use discount rate in just five instruments. These are listed below.

Terminology can be confusing. What we are calling 'discount rate' is also known in the USA as 'discount yield' or even just 'yield'. When we use the term 'yield' in this book, we always mean yield as we have described – also known as 'true yield', or 'investment yield'; we never mean discount rate.

Using a discount rate, the amount to be paid for a particular discount instrument is as follows:

$$\text{Amount paid} = \text{face value} \times \left(1 - \left(\text{discount rate} \times \frac{\text{days}}{\text{year}}\right)\right)$$

Since the difference between the start amount and the end amount can in theory be expressed as either a yield or a discount rate, it is possible to express one in terms of the other. This is useful when it is necessary to compare an instrument quoted with a yield (for example, US dollar commercial paper issued internationally) with an instrument quoted with a discount rate (for example, US dollar commercial paper issued domestically in the USA).

For instruments quoted on a discount rate

Amount paid = face value

$$\times \left(1 - \left(\text{discount rate} \times \frac{\text{days from settlement to maturity}}{\text{year}}\right)\right)$$

$$\text{Yield} = \frac{\text{discount rate}}{\left(1 - \left(\text{discount rate} \times \frac{\text{days to maturity}}{\text{year}}\right)\right)}$$

$$\text{Discount rate} = \frac{\text{yield}}{\left(1 + \left(\text{yield} \times \frac{\text{days to maturity}}{\text{year}}\right)\right)}$$

Instruments quoted on a discount rate include Treasury bills, domestic CP and trade bills/BAs in the USA, and sterling Treasury bills and trade bills/BAs in the UK. However, all loans/fixed deposits and CDs in dollars and sterling are quoted on a yield. Note that domestic CP in the UK, and US dollar CP issued in the Euromarket (i.e. dollar Euro-commercial paper) are all quoted on a yield. Note also that while the Treasury-bills issued by the UK government in sterling are quoted on a discount rate, the Treasury-bills it issues in euros are quoted on a yield, as are other international instruments in euros.

Instruments quoted on a discount rate

USA:		UK:	
	T-bill		T-bill (sterling only)
	BA		BA
			CP

Example 2

A dealer buys US domestic CP with face value USD 3 million at a discount rate of 5.17%, when it is issued with 30 days' maturity. What is the yield?

$$\text{Yield} = \frac{\text{discount rate}}{\left(1 - \left(\text{discount rate} \times \dfrac{\text{days}}{\text{year}}\right)\right)}$$

$$= \frac{0.0517}{\left(1 - \left(0.0517 \times \dfrac{30}{360}\right)\right)}$$

$$= 0.05192 = 5.192\%$$

The amount the dealer pays for it is:

$$\text{USD } 3{,}000{,}000 \times \left(1 - \left(0.0517 \times \frac{30}{360}\right)\right)$$

$$= \text{USD } 2{,}987{,}075.00$$

Seven days later, he sells it, again at a discount rate of 5.17%. It now has only 23 days to maturity, so the price he sells it for is:

$$\text{USD } 3{,}000{,}000 \times \left(1 - \left(0.0517 \times \frac{23}{360}\right)\right)$$

$$= \text{USD } 2{,}990{,}090.83$$

The return he has made on his investment over the 7 days is given by the same formula as before:

Yield over the holding period

$$= \left(\frac{\text{cashflow at the end}}{\text{cashflow at the start}} - 1\right) \times \frac{\text{year}}{\text{days held}}$$

$$= \left(\frac{2{,}990{,}090.83}{2{,}987{,}075.00} - 1\right) \times \frac{360}{7}$$

$$= 0.0519 = 5.19\%$$

In the previous example, the yield earned over the holding period of 7 days was calculated as shown in the section on 'Calculating the yield on an investment or the cost of a borrowing' in Chapter 2. In this case of discount rates rather than yields, an alternative is to use instead the following formula:

For instruments quoted on a discount rate

Yield over holding period

$$= \left(\frac{\left(1 - \left(\begin{array}{c} \text{discount} \\ \text{rate on sale} \end{array} \times \dfrac{\text{days from sale to maturity}}{\text{year}} \right)\right)}{\left(1 - \left(\begin{array}{c} \text{discount rate} \\ \text{on purchase} \end{array} \times \dfrac{\begin{array}{c}\text{days from purchase}\\\text{to maturity}\end{array}}{\text{year}} \right)\right)} - 1 \right) \times \frac{\text{year}}{\text{days held}}$$

In the previous example, this gives as before:

$$\text{Yield over holding period} = \left(\frac{\left(1 - \left(0.0517 \times \dfrac{23}{360}\right)\right)}{\left(1 - \left(0.0517 \times \dfrac{30}{360}\right)\right)} - 1 \right) \times \frac{360}{7}$$

$$= 0.0519 = 5.19\%$$

In Example 1, the dealer originally purchased at a yield of 5.17%. However, when he sold the investment at the same yield of 5.17%, it turned out that the yield he earned over the holding period was in fact 5.15%. It is always true that if you buy at a particular yield and then sell later at the same yield, then the yield earned is less.

In Example 2, however, the dealer originally purchased at a discount rate of 5.17%, which was equivalent to a yield of 5.19%. In this case, when he sold the investment at the same discount rate of 5.17%, it turned out that the yield he earned over the holding period was the same 5.19% at which he had originally invested. It is always true that if you buy at a particular discount rate and then sell later at the same discount rate, then the yield earned is the same as the original equivalent yield.

If you buy at particular discount rate and later sell at the same discount rate, the yield earned over the holding period is the same as the purchase yield.

Bond-equivalent yields for US Treasury bills

For trading purposes, a government Treasury bond which has less than a year left to maturity may be just as acceptable to a money market trader as a Treasury bill with the same remaining maturity. As the method used for quoting yields generally differs between the two instruments, the rate quoted for Treasury bills in the USA is often converted to a bond-equivalent yield for comparison.

The bond-equivalent yield of a Treasury bill is defined as the coupon of a theoretical US Treasury bond, trading at par, with the same maturity date, which would give the same return as the bill.

We show below the formulas for calculating this. If the bill has 182 days or less until maturity, the calculation is the same conversion from discount rate to yield as we have already seen above, except that it is also then converted to a 365-day year.

If the bill has more than 182 days until maturity, however, the calculation must take account of the fact that the equivalent bond would pay a coupon during the period as well as at the end. In either case, if 29 February falls in the 12-month period starting on the purchase date, 365 is conventionally replaced by 366.

Bond-equivalent yield for US Treasury bill

If there are 182 days or less to maturity:

$$\text{Bond-equivalent yield} = \left(\frac{\text{discount rate}}{\left(1 - \left(\text{discount rate} \times \frac{\text{days}}{360}\right)\right)} \right) \times \frac{365}{360}$$

If there are more than 182 days to maturity:

Bond-equivalent yield

$$= \frac{\left(\left(\left(\frac{\text{days}}{365}\right)^2 + \left(2 \times \left(\frac{\text{days}}{365} - 0.5\right)\right) \times \left(\frac{1}{\left(1 - \left(\text{discount rate} \times \frac{\text{days}}{360}\right)\right)} - 1 \right) \right)^{0.5} - \left(\frac{\text{days}}{365}\right) \right)}{\left(\frac{\text{days}}{365} - 0.5\right)}$$

If 29 February falls in the 12-month period starting on the purchase date, replace 365 by 366.

Example 3

What is the bond-equivalent yield for a US Treasury bill with 48 days left to maturity and trading at a discount rate of 5.24% on 15 April?

$$\text{Bond-equivalent yield} = \left(\frac{0.0524}{\left(1 - \left(0.0524 \times \frac{48}{360}\right)\right)} \right) \times \frac{365}{360}$$

$$= 0.05350 = 5.35\%$$

What is the bond-equivalent yield for a US Treasury bill with 248 days left to maturity and trading at a discount rate of 5.24% on 13 October 2003?

Bond-equivalent yield

$$= \frac{\left(\left(\frac{248}{366}\right)^2 + \left(2 \times \left(\frac{248}{366} - 0.5\right)\right) \times \left(\frac{1}{\left(1 - \left(0.0524 \times \frac{248}{360}\right)\right)} - 1 \right) \right)^{0.5} - \left(\frac{248}{366}\right)}{\left(\frac{248}{366} - 0.5\right)}$$

$$= 0.05487 = 5.487\%$$

Effective rates and Norwegian Treasury bills

In Chapter 2 we introduced the idea of an effective interest rate – i.e. an annual equivalent interest rate. In Norway, Treasury bills are quoted on the basis of an effective yield. This gives the following formula for the price of a Norwegian Treasury bill:

$$\text{Amount paid} = \frac{\text{face value}}{\left((1 + \text{effective yield})^{\left(\frac{\text{days to maturity}}{365}\right)}\right)}$$

$$\text{Effective yield} = \left(\left(\frac{\text{face value}}{\text{amount paid}}\right)^{\left(\frac{365}{\text{days to maturity}}\right)} \right) - 1$$

The following formula converts the effective yield to a simple yield on a 365-day basis as quoted in other markets, in order to facilitate a comparison with other instruments. This can then be converted to a 360-day basis in the usual way if necessary.

Simple yield on 365-day basis

$$= \left((1 + \text{effective yield})^{\left(\frac{\text{days to maturity}}{365} \right)} - 1 \right) \times \frac{365}{\text{days to maturity}}$$

Example 4

You purchase a Norwegian Treasury bill, face value NOK 10 million, with 87 days left to maturity, at an effective yield of 6.73%. How much do you pay? What is the simple yield of this bill?

$$\text{Price paid} = \frac{\text{NOK } 10,000,000}{\left(1.0673^{\left(\frac{87}{365} \right)} \right)} = \text{NOK } 9,845,952.49$$

Simple yield (365-day basis)

$$= \left(1.0673^{\left(\frac{87}{365} \right)} - 1 \right) \times \frac{365}{87} = 0.06564 = 6.564\%$$

Exercises

1 You own ECP with face value USD 10 million. The paper was issued at a yield of 4.50% on 15 March for 59 days, maturing on 13 May.

   It is now 17 April and you wish to sell the paper for value 19 April (24 days left until maturity). You are quoted 4.30/4.35% for the paper. How much money will you receive on the sale?

2 You own US domestic CP with face value USD 10 million. The paper was issued at a discount rate of 4.50% on 15 March for 59 days, maturing on 13 May.

   It is now 19 April and you wish to sell the paper for value 19 April (24 days left until maturity). You are quoted 4.30/4.35% for the paper. How much money will you receive on the sale?

3   A US Treasury bill with 147 days left to maturity is quoted in the market at 4.97%. What is the bill's yield on a 365-day basis?

4   A UK Treasury bill with 83 days left to maturity has a yield of 4.5567%. At what discount rate would it be quoted?

5   You buy sterling commercial paper with 163 days left to maturity, face value GBP 10 million, at a yield of 5.1%. You sell it one week later at a yield of 5.15%. What yield per annum have you made over the week?

6   You buy a US Treasury bill with 163 days left to maturity, face value USD 10 million, at a discount rate of 5.1%. You sell it one week later at a discount rate of 5.15%. What yield per annum have you made over the week?

7   What is the bond-equivalent yield for a US Treasury bill with 190 days left to maturity, trading at a discount rate of 4.99% on 10 July 2003?

8   You sell a Norwegian Treasury bill, with 103 days left to maturity, at a price of NOK 98.08 per NOK 100 face value. At what effective yield have you sold?

9   Which has the higher yield – a Norwegian Treasury bill with an effective yield of 5.7%, or a US Treasury bill quoted at a discount rate of 5.5%? Both have 119 days left to maturity.

10 Place the following instruments in ascending order of yield, given the rate quoted for each. All the instruments have exactly 91 days left to maturity.

UK sterling Treasury bill	4.98%
UK euro Treasury bill	4.98%
Sterling domestic CP	5.10%
Sterling ECP	5.10%
US dollar Treasury bill	4.81%
US dollar domestic CP	4.93%
US dollar ECP	4.93%

6

Forward interest rates, FRAs and introduction to futures

Overview

Forward-forwards, forward rate agreements (FRAs) and futures are very closely linked instruments, all relating to an interest rate applied to some period which starts in the future. We shall outline them first and then examine each more closely.

- A forward-forward is a cash borrowing or deposit which starts on one forward date and ends on another forward date. The term, amount and interest rate are all fixed in advance. Someone who expects to borrow or deposit cash in the future can use this to remove any uncertainty relating to what interest rates will be when the time arrives.
- An FRA is an *off-balance sheet* instrument which can be used to achieve the same economic effect as a forward-forward. Someone who expects to borrow cash in the future can buy an FRA to fix in advance the interest rate on the borrowing. When the time to borrow arrives, he borrows the cash in the usual way. Under the FRA, which remains quite separate, he receives or pays the difference between the cash borrowing rate and the FRA rate, so

that he achieves the same net effect as with a forward-forward borrowing.

Similarly, an investor or other lender can use an FRA to protect the return on a future investment.

There is of course no need to have any underlying borrowing or investment when trading an FRA. In this way, an FRA an be used speculatively, to take a view on whether interest rates will rise or fall, and also in arbitrage strategies.

• A futures contract is similar to an FRA. Futures are, however, traded only on an exchange, and differ from FRAs in a variety of technical ways.

Pricing a forward-forward

Example 1

I will need to borrow dollars for a 3-month period, starting in 2 months' time. I believe that interest rates will rise over the next 2 months, so that if I wait, I will have a higher borrowing cost than if I could borrow now.

The dollar interest rate now for 2 months (61 days) is 5.6/5.7% and the rate for 5 months (153 days) is 5.3/5.4%.

If I borrow now for 5 months at 5.4% and simultaneously deposit the cash borrowed at 5.6% for 2 months, the position over the first 2 months is a net zero one. I have therefore synthetically created a net borrowing which begins in 2 months and ends in 5 months – that is, a forward-forward borrowing. All the cashflows are known in advance, so it must be possible to calculate the cost of borrowing over the 3-month forward period. This rate is in fact given by the formula below.

If I am a bank customer, I could more simply ask the bank to provide the forward-forward loan from 2 months to 5 months at an agreed rate, rather than construct it myself as in Example 1. However, the bank would be able to construct it in exactly the same way and then present it to me as a forward-forward loan: the bank borrows for 5 months, lends the cash in the interbank market for 2 months and then has the cash available to lend to me for the forward period from 2 months to 5 months.

Forward-forward rate

$$
= \left(\frac{\left(1 + \left(\begin{array}{c} \text{interest rate for} \\ \text{longer period} \end{array} \times \frac{\text{days in longer period}}{\text{year}} \right) \right)}{\left(1 + \left(\begin{array}{c} \text{interest rate for} \\ \text{shorter period} \end{array} \times \frac{\text{days in shorter period}}{\text{year}} \right) \right)} - 1 \right)
$$

$$
\times \frac{\text{year}}{\text{days difference}}
$$

In the example above, this formula gives a forward-forward rate of:

$$
\left(\frac{\left(1 + \left(0.054 \times \frac{153}{360} \right) \right)}{\left(1 + \left(0.056 \times \frac{61}{360} \right) \right)} - 1 \right) \times \frac{360}{(153 - 61)} = 0.05218 = 5.218\%
$$

Note that this formula for a theoretical forward-forward rate applies only for periods up to one year. A money market deposit for longer than one year typically pays interim interest after one year (or each six months). This extra cashflow must be taken into account in calculating a forward-forward rate for any period ending after one year.

Forward-forwards and FRAs are referred to by the beginning and end dates of the forward period, compared with the dealing date or *spot* value date. Thus the forward-forward described here is a '2v5' (or '2x5', or 2/5, or 'twos against fives'), meaning that the forward period starts 2 months from now and ends 5 months from now.

Break-even on a forward position

If a dealer has borrowed for a longer period than he has lent – for example, he has borrowed USD 10 million for 8 months and lent USD 10 million for two months – he is said to be *over-borrowed*, because at a future point (in 2 months' time in this case), his borrowing will be greater than his lending. He will therefore need to lend again in the future to square his book. Similarly, a dealer who has lent for a longer period than he has borrowed is said to be *over-lent*.

The forward-forward formula is useful for calculating the break-even rate which a dealer needs to achieve to cover such an unmatched position, because the forward-forward rate is exactly the rate which is consistent with the rate for the shorter period and the rate for the longer period.

Example 2

A dealer borrows USD 10 million for 8 months (244 days) at 4.95% and lends USD 10 million for 2 months (92 days) at 4.91%. At what 6-month rate does the dealer need to lend again in the future in order just to break even?

Break-even rate

$$= \left(\left(\frac{\left(1 + \left(\begin{array}{c} \text{interest rate for} \\ \text{longer period} \end{array} \times \begin{array}{c} \text{days in longer period} \\ \text{year} \end{array} \right) \right)}{\left(1 + \left(\begin{array}{c} \text{interest rate for} \\ \text{shorter period} \end{array} \times \begin{array}{c} \text{days in shorter period} \\ \text{year} \end{array} \right) \right)} \right) - 1 \right)$$

$$\times \frac{\text{year}}{\text{days difference}}$$

$$= \left(\left(\frac{\left(1 + \left(0.0495 \times \frac{244}{360} \right) \right)}{\left(1 + \left(0.0491 \times \frac{92}{360} \right) \right)} \right) - 1 \right) \times \frac{360}{152} = 0.04913 = 4.913\%$$

Forward rate agreement (FRA)

An FRA is an off-balance sheet agreement to make a settlement in the future which, when combined with a cash borrowing in the future, can be used to have the same economic effect as a forward-forward. It is an agreement to pay or receive, on an agreed future date, the difference between a fixed interest rate agreed at the outset and the interest rate actually prevailing at that future date, calculated on an agreed notional principal amount. The principal itself is not transferred in either direction.

Example 3

I will need to borrow cash for a 3-month period, starting in 2 months' time. I have an arrangement with a bank which will allow me to borrow at LIBOR plus 0.50%.

I believe that interest rates will rise over the next 2 months, so that if I wait, I will have a higher borrowing cost than if I could borrow now.

I therefore arrange a 2v5 FRA, whereby I will pay a fixed rate, which is agreed with the bank at 5.22%, and receive LIBOR for the 2v5 period.

The net result will be a cost fixed at 5.72%, as follows:

pay to the lending bank	LIBOR + 0.50%
receive in the FRA	LIBOR
pay in the FRA	5.22%.
net cost	5.72%

Although I do not know what LIBOR will be when the forward 3-month period starts, I know that the LIBOR I pay will be offset exactly by the LIBOR I receive.

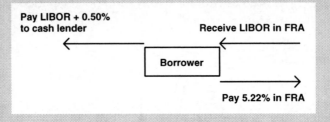

Pricing

In calculating a theoretical FRA price, we can apply exactly the same ideas as in the forward-forward calculation earlier. As we are not actually borrowing cash with the FRA, however, we could calculate using middle rates for both the 5-month and 2-month periods – rather than separate bid and offered rates. This calculation produces a theoretical FRA rate which is comparable to LIMEAN. By convention, however, FRAs are always settled against LIBOR rather than LIMEAN. We therefore need to add the difference between LIMEAN and LIBOR – generally around 0.05% – to this theoretical rate. An alternative approach is to base the theoretical price calculation on LIBOR for both periods, rather than LIMEAN. The result is different, but generally only very slightly.

Theoretical FRA rate

$$= \left(\frac{\left(1 + \left(\frac{\text{LIBOR for}}{\text{longer period}} \times \frac{\text{days in longer period}}{\text{year}} \right) \right)}{\left(1 + \left(\frac{\text{LIBOR for}}{\text{shorter period}} \times \frac{\text{days in shorter period}}{\text{year}} \right) \right)} - 1 \right)$$

$$\times \frac{\text{year}}{\text{days difference}}$$

In practice, a dealer generally prices an FRA from the futures market (see below) rather than from cash forward-forwards, because futures are very liquid and cash is expensive on the balance sheet. However, futures pricing theory still comes back to forward-forward pricing and in any case, FRAs in minor currencies where there is no futures market do need to be priced from, and hedged by, cash forward-forwards.

Having established a theoretical FRA price, a dealer would then build a spread round this price to give a two-way price with a bid and an offer. Based on this two-way price, a customer or bank wishing to pay the fixed FRA rate (as in Example 3) would pay the offer (the higher rate). This is known as buying an FRA. A customer wishing to receive the fixed FRA rate would receive the bid (the lower rate). This is known as selling an FRA. The terminology of buying or selling an FRA has nothing to do with the customer/bank relationship; it is merely a way of distinguishing who is the fixed rate payer from who is the fixed rate receiver.

> The buyer in an FRA is the party paying the FRA rate and receiving LIBOR.
> The seller in an FRA is the party receiving the FRA rate and paying LIBOR.

Settlement

The settlement on an FRA – of the difference between the FRA rate and LIBOR at the beginning of the period – is in fact settled net rather than gross. That is, the difference is paid in one direction or the other, rather than having two payments, one in each direction. By convention, this difference is paid or received at the beginning of the forward period to which it relates, rather than at the end as is normal for interest payments. It is therefore discounted to a present value (see Chapter 2) in order to calculate the actual settlement amount paid. Taking this into account, the settlement amount is as follows:

$$\text{FRA settlement amount} = \text{notional principal amount}$$

$$\times \frac{(\text{FRA rate-LIBOR}) \times \dfrac{\text{days in FRA period}}{\text{year}}}{\left(1 + \left(\text{LIBOR} \times \dfrac{\text{days in FRA period}}{\text{year}}\right)\right)}$$

The direction of payment depends simply on which of the two flows would be bigger if they were instead paid gross. This means:

The buyer pays the seller if LIBOR is fixed lower than the FRA rate.

The seller pays the buyer if LIBOR is fixed higher than the FRA rate.

The LIBOR used to calculate the settlement amount depends on the currency. With a sterling FRA, it is generally the LIBOR for the forward period that prevails on the *effective* date of the FRA – that is, the first day of the forward period. LIBOR is therefore fixed on the settlement date itself. This is also sometimes the case with Canadian dollars and Hong Kong dollars.

With an FRA in other currencies, it is generally the LIBOR that prevails two business days earlier. This is because the LIBOR for a currency other than sterling is for value spot. In domestic markets in other currencies, as opposed to the international market, FRAs can be traded for settlement against a same-day value reference, as with sterling.

Suppose that an FRA is traded for a regular period – for example, 7 months against 10 months. In the case of foreign currency FRAs, both the effective date (7 months) and the end date (10 months) are generally taken from the spot date. Because of non-business days, however, it might be that, when LIBOR is fixed, the period between the two dates turns out not to be a regular period. The following example demonstrates this.

Example 4

It is now Thursday 13 March 2003. I will need to borrow USD 1 million for a 3-month period, starting in 2 months' time. I purchase a 2v5 FRA at 5.22% on a notional amount of USD 1 million.

Spot value date is Monday 17 March. The 2-month value date is Monday 19 May (because 17 and 18 May are non-business days). The 5-month value date is Monday 18 August (because 17 August is a non-business day). I have therefore purchased an FRA from 19 May to 18 August (a 91-day period).

LIBOR on 15 May for the period from 19 May to 18 August is not exactly the 3-month LIBOR fixing on that day, because 3-month LIBOR would be from 19 May to 19 August. It is therefore necessary on 15 May to interpolate between the 2-month LIBOR and 3-month LIBOR fixings, although the difference would be rather slight. Assume that the LIBOR so calculated for the period 19 May to 18 August is 5.05%. The FRA settlement amount is then USD 424.31:

$$\text{USD } 1,000,000 \times \frac{(0.0522 - 0.0505) \times \dfrac{91}{360}}{\left(1 + \left(0.0505 \times \dfrac{91}{360}\right)\right)} = \text{USD } 424.31$$

Because I purchased the FRA and rates went down, I will pay the FRA settlement rather than receive it.

Assuming that on 15 May, I arrange a 3-month borrowing of USD 1 million, this would normally be from 19 May to 19 August, so that, as well as being based on a slightly different LIBOR from the FRA settlement, the borrowing would be for one day longer than the FRA. It would have been possible instead to have arranged the FRA originally for the exact dates I wanted.

FRA periods longer than one year

If the period of the FRA is longer than one year, the corresponding LIBOR rate used for settlement relates to a period where interest is conventionally paid at the end of each year as well as at maturity. A 6v24 FRA, for example, covers a period from 6 months to 24 months and will be settled against an 18-month LIBOR rate at the beginning of the FRA period.

An 18-month deposit would, however, typically pay interest at the end of one year and again after 18 months. As FRA settlements are paid at the beginning of the period on a discounted basis, each of these amounts needs to be discounted separately. Strictly, the net settlement payment calculated for the end of 18 months should be discounted at an appropriate compounded 18-month rate and the net settlement amount calculated for the end of the first year should be discounted at 1-year LIBOR. In practice, the FRA settlement LIBOR is generally used for both. The final discounted settlement amount is therefore as follows:

For periods longer than a year but less than 2 years

FRA settlement amount = notional principal amount

$$\times \left(\frac{(\text{FRA rate-LIBOR}) \times \dfrac{\text{days of FRA period in first year}}{\text{year}}}{\left(1 + \left(\text{LIBOR} \times \dfrac{\text{days of FRA period in first year}}{\text{year}}\right)\right)} \right.$$

$$\left. + \left(\frac{(\text{FRA rate-LIBOR}) \times \dfrac{\text{days of FRA period in second year}}{\text{year}}}{\left(1 + \left(\text{LIBOR} \times \dfrac{\text{days of FRA period in first year}}{\text{year}}\right)\right) \times \left(1 + \left(\text{LIBOR} \times \dfrac{\text{days of FRA period in second year}}{\text{year}}\right)\right)} \right) \right)$$

This same principle can be applied to the settlement of FRAs covering any period.

Introduction to futures

In general, a *futures* contract in any market is a contract in which the commodity being bought and sold is considered as being delivered (even though this may not physically occur) at some future date rather than immediately – hence the name. The significant differences between a futures contract and a *forward* arise in two ways.

Firstly, a futures contract is traded on a particular exchange (although two or more exchanges might trade identically specified contracts). A forward, however, which is also a deal for delivery on a future date, is dealt *over the counter* (*OTC*) – a deal made between any two parties, but not on an exchange.

Secondly, futures contracts are generally standardized, while forwards are not. The specifications of each futures contract are laid down precisely by the relevant exchange and vary from instrument to instrument and from exchange to exchange. Some contracts, for example, specifically do not allow for the instrument to be delivered; although their prices are calculated as if future delivery does take place, the contracts must be reversed before the notional delivery date, thereby capturing a profit or a loss. Short-term interest rate futures (*STIR* futures), for example, cannot be delivered.

The theory underlying the pricing of a futures contract depends on the underlying instrument on which the contract is based. For a futures contract based on 3-month interest rates, the pricing is therefore based on the same forward-forward pricing theory explained earlier.

Example 5

3-month EURIBOR futures contract traded on LIFFE:

Exchange: LIFFE (London International Financial Futures and Options Exchange).

Underlying: The basis of the contract is a 3-month deposit of EUR 1 million based on an ACT/360 year.

Delivery: It is not permitted for this contract to be delivered; if a trader buys such a contract, he cannot insist that, on the future delivery date, his counterparty makes arrangements for him to have a deposit for 3 months from then onwards at the interest rate agreed. Rather, the trader must reverse his futures contract by delivery, thereby taking a profit or loss.

Delivery months: The nearest 3 months following dealing and March, June, September and December thereafter.

Delivery day: First business day after the Last Trading Day.

Last trading day: 10.00 a.m. 2 business days prior to the third Wednesday of the delivery month.

Settlement price: On the last day of trading – usually the third Monday of the month – LIFFE declares an 'exchange delivery settlement price' (EDSP) which is the closing price at which any contracts still outstanding will be automatically reversed. The EDSP is 100 minus the European Bankers Federation/ACI 3-month offered rate (EURIBOR) at 11:00 a.m. Brussels time.

Price: The price is determined by the free market and is quoted as an index rather than an as interest rate. The index is expressed as 100 minus the implied interest. Thus a price of 94.52 implies an interest rate of 5.48% (100 − 94.52 = 5.48).

Price movement: Prices are quoted in units of 0.005. This minimum movement is called a tick.

Profit and loss value: The P&L is defined as being calculated on exactly 3/12 of a year, regardless of the number of days in a calendar quarter. The profit or loss on a single contract is therefore:

$$\text{Contract amount} \times \text{price movement} \times \frac{3}{12}$$

Therefore the value of a 1 basis point movement is EUR 25.00 and the value of a 1 tick movement (the tick value) is EUR 12.50:

$$\text{EUR 1 million} \times 0.01\% \times \frac{3}{12} = \text{EUR 25.00}$$

$$\text{EUR 1 million} \times 0.005\% \times \frac{3}{12} = \text{EUR 12.50}$$

There are relatively minor differences between futures exchanges, and even between different STIR contracts on the same exchange:

- **Underlying** The typical contract specification for short-term interest rate futures is for a 3-month interest rate, although 1-month contracts also exist in some currencies on some exchanges (for example, US dollar and euro futures contracts). The precise specification varies from exchange to exchange but is in practice for exactly one quarter of a year (or exactly one twelfth of a year for 1-month contracts). Thus settlement on the sterling 3-month interest rate futures contract traded on LIFFE, is effectively equivalent to $91\frac{1}{4}$ days' settlement because sterling is based on a year of 365 days:

$$\frac{91\frac{1}{4}}{365} = \frac{3}{12}$$

The size of the contract varies. For example, the US dollar and euro 3-month contracts are USD 1 million and EUR 1 million, the US dollar and euro 1-month contracts are USD 3 million and EUR 3 million, the sterling 3-month contract is GBP 500,000 and the yen 3-month contract is JPY 100 million.

- **Delivery date** STIR contracts worldwide are generally based on the delivery month cycle of March, June, September and December as described above. Some contracts include *serial months* (as in the example above) but others do not. Serial months are additional delivery months other than these four, added so that the three nearest possible months are always available. For example, on 5 June, the delivery months available would be June, July, August, September, December, March.... On 25 July, the delivery months available would be August, September, October, December, March....

  In the case of sterling futures, both the last trading day and the LIBOR fixing used for settlement are the third Wednesday of the delivery month (or the next following business day), rather than two business days earlier.

- **Trading** Trading times vary. Some contracts are traded by open outcry (see below) – notably on the *IMM* (the International Monetary Market, the financial sector of the Chicago Mercantile Exchange (*CME*)) – and some are traded electronically.

- **Price movement** Tick sizes, and hence tick values, vary. For example, the minimum price movement on sterling is 1 basis point. The minimum price movement for US dollars varies from $\frac{1}{4}$ basis point for the nearest-dated futures contact, through $\frac{1}{2}$ basis point for subsequent ones, to 1 basis point for later ones.

- **Settlement price** The settlement price varies according to both currency and exchange.

Example 6

A dealer expects interest rates to fall (futures to rise) and takes a speculative position. He therefore buys 20 EUR 1-month futures contracts at 95.27. He closes them out subsequently at 95.20. What is his profit or loss?

The price has fallen, so he makes a loss of EUR 3,500:

$$\text{Number of contracts} \times \text{contract amount} \times \text{price movement} \times \frac{1}{12}$$

$$= 20 \times \text{EUR } 3,000,000 \times 0.07\% \times \frac{1}{12} = \text{EUR } 3,500$$

Short-term interest rate futures

$$\text{Price} = 100 - (\text{implied forward-forward interest rate} \times 100)$$

Profit on a long position in a 3-month contract

$$= \text{contract amount} \times \frac{(\text{sale price} - \text{purchase price})}{100} \times \frac{3}{12}$$

The mechanics of futures

Market participants

The users of an exchange are its members and their customers. An exchange also has *locals*, private traders dealing only for their own account. Each member may enter into transactions either on his own account or, if he is a *public order member*, also on behalf of customers. Certain members may also act as floor dealers executing transactions on behalf of other members.

Open outcry versus screen-trading

There are two methods of dealing. The first, traditional, method is *open outcry*, whereby the buyer and seller deal face to face in public in the exchange's trading pit. This should ensure that a customer's order is always transacted at the best possible rate and ensures complete transparency of all dealing. The second method is electronic screen-trading, designed to simulate open outcry but with the advantage of lower costs and wider access. Some exchanges use only screen-based trading and there is a general trend away from open outcry because of its higher costs.

Clearing

The futures exchange is responsible for administering the market, but all transactions are cleared through a clearing house, which may be separately owned. On LIFFE, for example, this function is performed by the London Clearing House (LCH). Following confirmation of a transaction, the clearing house substitutes itself for each counter-party and becomes the seller to every buyer and the buyer to every seller.

Only clearing members of an exchange are entitled to clear their transactions directly with the clearing house. In order to become a clearing member, certain conditions set by the exchange and the clearing house have to be satisfied, including a minimum net worth requirement. Non-clearing members have to clear all their transactions through a clearing member.

Margin requirements

In order to protect the clearing house, clearing members are required to place collateral with it for each deal transacted. This collateral is called *initial margin*.

Members are then debited or credited each day with *variation margin* which reflects the day's loss or profit on contracts held. Customers, in turn, are required to pay initial margin and variation margin to the member through whom they have cleared their deal. The initial margin is intended to protect the clearing house for the short period until a position can be revalued and variation margin called for if necessary. As variation margin is paid each day, the initial margin is relatively small in relation to the potential price movements over a longer period.

The calculation of variation margin is equivalent to *marking to market* – that is, revaluing a futures contract each day at the closing price. The variation margin required is the tick value multiplied by the number of ticks price movement since the close the previous day. For example, if the tick value is EUR 12.50 on each contract, and the price moves from 94.730 to 94.215 (a fall of 103 ticks), the loss on a long futures contract is EUR (12.50×103) = EUR 1,287.50. Depending on the size of initial margin already placed with the exchange, and the exchange's current rules, a variation margin may not be called for below a certain level.

Initial margin requirements need to be funded by members for as long as positions are held open. It is therefore in the interests of promoting market liquidity to keep this margin as low as possible while maintaining adequate protection for the clearing house. For example, the LCH's system for calculating margin, known as SPAN (standard portfolio analysis of risk), recognizes that a combination of futures (and options) may have less risk than the sum of the risks attached to each element of the position individually, and therefore require less margin.

Closing out

A futures position can be closed out by means of an exactly offsetting transaction. Contracts which are not settled before maturity are required to be reversed automatically at maturity and the price difference paid or received.

All contracts are completely *fungible*; once a purchase of a certain quantity of a particular contract is added to an existing holding of the same contract, there is no distinction whatever between the two purchases; they simply become a single, larger holding of the contract.

Limit up/down

Some markets impose limits on trading movements in an attempt to prevent wild price fluctuations and hence limit risk to some extent.

Basis

In practice, the actual futures price trading in the market is unlikely to be exactly the same as the fair theoretical value which can be calculated according to the underlying cash market forward-forward. The difference between the actual price and the theoretical fair price is termed the *value basis*.

Basis is the difference between what the futures price would be, based on the current cash interest rate, and the actual futures price. This difference should tend towards zero on the last trading day for the futures contract.

Basis risk is the risk arising from the basis on a futures position. Suppose, for example, that on 2 April a futures trader sells a 1v4 FRA to a customer which will settle on 4 May and that he hedges this by selling futures contracts for delivery on 18 June. The trader cannot be perfectly hedged because on 4 May the cash market 3-month LIBOR against which the FRA will be settled will not necessarily have moved since 2 April to the same extent as the futures price. He thus has a basis risk.

Value basis = theoretical futures price – actual futures price
Basis = implied cash price – actual futures price
Basis risk is the risk arising from the basis

Example 7

It is now mid-February and the current 3-month GBP LIBOR is 5.32%; the current June futures price is 94.37 and the theoretical June futures price based on the current cash market is 94.39.

Value basis = 94.39 – 94.37 = 0.02 = 2 basis points

Basis = (100 – 5.32) – 94.37 = 94.68 – 94.37 = 0.31

= 31 basis points

Futures compared with FRAs

It is worth summarizing the differences between an FRA and a futures contract:

- **Standardization versus flexibility** For each futures contract, the amount, delivery date and period are all standardized. With an FRA, they are entirely flexible.
- **Margin versus credit risk** Dealing in futures requires the payment of collateral (initial margin) as security. In addition, variation margin is paid or received each day to reflect the day's loss or profit on contracts held. The margin system ensures that the exchange clearing house is generally fully protected against the risk of default. There is therefore usually virtually no credit risk in dealing futures. When trading OTC, however, professional traders usually deal on the basis of credit lines, with no security required.
- **Settlement** An important practical difference between FRAs and futures is in the settlement mechanics. An FRA settlement is paid at the beginning of the forward period, and the settlement formula incorporates discounting to a present value. The futures settlement – the profit or loss on the contract – is also all settled by the same date, via the variation margin payments made during the period from transaction until the futures delivery date. However, in most futures markets, this settlement is not discounted. A 90-day FRA is not therefore exactly matched by an offsetting futures contract even if the amounts and dates are the same.
- **Liquidity and spread** Standardization and transparency generally ensure a liquid market in futures contracts, together with narrower spreads between bid and offer than in FRAs. For delivery dates far in the future, on the other hand, there may be insufficient liquidity in the futures market, whereas an FRA price might be available.
- **Underlying commodity** Futures contracts are not available in all currencies, whereas an FRA might be available, albeit at an unattractive price.
- **Taking a position** FRAs and futures are in opposite directions. A buyer of an FRA will profit if interest rates rise. A buyer of a futures contract will profit if interest rates fall. If a trader sells an FRA to a counterparty, he might therefore also sell a futures contract to cover his position.

The yield curve

In Chapter 3 we discussed the yield curve – how interest rates vary with term to maturity.

Rather than this normal yield curve, a more useful curve to look at might be one that shows what the market expects rates to be at certain times in the future. For example, what is the 3-month rate now, what will the 3-month rate be after 1 month, after 2 months, after 3 months etc.? Given enough such rates, it is in fact possible to work backwards to construct the normal yield curve.

Suppose, for example, that the 3-month rate now is 5.0% and the market expects that rates will fall slightly during the next 3 months – so that at the end of 3 months, the new 3-month rate will be 4.94%. Given these data, what should the 6-month rate be now?

The answer must be the rate achieved by taking the 3-month rate now, compounded with the expected 3-month rate in 3 months' time; otherwise there would be an expected profit in going long for 3 months and short for 6 months, or vice versa, and the market would tend to move the rates. In this way, the 6-month rate now can be calculated using a strip (see Chapter 2):

$$\left(\left(\left(1+\left(0.0500\times\frac{91}{360}\right)\right)\times\left(1+\left(0.0494\times\frac{92}{360}\right)\right)-1\right)\times\frac{360}{183}\right.$$

$$= 0.0500 = 5.00\%$$

If we now work in the other direction, we would find that the 3v6 forward-forward rate is 4.94% as expected:

$$\left(\frac{\left(1+\left(0.0500\times\frac{183}{360}\right)\right)}{\left(1+\left(0.0500\times\frac{91}{360}\right)\right)}-1\right)\times\frac{360}{92}=0.0494=4.94\%$$

This shows that a flat short-term yield curve – in our example, the 3-month and 6-month rates are the same at 5.00% – does not imply that the market expects interest rates to remain stable. Rather, it expects them to fall.

An important point here is to consider the question of which comes first. Are forward-forward rates (and hence FRA rates and futures prices) the mathematical result of the yield curve? Or are the market's expectations of future rates (i.e. forward-forwards, FRAs and futures) the starting point, and from these it is possible to create the yield curve? The question is a circular one to some extent, but market traders increasingly look at constructing a yield curve from expected future rates for various periods and maturities – in other words, the futures market is the driving force.

Applications of FRAs and futures

As with any instrument, FRAs may be used for hedging, speculating or arbitrage, depending on whether they are taken to offset an existing position or taken as new positions themselves.

Hedging

As we have discussed above, a future borrower wishing to hedge against the possibility of higher interest rates would buy an FRA or sell futures. A future investor or lender wishing to hedge against the possibility of lower interest rates would sell an FRA or buy futures.

Example 8

A dealer has lent USD 3 million for 1 month and borrowed USD 3 million for 9 months. He is therefore over-borrowed and wishes to hedge this position with an FRA.

1v9 FRAs are quoted to him as 4.50/4.60%. He therefore sells an FRA at 4.50% and, after 1 month rolls over the lending at LIBID. The net result will be as follows:

earn on rollover	LIBID
pay in the FRA	LIBOR
receive in the FRA.	4.50%
net income	4.50% – spread between LIBID and LIBOR

In this case, the result is not known exactly because FRAs are always priced and settled against LIBOR but the rollover will be at LIBID. The dealer can estimate, however, what the spread is likely to be.

In practice, the amount of the FRA dealt will probably be USD 3 million. If the dealer wishes to hedge the position exactly however, he can calculate the maturing amount of the lending at the end of 1 month, including principal and interest. This is the amount which he will have available to relend at that time, and is therefore the amount to be protected by the FRA if he wishes to be precise.

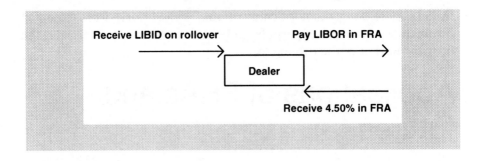

In Chapter 2 we used a strip to calculate a borrower's overall cost when he rolls over a loan. We have repeated the strip formula below. Exactly the same approach works when using FRAs or futures, as in the next example.

Creating a strip

The simple interest rate for a period up to one year

$$
= \left(
\begin{array}{l}
\left(1 + \left(\text{first interest rate} \times \dfrac{\text{days in first period}}{\text{year}}\right)\right) \\
\times \left(1 + \left(\text{second interest rate} \times \dfrac{\text{days in second period}}{\text{year}}\right)\right) \\
\times \ldots \ldots \\
\times \left(1 + \left(\text{last interest rate} \times \dfrac{\text{days in last period}}{\text{year}}\right)\right) - 1
\end{array}
\right)
$$

$$
\times \frac{\text{year}}{\text{total days}}
$$

Example 9

It is now mid-September and an investor wishes to deposit USD 1 million for nine months. Given the following rates, and assuming that he can always place cash at LIBID, what is the best way of doing so?

3 months (91 days)	5.23/5.33%
6 months (181 days)	5.25/5.35%
9 months (273 days)	5.25/5.35%
3v6 FRA	5.28/5.33%
6v9 FRA	5.24/5.29%
December futures	94.68/94.69
March futures	94.77/94.78

If the 3v6 period is covered separately, it is better to buy December futures at 94.69 (implied interest rate 5.31%) than to sell an FRA at 5.28%.

If the 6v9 period is covered separately, it is better to sell an FRA at 5.24% than to buy March futures at 94.78 (implied interest rate 5.22%).

It is important to remember that, even for an investor, an FRA or a futures contract is still settled against LIBOR, not LIBID. If the investor covers the 3v6 period with futures at 5.31%, for example, his return for that period will not be 5.31% but rather 5.31% less the LIBID/LIBOR spread. If this is 10 basis points, his return will be only 5.21% for that period. Similarly, if he covers the 6v9 period with an FRA, his return would be say 5.14%, not 5.24%

The choices are therefore reduced to:

- Deposit 9-month cash at 5.25%.
- Deposit 6-month cash at 5.25%, sell a 6v9 FRA at 5.24% and roll over the deposit at LIBID after 6 months, to give a compound return of 5.259%:

$$\left(\left(1 + \left(0.0525 \times \frac{181}{360}\right)\right) \times \left(1 + \left(0.0514 \times \frac{92}{360}\right)\right) - 1\right)$$

$$\times \frac{360}{273} = 0.05259 = 5.259\%$$

- Deposit 3-month cash at 5.23%, buy December futures at 5.31%, sell a 6v9 FRA at 5.24% and roll over the deposit at LIBID after 6 months and again after 9 months, to give a compound return of 5.262%:

$$\left(\begin{array}{c}\left(\left(1 + \left(0.0523 \times \frac{91}{360}\right)\right) \times \left(1 + \left(0.0521 \times \frac{90}{360}\right)\right)\right) \\ \times \left(1 + \left(0.0514 \times \frac{92}{360}\right)\right) - 1\end{array}\right)$$

$$\times \frac{360}{273} = 0.05262 = 5.262\%$$

Of these, the last is the best, although the difference is so small that the administrative burden, and uncertainty of cashflow timing, arising from the futures trade might well make the strategy not worth while. On the other hand, there could be an advantage from the reduced credit risk and capital adequacy requirements compared with a straightforward 9-month deposit.

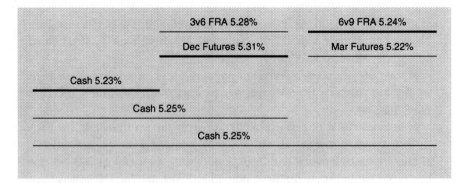

Hedging an FRA position with futures

We have already mentioned that a trader is likely to generate an FRA price from futures prices rather than from cash forward-forwards. Similarly, he is likely to hedge the resulting position by buying or selling futures.

If the FRA period coincides exactly with one futures period, then the dealer can hedge the FRA with that futures contract – if he is long of FRAs, then he buys futures to hedge; if he is short of FRAs then he sells futures to hedge. He can price the FRA as the interest rate implied by the futures price, together with an appropriate bid/offer spread.

Example 10

A dealer sells an FRA for GBP 12 million for a 3-month period from mid-March to mid-June.

The number of futures contracts used for the hedge should be such that a 1 basis point change has equal but opposite effects on the FRA position and the futures hedge. Ignoring exact day counts and the present value component of the FRA settlement formula, the profit or loss on the FRA arising from a 1 basis point change in rates would be:

$$\text{GBP 12 million} \times 0.01\% \times \frac{3}{12} = \text{GBP 300}$$

The value of 1 basis point on a sterling futures contract is GBP 12.50. Therefore the dealer sells 24 March futures contracts as a hedge:

$$\frac{\text{GBP 300}}{\text{GBP 12.50}} = 24$$

If the FRA period coincides with a strip of futures, then he hedges with a strip of futures.

Example 11

A dealer buys from a customer a GBP 12 million FRA for the 9-month period from mid-September to mid-June. Futures prices at the time are:

September: 95.36 (implied rate 4.64%)
December: 95.43 (implied rate 4.57%)
March   95.65 (implied rate 4.35%)

The interest rate implied by the strip of futures is 4.57%:

$$\left(\left(\left(1 + \left(0.0464 \times \frac{91}{365} \right) \right) \times \left(1 + \left(0.0457 \times \frac{90}{365} \right) \right) \times \left(1 + \left(0.0435 \times \frac{92}{365} \right) \right) - 1 \right) \times \frac{365}{273} \right)$$

$$= 0.0459 = 4.59\%$$

The dealer will therefore quote a rate for the FRA of 4.59% less a spread. He hedges the position by buying 24 September contracts, 24 December contracts and 24 March contracts). When the FRA is settled in mid-September, the September futures contract expires at the same time and he closes out the December and March contracts.

If the FRA period does not coincide exactly with futures periods, however, the dealer must use overlapping futures contracts. Suppose, for example, that the FRA is for GBP 12 million for a 6-month period from mid-April to mid-October. This could be hedged by a combination of some March futures, some June futures and some September futures (see Figure 6.1).

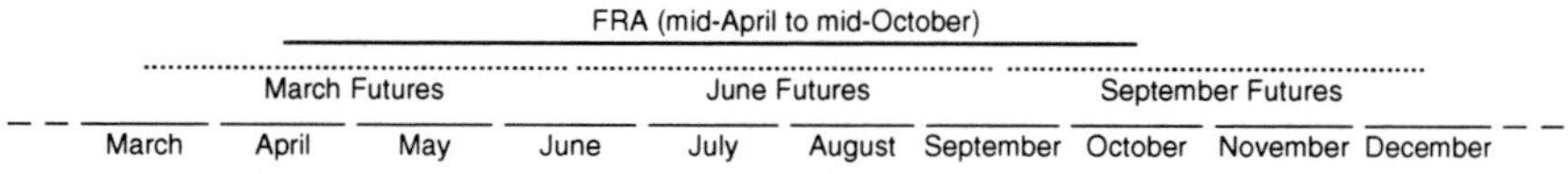

Figure 6.1

This period overlaps 2 months out of 3 of the March futures contract (i.e. mid-April to mid-June, 3 months out of 3 of the June contract (mid-June to mid-September) and 1 month out of 3 of the September contract (mid-September to mid-October). For each futures contract where the overlap is complete, the hedge should be complete – i.e. 24 contracts. For each end where the overlap is not complete, the hedge should be pro-rata. Therefore the hedge should be 16 March contracts, 24 June contracts and 8 September contracts.

The total number of futures contracts used for the hedge in this case should still be such that a 1 basis point change has equal but opposite effects on the FRA position and the futures hedge. The approximate profit or loss on the FRA arising from 1 basis point change in rates in this case would be:

$$\text{GBP 12 million} \times 0.01\% \times \frac{6}{12} = \text{GBP 600}$$

The number of futures contracts required for the hedge is therefore 48:

$$\frac{\text{GBP 600}}{\text{GBP 12.50}} = 48$$

This agrees with the hedge of 16 March contracts, 24 June contracts and 8 September contracts.

Example 12

In January, a dealer buys a 4v9 FRA from a customer for the 5-month period from 12 May to 12 October for EUR 10 million and needs to hedge this with futures.

If the FRA were for a 3-month period, the approximate value of a 1 basis point change on the FRA would be EUR 250:

$$\text{EUR } 10,000,000 \times 0.01\% \times \frac{3}{12} = \text{EUR 250}$$

The value of a 1 basis point change on a single EUR futures contract is EUR 25. Therefore 10 contracts would be required. However, the FRA period is in fact 5 months and overlaps approximately 5 weeks out of 12 of the March futures period, all of the June futures period and approximately 3 weeks out of 12 of the September futures period (see Figure 6.2).

		FRA (12 May to 12 October)							
	March Futures			June Futures			September Futures		
March	April	May	June	July	August	September	October	November	December

Figure 6.2

The hedge required is therefore 4.2 (= approximately $\frac{5}{12} \times 10$) March contracts, 10 June contracts and 2.5 (= approximately $\frac{3}{12} \times 10$) September contracts.

The approximate value of a 1 basis point change on the 5-month FRA would be EUR 417:

$$\text{EUR } 10,000,000 \times 0.01\% \times \frac{5}{12} = \text{EUR } 417$$

The total number of contracts required for the hedge is therefore 16.7:

$$\frac{\text{EUR } 417}{\text{EUR } 25} = 16.7$$

As futures must be traded in round amounts, the dealer therefore buys 4 March contracts, 10 June contracts and 3 September contracts.

In mid-March, the hedge must be adjusted because the March futures contracts expire. They are therefore replaced by 4 more June contracts. This creates a bias, however. The FRA is for a period starting in mid-May but the futures strip is for a period starting in mid-June. The hedge is satisfactory if the forward yield curve moves up or down in parallel. However, if it also twists anti-clockwise, the loss on the FRA position could be greater than the profit on the futures hedge (or the profit on the FRA less than the loss on the futures). In order to reduce this risk, the dealer could superimpose a further hedge, by buying a further 4 June contracts and selling 4 September contracts. This is essentially the same strategy as a spread – see below. He would then be left with a hedge of long 18 June contracts and short 1 September contract.

On 10 May, when LIBOR is fixed for the FRA settlement, all the futures contracts are closed.

The hedge in the previous example is not perfect, for various reasons:

- Futures contracts are for standardized notional amounts only.
- Futures profit/loss is based on exactly $\frac{3}{12}$ year, rather than 90, 91 or 92 calendar days etc.
- FRA settlements are discounted but futures settlements are not and also the timing of the futures variation margin cashflows is unknown.
- There is basis risk because the futures dates do not coincide with the FRA date.

Quoting for fixed deposits with delayed interest settlement

A fixed deposit for longer than 1 year conventionally pays interest at the end of each year and then at maturity. Sometimes a customer asks for all the interest to be paid at maturity instead. Effectively in this case, the bank is keeping the interim interest payments, reinvesting them until maturity, and then giving them to the customer. In quoting to the customer in such a case, account must therefore be taken of the rate at which it is possible to reinvest the interim cashflows. Since this reinvestment rate can be fixed in advance by using FRAs or futures, the FRA or futures rates can be used for the calculation.

Example 13

You are a dealer. You quote a customer 5.13% for a deposit of GBP 1 million for 18 months, with interest paid at the end of 1 year and again at maturity. The customer asks to have all the interest paid at the end and asks for a quote on that basis instead. What rate do you quote? 12v18 FRAs are currently quoted at 4.55/4.65%. The 1-year period has 365 days and the 18-month period has 548 days.

Effectively, you will need to take the interest amount at the end of 1 year and invest it for 6 months – which you can protect at the FRA bid rate of 4.55% – and then add it to the remaining interest due at the end of 18 months.

The interest amount normally due at the end of 365 days is:

$$\text{GBP } 1,000,000 \times 0.0513 \times \frac{365}{365} = \text{GBP } 51,300.00$$

Reinvest this amount of GBP 51,300 for the remaining 183 days at 4.55%, to give a total of:

$$\text{GBP } 51,300 \left(1 + \left(0.0455 \times \frac{183}{365}\right)\right) = \text{GBP } 52,470.27$$

The interest amount normally due at the end of 548 days is:

$$\text{GBP } 1{,}000{,}000 \times 0.0513 \times \frac{183}{365} = \text{GBP } 25{,}720.27$$

The total interest therefore payable at the maturity is:

$$\text{GBP } 52{,}470.27 + \text{GBP } 25{,}720.27 = \text{GBP } 78{,}190.54$$

This represents an interest rate of:

$$\frac{78{,}190.54}{1{,}000{,}000} \times \frac{365}{548} = 0.05208 = 5.208\%$$

Speculation

The most basic trading strategy is to speculate on whether the cash interest rate when the forward period begins is higher or lower than the FRA rate or implied futures rate. If the trader expects interest rates to rise, he buys an FRA or sells a futures contract; if he expects rates to fall, he sells an FRA or buys a futures contract. In example 6, we considered speculation using futures contracts. Here is the same strategy using FRAs:

Example 14

On 15 May, a dealer expects interest rates to fall and takes a speculative position. He therefore sells a 2v3 FRA (from 17 July to 17 August) for EUR 60 million at 4.73%. On 15 July, 1-month EURIBOR is fixed at 4.80%. What is his profit or loss?

The interest rate has risen so he makes a loss of EUR 3,601.78:

$$\text{EUR } 60{,}000{,}000 \times \frac{(0.0473 - 0.048) \times \dfrac{31}{360}}{\left(1 + \left(0.048 \times \dfrac{31}{360}\right)\right)} = \text{EUR } 3{,}601.78$$

The result is not exactly the same as in example 6 using futures, for 2 reasons:

(i) The FRA settlement is based on a period of 31 days and a year of 360 days, whereas a 1-month futures contract is always based on exactly $\frac{1}{12}$ year.

(ii)   The FRA settlement amount is discounted to a present value, but is received or paid correspondingly earlier

Strip trading

In the same way, if a trader is using futures and wishes to speculate on a longer-term rate than the 3-month rate, he would sell or buy a strip of futures.

Example 15

It is now February. A dealer with no position expects 12-month interest rates to rise. He therefore sells a strip of March, June, September and December futures. If he is correct and the 12-month rate rises above the 12-month interest rate implied by stripping these four prices together, he will be able to reverse the four contracts at an overall profit.

Calendar spread

A spread is a strategy whereby the trader buys a shorter-dated FRA or futures contract and sells a longer-dated one, because he expects the difference between them to change – a twist in the shape of the yield curve – but does not necessarily have any expectation about the whole yield curve moving up or down.

Example 16

Interest rates for euros are now as follows (for simplicity, we have ignored bid/offer spreads in this example):

2 months (61 days)	5.00%
5 months (153 days)	5.00%
8 months (245 days)	5.00%
11 months (337 days)	5.00%
2v5 FRA	4.96%
8v11 FRA	4.84%

A trader expects the yield curve to become positive. He therefore sells a 2v5 FRA and buys a 8v11 FRA.

Later that day, rates are as follows:

2 months (61 days)	5.01%
5 months (153 days)	5.04%
8 months (245 days)	5.07%
11 months (337 days)	5.10%
2v5 FRA	5.02%
8v11 FRA	5.01%

The dealer has lost 6 basis points on the 2v5 FRA but gained 17 basis points on the 8v11 FRA – a net gain of around 11 basis points because the yield curve has twisted as he expected.

Calendar spread

A dealer expecting the yield curve to twist anti-clockwise sells a shorter-date FRA and buys a longer-dated FRA (or buys a shorter-dated futures and sells a longer-dated futures).

A dealer expecting the yield curve to twist clockwise buys a shorter-date FRA and sells a longer-dated FRA (or sells a shorter-dated futures and buys a longer-dated futures).

A longer-term spread can be taken if a trader has a view on short-term yields compared with bond yields – for example, a spread between a 3-month Eurodollar futures and long-term USD bond futures. In this case an adjustment has to be made for the difference in maturity of the underlying instrument. Settlement on the short-term futures relates to a 90-day instrument, while settlement on the bond futures relates to a notional 15-year bond. For a given change in yield therefore, there will be a far greater profit or loss on the bond futures than on the short-term futures. To balance this, the trader would buy or sell a much smaller notional amount of the bond futures than of the short-term futures.

Cross-market spread

A spread can similarly be taken on the difference between two markets. For example, if sterling interest rates are above dollar rates and a trader believes that the spread between them will narrow, he could sell sterling FRAs and buy dollar FRAs, or buy sterling futures and sell dollar futures.

Arbitrage

Because FRAs and futures are essentially the same instrument traded in different ways, there is a straightforward arbitrage between them if prices move out of line – either buy a FRA and buy futures, or sell a FRA and sell futures.

Because of the close link between the two instruments, and the fact that dealers will hedge positions in one against the other, FRAs are often dealt to coincide with futures dates – that is, with effective dates on the third Wednesday of March, June, September or December and a forward period of 3 months. These futures dates are known as IMM dates, after the IMM, the oldest financial futures exchange.

Example 17

It is mid-March and rates for US dollars are as follows:

3v6 FRA:	4.75/4.80%
June futures	95.17/95.18

A dealer buys a USD 1 million 3v6 FRA at 4.80% and at the same time he buys 1 futures contract at 95.18. The implied interest rate of the futures contract is 4.82%. The dealer has therefore locked in a profit of 2 basis points.

There are at least two possible problems for the dealer, even if the effective date of the FRA exactly matches the futures date. Firstly, if interest rates rise at all significantly, he will make a profit on the FRA and a loss on the futures contract. The profit will be discounted to a present value but the loss will not be. The loss will also arise earlier (because of the mechanics of variation margin payments), which effectively increases the value of the loss even further.

Secondly, if interest rates fall, he will make a loss on the FRA and a profit on the futures. If the FRA is for a 3-month period of, say, 92 days, this would magnify the loss compared to the futures profit which is based effectively on 90 days.

Either of these effects could offset his apparent profit of 2 basis points.

Arbitraging and creating FRAs

It is possible to make use of FRAs and futures in covering forward FX positions, and also to construct synthetically an FRA in one currency from an FRA in another. These topics are covered in the FX section, in Chapter 9.

Exercises

1   Based on the following cash market rates for Swedish kronor, what is the theoretical rate at which a dealer would take a 6v9 forward-forward deposit from a customer?

    3 months (91 days)   4.87/5.00%
    6 months (182 days)   5.12/5.25%
    9 months (273 days)   5.00/5.12%

2   On Friday, you lend EUR 10 million for 1 week at 4.3% and borrow the same amount overnight at 4.25%. What is the break-even rate for the remaining period?

3   You sold a 2v5 GBP 2,000,000 FRA when rates were quoted to you as 7.30/7.40%. Settlement is now due and 3-month (91 days) GBP LIBOR is 7.15%. What amount do you pay or receive?

4   You are a dealer. You are given a deposit of EUR 7 million at 4.9% for 9 months (273 days). You also lend EUR 7 million at 4.9% for 3 months (92 days). You cover the mismatch with a 3v9 FRA, quoted to, you as 4.80/4.85%.

    a.   Do you buy or sell the FRA?
    b.   At what price do you deal?
    c.   What notional principal amount do you deal for the FRA, assuming that you wish to match your exposure as closely as possible and that you can deal exactly the right amount?
    d.   When the time comes to settle the FRA, the 6-month interest rate is 4.95%/5.05%. What is the settlement amount on the FRA, and who pays whom?
    e.   You always borrow at LIBOR and lend at LIBID. What is your overall cash profit or loss in euros at the end of nine months?

5   You sell 10 December euro futures contracts at 95.32. In which direction do you expect euro interest rates to move? You buy them back at 95.43. What is your profit or loss?

6   It is now the middle of March. You fund yourself at LIBOR flat and need to borrow euros for 9 months. What is the cheapest way of achieving this, given the following rates?

    3-month cash: 5.10/5.20%
    6-month cash   5.25/5.35%
    9-month cash: 5.35/5.45%
    3v6 FRA: 5.34/5.39%
    3v9 FRA: 5.42/5.47%
    6v9 FRA: 5.40/5.45%

June futures: 94.60/94.61
September futures: 94.57/94.58

7 It is now the middle of October. You are a dealer and sell a 7v12 FRA to a customer. Which futures contracts might you use to hedge your position?

8 You have taken a deposit from one customer for 6 months and lent to another for 3 months. Assuming all the dates match, what is the best hedge for the mismatched position, given the following prices available to you?

3v6 FRA: 6.51/6.56%
futures   93.50/93.51

9 It is now the middle of April. What is the theoretical 2v8 FRA rate in US dollars consistent with the following futures prices?

March   95.23
June   95.61
September   95.84
December   95.93

10 It is now March and the yield curve is negative. You expect it to become less negative over the next few months but have no view on whether interest rates will rise or fall overall. What might be an appropriate trading strategy?

Part 3
Foreign Exchange

Spot foreign exchange

Introduction

The uses of spot foreign exchange

A *spot* transaction is a straightforward purchase or sale of one currency against another. For an end-user, such a transaction is generally used simply for converting one currency to another. For example, if an industrial company in the UK has received US dollars for its exports to the USA, it probably needs to convert them to sterling, which it will do using a spot transaction.

Banks and other financial institutions, however, often use the spot market for *speculation* – that is, deliberately taking a risk in the hope of making a profit. For example, a German bank (with the euro as its domestic currency) might believe that the Japanese yen will strengthen during the day. It will therefore undertake a spot transaction to buy yen against euros. As it does not actually need the yen, it will sell them back again into euros later the same day, so that there is no net inflow or outflow of yen, other than possibly a profit or loss between the two transactions.

Some banks present themselves to the market as *market makers*. This means that they are prepared to quote a spot price for buying and selling, to anyone who asks (as long as they are creditworthy) – both customers and other financial institutions.

In practice, the market is of course less segmented than this. Individuals and corporate users also take speculative positions. Conversely, banks also use spot transactions to convert cash into another currency other than for speculation. Also, a bank which deals with a customer at the customer's request – for example, selling Australian dollars to the customer – has created a risk for itself. If it wishes to remove this risk, it will *close* the position by buying the same amount of Australian dollars from another bank, in another transaction.

The value date

A *spot* transaction is for delivery two working days after the dealing date (the date on which the contract is made). This allows time for the necessary paperwork and cash transfers to be arranged. Normally therefore, if a spot deal is contracted on Monday, Tuesday or Wednesday, delivery will be two days after (i.e. Wednesday, Thursday or Friday respectively). If a spot deal is contracted on a Thursday or Friday, the delivery date is generally on Monday or Tuesday respectively, as neither Saturday nor Sunday are working days in the major markets.

There are, however, some exceptions. For example, a price for the US dollar against the Canadian dollar in the professional interbank market generally implies delivery on the next working day after the dealing day. This is referred to as *funds* rather than spot. A spot price (value two working days after the dealing day, as usual) can generally be requested as an alternative. The rate for the US dollar against the Hong Kong dollar is also often traded for value the next working day. The US dollar/ Turkish lira rate is generally traded for value on either the same day as the deal is done, or the next day. A problem arises in trading Middle East currencies where the relevant markets are closed on Friday but open on Saturday. A spot deal on Wednesday between the US dollar and the Saudi riyal, for example, would need to have a split settlement date: the dollars would be settled on Friday, but the riyals on Saturday.

If the spot date falls on a public holiday in one or both of the centers of the two currencies involved, the next working day is taken as the value date. For example, if a spot deal between sterling and the US dollar is transacted on Thursday 31 August, it would normally be for value Monday 4 September. If this date is a holiday in the UK or the USA, however, all spot transactions on Thursday 31 August are for value Tuesday 5 September. If the intervening day (between today and spot) is a holiday in one of the two centers, the spot value date is again usually delayed by one day.

The recognized opening and closing times for the foreign exchange market each week are 5:00 a.m. Monday, Sydney time and 5:00 p.m. Friday, New York time.

How spot rates are quoted

Base currency and variable currency

Throughout this book, we have generally used ISO codes (also used by the SWIFT system) to abbreviate currency names. You can find a list of the codes in Appendix C.

In the spot market, a variable number of units of one currency is quoted per one unit of another currency. In this book, we have used the usual convention that, for example, the US dollar/Japanese yen exchange rate is written as 'USD/JPY' if it refers to the number of yen equal to 1 US dollar but as 'JPY/USD' if it refers to the number of US dollars equal to 1 yen. The currency code written on the left is the *base* currency; there is always 1 of the base unit. The currency code written on the right is the *variable* currency (or *counter* currency or *quoted* currency); the number of units of this currency equal to 1 of the base currency varies according to the exchange rate.

When quoting against the euro, it is the practice in the interbank market to quote all currencies in terms of a varying number of units of that currency per 1 euro. In other words, the euro is, by convention, always the base currency if it is one of the two currencies involved. Similarly, apart from the euro, it is the interbank convention to quote all currencies against sterling using sterling as the base currency. Again, apart from the euro, sterling, Australian dollar and New Zealand dollar, all rates against the US dollar are always quoted interbank with the US dollar as the base currency.

The Canadian dollar is generally quoted as the variable currency against the US dollar, although the other way round is possible.

In the currency futures markets, as opposed to the interbank market, quotations against the USD usually have USD as the variable currency.

In other cases, there is not a universal convention for which way round to quote a cross-rate – that is, which is the base currency and which the variable currency.

Cross-rates

Although dealing is possible between any two convertible currencies – for example, New Zealand dollars against euros or Swiss francs against Japanese yen – the interbank market has historically quoted mostly against US dollars, so reducing the number of individual rates that needed to be quoted. The exchange rate between any two non-US dollar currencies could then be calculated from the rate for each currency against US dollars. Such a rate between any two currencies, neither of which is the dollar, is known as a cross-rate.

Some of these cross-rates (for example, euro/sterling, euro/yen, euro/Swiss franc) have, however, increasingly been traded between banks in addition to the dollar-based rates. This sometimes reflects the importance of the relationship between the pair of currencies. The economic relationship between the Swiss franc and the euro, for example, is closer than the relationship between the Swiss franc and the dollar. It is therefore more true nowadays to say that the dollar/franc exchange rate is a function of the euro/dollar rate and the euro/franc rate, rather than that the euro/franc rate is a function of the euro/dollar rate and the dollar/franc rate. The principle of calculating one rate from two others remains the same, however. The calculations are explained below.

Bid and offer rates

As in other markets, a bank normally quotes a two-way price, whereby it indicates both at what level it is prepared to buy the base currency against the variable currency (the *bid* for the base currency – a cheaper rate), and at what level it is prepared to sell the base currency against the variable currency (the *offer* of the base currency – a more expensive rate). For example, if a bank is prepared to buy 1 US dollar for 1.6375 Swiss francs, and sell 1 US dollar for 1.6385 Swiss francs, the USD/CHF rate would be quoted as '1.6375/1.6385'.

In the spot market, the price is always quoted so that the quoting bank buys the base currency on the left. This is the quoting bank's bid for the base currency, which is the lower number. Similarly, the quoting bank always sells the base currency – its offer for the base currency, which is the higher number – on the right. If the bank quotes such a rate to a company or other counterparty, the counterparty would sell the base currency on the left, and buy the base currency on the right – the opposite of how the bank itself sees the deal. The universal rule is that the party quoting the price deals on the side which is more advantageous to it, while the party asking for the price – if it decides to deal – is obliged to deal on the side which is less advantageous to it.

As the market moves very quickly, dealers need to deal with great speed and therefore abbreviate when dealing. For example, if one dealer wishes to buy USD 5 million from another who is quoting him a USD/CHF price, he will say simply "5 mine"; this means "I wish to buy from you 5 million of the base currency and sell the other currency, at your offered price". Similarly, if he wishes to sell USD 5 million, he will say simply "5 yours", meaning "I wish to sell you 5 million of the base currency and buy the other currency, at your bid price".

Example 1

Bank A asks Bank B and Bank C each for a price in EUR/USD.

Bank B quotes 0.9349/54.
Bank C quotes 0.9350/55.

> Bank A wishes to buy EUR 5 million. The quoting bank will therefore be selling EUR, the base currency. If Bank A chooses to deal on either of these prices, it will therefore deal on the right side. Bank A is therefore looking for the most attractive right side price, which in this case is Bank B's price at 0.9354.
>
> Bank B therefore replies "Nothing thanks." to Bank C and replies "5 mine" to Bank B. He has then bought EUR 5 million from Bank B at 0.9354.

The difference between the two sides of the quotation is known as the *spread* and represents the dealer's profit for being willing to take the risk of quoting prices to other parties. Historically, a two-way price in a cross-rate would have a wider spread than a two-way price in a dollar-based rate, because the cross-rate constructed from the dollar-based rates would combine both the spreads. Now, however, the spread in say a euro/Swiss franc price might be proportionally narrower than a dollar/franc spread, because it is more the euro/franc price that is driving the market, as noted above, than the dollar/franc price.

Dealers generally operate on the basis of small percentage profits but large turnover. These rates will be good for large, round amounts. For very large amounts, or for smaller amounts, a bank would normally quote a wider spread. The amount for which a quotation is *good* (i.e. a valid quote on which the dealer will deal) will vary to some extent with the currency concerned and market conditions.

Rates are often quoted to 1/100th of a cent etc. (known as a *point* or a *pip*). For example, the US dollar/Swiss franc rate would usually be quoted to four decimal places – for example, "1.5375/1.5385". This depends on the size of the number, however, and in the case of USD/JPY, for example, which might be quoted say "105.05/105.15", "15 points" means 0.15 yen. One point is thus one unit of the last decimal place quoted.

Example 2

You buy USD 1 million against CHF at 1.6920 and sell USD 1 million against CHF at 1.6921. You have made 1 point profit, which is CHF 100:

$$1,000,000 \times 0.0001 = 100$$

You also buy USD 1 million against JPY at 109.20 and sell USD 1 million against JPY at 109.21. Again, you have made

> 1 point profit, which is JPY 10,000:
>
> $1,000,000 \times 0.01 = 10,000$

As the first three digits of the exchange rate (known as the *big figure*) do not change in the short term, dealers generally do not mention them when dealing in the interbank market. In the example above (1.6375/1.6385) the quotation would therefore be given as simply "75/85". However, when dealers are quoting a rate to a corporate client they will often mention the big figure also. In this case, the quotation would be "1.6375/55".

If the bid and offer prices are close to a round number, it can sometimes appear that the right side is smaller than the left side. For example, the price might be abbreviated as "1.6395/05". This in fact means "1.6395/1.6405" and might be expressed as "Ninety-five/o five, around one sixty-four". Similarly, a price of "1.6390/00" means "1.6390/1.6400" and might be expressed as "One sixty-three, ninety/the figure", where "the figure" means "00".

Some more terminology

A *long* position is a surplus of purchases over sales of a given currency – i.e., a position which benefits from a strengthening of that currency. Similarly, a *short* position is a surplus of sales over purchases of a given currency, which benefits from a weakening of that currency. A *square* position is one which is neither long nor short – i.e. one in which the sales and purchases are equal.

A *yard* of a currency is an American billion units of that currency (i.e. 1,000,000,000 units).

Cable is a nickname for the sterling/US dollar exchange rate.

If one party asks another for a two-way price and then chooses to deal on the bid side of the price, he is said to *hit* the bid. If he chooses to deal on the offer side of the price, he is said to *lift* the offer.

Occasionally a dealer will narrow the bid/offer spread to zero – i.e. he will quote a single price and the party asking for the price can choose whether he will buy or sell at that price. This is known as a *choice* price.

If a dealer quoting puts his price *under reference*, it means that the counterparty must ask again for a reconfirmation of the price before dealing on it.

If a party who has asked for a price says "My risk", he is acknowledging that the price may change before he has accepted it – generally because he knows that he may not be able to respond immediately as to whether or not he will choose to deal on the price. If a dealer says "Off!", he means that the last price he quoted is no longer valid.

Position-keeping

To earn profit from dealing, the bank's objective is clearly to sell the base currency at the highest rate it can against the variable currency and buy the base currency at the lowest rate.

Example 3

You are a dealer and are long of USD 4 million against CHF at 1.6612. You want to close this position because you expect the dollar to weaken.

You therefore ask another bank for a USD/CHF price and are quoted 1.6610/15. You decide that you will deal on this price. You need to sell US dollars, so that the quoting dealer is buying dollars, the base currency. You therefore hit his bid at 1.6610. You have a net loss of CHF 800:

	USD		CHF
Original position:	+4,000,000	at 1.6612:	−6,644,800
Deal to close:	−4,000,000	at 1.6610:	+6,644,000
Net result:			−800

Example 4

You have the same original situation as in the previous example. This time, however, another bank calls you to ask for a price. The market is currently 1.6610/15. What price should you quote in order to encourage the other bank to buy dollars from you, so that your position will be squared up, which is what you want?

You hope that the other dealer will lift your offer and not hit your bid. You should therefore show him a two-way price with a more attractive offer than the market generally, but an unattractive bid. You might therefore quote, say, 1.6608/13 to encourage him to deal at 1.6613.

At any time, a dealer needs to know what is his position resulting from the net of all the deals he has undertaken during the day so far. He also needs to know what is the average exchange rate of this net position, so that he can compare it with the current market rate to see whether or not the position is profitable. At the end of the day, he might not close out the position, but will in that case need to *mark to market* the position – i.e. calculate the unrealized profit or loss on the position so far. This is achieved by calculating what the profit or loss would be if he did in fact close out the position out at the current rate (i.e. the end-of-day closing market rate).

Example 5

You undertake three spot deals in USD/CHF as follows.

Sell USD 4 million at 1.6723
Buy USD 1 million at 1.6732
Buy USD 5 million at 1.6729

The market closes at 1.6730.

What is your position? What is the average rate of this position? What is your net profit or loss?

	USD		CHF
	−4,000,000	at 1.6723:	+6,689,200
	+1,000,000	at 1.6732:	−1,673,200
	+5,000,000	at 1.6729:	−8,364,500
Position:	+2,000,000		−3,348,500
Average rate:		$\dfrac{3,348,500}{2,000,000}$ $=1.67425$	
	−2,000,000	at 1.6730:	+3,346,000
Loss:			−2,500

The position is therefore long USD 2 million. The average rate is 1.67425. The loss is CHF 2,500. This loss could be expressed in US dollars by converting it into US dollars at the spot rate, or in any other currency by converting it at the appropriate spot rate.

Reciprocal rates

Any quotation with a particular currency as the base currency can be converted into the equivalent quotation with that currency as the variable currency by taking its reciprocal. Thus a USD/CHF quotation of 1.4375/1.4385 can be converted to a CHF/USD quotation of $(1 \div 1.4375)/(1 \div 1.4385)$. However, this would still be quoted with a smaller number on the left, so that the two sides of the quotation are reversed: 0.6952/0.6957. In every case, the bank buys the base currency against the variable currency on the left, and sells the base currency against the variable currency on the right.

Example 6

The AUD/CAD rate is 0.7954/0.7959. What is the CAD/AUD rate?

$1 \div 0.7954 = 1.2572$
$1 \div 0.7959 = 1.2564$

Therefore the CAD/AUD rate is 1.2564/1.2572

Cross-rate calculations

As mentioned earlier, it is often necessary to calculate an exchange rate between two currencies from two other rates, because only a small proportion of possible currency pairs are regularly traded interbank. Frequently, but not always, it is the dollar-based rates which serve as the starting point for these calculations.

Example 7

Given the following rates, what is the CAD/CHF rate?

USD/CHF   1.6348/53
USD/CAD   1.5497/02

The left side (i.e. the bid side) of the resulting CAD/CHF rate is where the quoting bank buys CAD and sells CHF. The bank's USD/CAD dealer buys CAD (the same as selling USD) on the right side of his own price – i.e. 1.5502. The bank's USD/CHF dealer sells CHF (the same as buying USD) on the left side of his own price – i.e. 1.6348.

Each USD 1 is worth CAD 1.5502 and is also worth CHF 1.6348. Therefore the rate between CAD and CHF is the ratio between these two numbers:

$1.6348 \div 1.5502 = 1.05457$

1.0546 is therefore the left side of the resulting CAD/CHF price. Similarly, the right side is derived from the right side of the USD/CHF price and the left side of the USD/CAD price:

$1.6353 \div 1.5497 = 1.05524$

The CAD/CHF price is therefore 1.0546/52. **Note that in practice a dealer would probably round down the left price (to 1.0545 in this example) and round up the right price (to 1.0553) to ensure that he does not make a loss. For simplicity however, we have used normal rounding rules in this book.**

In summary, to calculate a spot rate from two other rates which share the same base currency (in our example this was USD), divide opposite sides of the exchange rates. Following the same logic shows that to calculate a spot rate from two other rates which share the same variable currency (in the following example this is also USD), we again need to divide opposite sides of the exchange rates:

Example 8

Given the following rates, what is the GBP/NZD rate?

GBP/USD   1.4320/25
NZD/USD   0.4460/65

The left side (i.e. the bid side) of the resulting GBP/NZD rate is where the quoting bank buys GBP and sells NZD. The bank's GBP/USD dealer buys GBP on the left side of his own price – i.e. 1.4320. The bank's NZD/USD dealer sells NZD on the right side of his own price – i.e. 0.4465.

Each GBP 1 is worth USD 1.4320. Each NZD 1 is worth USD 0.4465. Therefore the rate between GBP and NZD is the ratio between these two numbers:

$1.4320 \div 0.4465 = 3.2072$

3.2072 is therefore the left side of the resulting GBP/NZD price. Similarly, the right side is derived from the right side of the

GBP/USD price and the left side of the NZD/USD price:

$1.4325 \div 0.4460 = 3.2119$

The GBP/NZD price is therefore 3.2072/19

Finally, to calculate a cross-rate from two rates where the common currency is the base currency in one quotation but the variable currency in the other, following the same logic through shows that we multiply the same sides of the exchange rates:

Example 9

Given the following rates, what is the GBP/CHF rate?

GBP/USD   1.4320/25
USD/CHF   1.6348/53

The left side (i.e. the bid side) of the resulting GBP/CHF rate is where the quoting bank buys GBP and sells CHF. The bank's GBP/USD dealer buys GBP on the left side of his own price – i.e. 1.4320. The bank's USD/CHF dealer sells CHF (the same as buying USD) on the left side of his own price – i.e. 1.6348.

Each GBP 1 is worth USD 1.4320. Each of these USD is worth CHF 1.6348. Therefore the rate between GBP and CHF is the product of these two numbers:

$1.4320 \times 1.6348 = 2.3410$

2.3410 is therefore the left side of the resulting GBP/CHF price. Similarly, the right side is derived from the right side of the GBP/USD price and the right side of the USD/CHF price:

$1.4325 \times 1.6353 = 2.3426$

The GBP/CHF price is therefore 2.3410/26

To calculate an exchange rate by combining two others

From two rates with the same base currency or the same variable currency: divide opposite sides of the exchange rates. See the next box for deciding which exchange rate to divide by which

From two rates where the base currency in one is the same as the variable currency in the other: multiply the same sides of the exchange rates.

The construction of one exchange rate from two others in this way can be seen algebraically:

> Given two exchange rates A/B and A/C, they can be combined as follows:
>
> $$B/C = A/C \div A/B$$
>
> Given two exchange rates B/A and C/A, they can be combined as follows:
>
> $$B/C = B/A \div C/A$$
>
> Given two exchange rates B/A and A/C, they can be combined as follows:
>
> $$B/C = B/A \times A/C$$
>
> and $\qquad\qquad C/B = 1 \div (B/A \times A/C)$
>
> When dividing, use opposite sides. When multiplying, use the same sides.

The examples above all construct exchange rates from two other rates involving the US dollar (which is often the case). The same approach applies when constructing any rate from any other two rates. Considering the way in which each of the two separate dealers will deal to create the combined rate, gives the construction:

Example 10

Given the following rates, what are the USD/CHF and EUR/JPY rates?

EUR/CHF	1.5348/53
EUR/USD	0.9497/02
EUR/GBP	0.6378/83
GBP/JPY	175.95/05

$1.5348 \div 0.9502 = 1.6152$

$1.5353 \div 0.9497 = 1.6166$

Therefore the USD/CHF rate is 1.6152/66

$0.6378 \times 175.95 = 112.22$

$0.6383 \times 176.05 = 112.37$

Therefore the EUR/JPY rate is 112.22/37

The market environment

It is useful to have an idea of the size of the foreign exchange market. The total average daily volume of transactions worldwide is around USD 1,200 billion. Of this total, only a tiny proportion represents deals to convert the cashflows of international commercial trade; the vast majority represents position-taking and financial flows.

Around 32% of the total is spot transactions and 68% is forward swaps and outrights (covered in the next chapter). By far the largest turnover – around one third of the total world volume – takes place in the London market, followed by New York in second place and Tokyo in third place. Around 57% of the total volume involves cross-border transactions – i.e. deals where the two banks are in different countries.

As has been the case historically, around 90% of all transactions involve the US dollar as one of the two currencies. Other important traded currencies, in decreasing order of volume, are the euro, the yen and sterling. The Swiss franc, Canadian dollar and Australian dollar are also traded in reasonable volume.

Exercises

1 The SGD/NOK exchange rate is quoted as 2.9584. Does this exchange rate express the number of Norwegian kroner equal to 1 Singapore dollar, or the number of Singapore dollars equal to one Norwegian krone?

2 You wish to sell US dollars against sterling and are given the following quotes from two banks. At what price will you deal?
   - 1.4356/61
   - 1.4358/63

3 You are a dealer and a counterparty asks you for you price in EUR/USD. You quote "0.9503/08" and the counterparty replies "5 yours". What have you sold or bought, how much, and at what rate?

4 If the spot AUD/USD exchange rate is quoted as 0.5413, what is the value of 1 'point' on a deal of 1 million of the base currency? If the spot USD/JPY exchange rate is quoted as 107.13, what is the value of 1 'point' on a deal of 1 million of the base currency?

5 You buy USD 10 million against Canadian dollars at 1.3785 and sell USD 10 million at 1.3779. What is your profit or loss?

6   You are a dealer with a short position in US dollars against euros.
    A counterparty calls you for a price in EUR/USD. The market
    is currently 0.9503/08. Which of the following prices might you
    quote if you now wish to reduce the size of your position?

    • 0.9502/07
    • 0.9503/08
    • 0.9504/09

7   You are a dealer. A customer asks you for a CHF/USD price. You
    quote him 0.6330/38 and he buys CHF 5 million from you. You
    want to cover this position in the market and therefore deal on
    a price of USD/CHF 1.5783/88 quoted to you by another bank,
    for exactly the same amount of CHF 5 million. What profit or loss
    in USD have you made?

8   You sell EUR 5 million against USD at 0.9320, you buy
    EUR 2 million at 0.9325, you buy EUR 4 million at 0.9330 and
    you sell EUR 3 million at 0.9327. The market closes at 0.9328
    and the closing rate for GBP/USD is 1.4730. At the end of the
    day, what is your EUR/USD position? What is the average rate
    of this position? What is your total net profit or loss in GBP?

9   The SEK/NOK exchange rate is 1.0523/28. What is the recip-
    rocal rate?

10 Current spot rates are as follows:

    USD/CHF   1.5384/89
    USD/SGD   2.3895/05
    EUR/USD   0.9678/83
    AUD/USD   0.5438/43

    (a) What is the two-way price for CHF/SGD? On which side of
         this price would the customer sell SGD?
    (b) What is the two-way price for EUR/AUD? On which side of
         this price would the customer buy EUR?
    (c) What is the two-way price for EUR/CHF? On which side of
         this price would the customer buy CHF?
    (d) What is the two-way price for CHF/AUD? On which side of
         this price would the customer sell CHF?

Forward outrights and swaps

At the end of this chapter, we have summarized the uses of the various instruments described in it. You might find it useful to glance through this summary before reading the rest of the chapter.

Forward outrights

Although *spot* is settled 2 working days in the future, it is not considered in the foreign exchange market as 'future' or 'forward', but as the baseline from which all other dates (earlier or later) are considered.

An *outright* is an outright purchase or sale of one currency in exchange for another currency for settlement on a fixed date other than the spot value date. Rates are quoted in a similar way to those in the spot market, with the quoting bank buying the base currency on the left side and selling it on the right side. The term *short date* (see later in this chapter) is used for settlement on a date other than spot but less than 1 month after spot, and the term *forward outright* is therefore generally reserved for settlement later than that – i.e. at least one month after spot – although short dates are really only a particular range of forward outrights.

> ### Example 1
>
> The spot USD/CHF rate is 1.7166/1.7171, but the rate for value 3 months after the spot value date is 1.7144/1.7151.

> The spread (the difference between the bank's buying price and the bank's selling price) is wider in the forward outright quotation than in the spot quotation. Also, in this example, the dollar is worth less for delivery in the future than for delivery on the spot date. USD 1 buys CHF 1.7144 in 3 months' time, as opposed to CHF 1.7166 spot. In a different example, the dollar might be worth more for delivery in the future than on the spot date.

Where does the forward outright rate come from?

The forward outright rate may be seen both as the market's assessment of where the spot rate will be in the future and as a reflection of current interest rates in the two currencies concerned.

Consider, for example, the following round-trip transactions, all undertaken simultaneously:

(i)   Borrow Swiss francs for 3 months starting from spot value date.
(ii) Sell the Swiss francs and buy dollars for value spot.
(iii) Deposit the purchased dollars for 3 months starting from spot value date.
(iv) Sell forward now the dollar principal and interest which mature in 3 months' time, into Swiss francs; use these Swiss francs to repay the borrowing in (i).

In general, the market will adjust the forward price for (iv) so that these simultaneous transactions generate neither a profit nor a loss. When the four rates involved are not in line (Swiss franc interest rate, USD/CHF spot rate, dollar interest rate and USD/CHF forward rate), there is in fact opportunity for making a profit by round-tripping. That is, either the transactions as shown above will produce a profit, or exactly the reverse transactions (borrow dollars, sell dollars spot, deposit Swiss francs and sell Swiss francs forward) will produce a profit. The supply and demand effect of this arbitrage activity is such as to move the rates back into line. If in fact this results in a forward rate which is out of line with the market's average view, supply and demand pressure will tend to move the spot rate or the interest rates until this is no longer the case.

In more detail, the transactions might be as follows:

(i)   Borrow CHF 100 for 92 days at 3%
      The total repayment (principal plus interest) at maturity will be:

$$\text{CHF } 1,000,000 \times \left(1 + \left(0.03 \times \frac{92}{360}\right)\right) = \text{CHF } 1,007,667$$

(ii) Sell CHF 1 million for dollars at a spot rate of 1.7300 to give:

$$\text{USD} \left(\frac{1,000,000}{1.7300} \right) = \text{USD } 578,035$$

(iii) Invest USD 578,035 at an interest rate of 4% per annum.
The total repayment (principal plus interest) at maturity will be:

$$\text{USD } 578,035 \times \left(1 + \left(0.04 \times \frac{92}{360} \right) \right) = \text{USD } 583,943$$

(iv) Sell USD 583,943 forward into Swiss francs to give:

$$\text{CHF} \left(583,943 \times \text{forward outright exchange rate} \right)$$

Arbitrage activity will tend to make this last amount the same as that in (i), so that:

$$583,943 \times \text{forward outright exchange rate} = 1,007,667$$

Therefore, the forward outright exchange rate must be:

$$\frac{1,007,667}{583,943} = 1.7256$$

This arbitrage idea gives the following formula for the theoretical forward outright exchange rate:

$$
\text{Forward outright} = \text{spot} \times \frac{\left(1 + \left(\text{variable currency interest rate} \times \dfrac{\text{days}}{\text{variable year}}\right)\right)}{\left(1 + \left(\text{base currency interest rate} \times \dfrac{\text{days}}{\text{base year}}\right)\right)}
$$

Notice that the length of the year may be 360 or 365, depending on each currency (see Chapter 2).

Applying the formula to the example above gives 1.7256 as expected:

$$1.7300 \times \frac{\left(1 + \left(0.03 \times \dfrac{92}{360}\right)\right)}{\left(1 + \left(0.04 \times \dfrac{92}{360}\right)\right)} = 1.7256$$

Example 2

What should the mid-rate theoretically be for the GBP/USD 3-month outright, given the following? The 6-month period is 183 days.

GBP/USD spot: 1.4120/26
GBP 6-month interest rate: 5.10/5.20%
USD 6-month interest rate: 4.30/4.40%

Note that sterling interest rates are on a 365-day year and dollar rates are on a 360-day year. Using middle rates both for spot, and for the interest rates, we have:

$$1.4123 \times \frac{\left(1 + \left(0.0435 \times \frac{183}{360}\right)\right)}{\left(1 + \left(0.0515 \times \frac{183}{365}\right)\right)} = 1.4072$$

   Forward outright prices can be quoted as two-way prices in the same way as other prices. One could use the bank's bid rate for the spot, its offered rate for sterling (5.20%) and its bid rate for dollars (4.30%) in the above example, to calculate the price where the bank buys sterling from the customer against dollars for delivery in 6 months' time, and use the bank's offered rate for spot, its bid rate for sterling (5.10%) and its offered rate for dollars (4.40%) to determine the other side of the price, as in the following example.

Example 3

What two-sided price can be constructed for the GBP/USD 3-month outright, given the following? The 6-month period is 183 days.

GBP/USD spot: 1.4120/26
GBP 6-month interest rate: 5.10/5.20%
USD 6-month interest rate: 4.30/4.40%

For the bid side:

$$1.4120 \times \frac{\left(1 + \left(0.0430 \times \frac{183}{360}\right)\right)}{\left(1 + \left(0.0520 \times \frac{183}{365}\right)\right)} = 1.4062$$

For the offer side:

$$1.4126 \times \frac{\left(1 + \left(0.0440 \times \dfrac{183}{360}\right)\right)}{\left(1 + \left(0.0510 \times \dfrac{183}{365}\right)\right)} = 1.4082$$

The two-sided outright price is therefore 1.4062/1.4082

In minor markets where the price does need to be constructed and hedged in this way, this calculation might be necessary. In a well-established market, however, this would generally produce a rather larger bid/offer spread than is realistic. In this case, it might be better to use middle prices throughout to calculate a middle price, as in Example 2, and then to spread the two-way price around this middle price. In practice, a dealer does not recalculate forward prices continually in any case, but takes them from the market just as the spot dealer takes spot prices.

Forward swaps

Forward outrights are an important instrument because they enable a bank's customer to lock in an exchange rate for the future. However, trading banks generally do not deal between themselves in forward outrights, but rather in forward *swaps*, where a forward swap is the difference between the spot and the forward outright. The reason for not dealing in outrights will become clear later. The forward outright rate can therefore be seen as a combination of the current spot rate and the forward swap rate added together.

Forward outright = spot + forward swap

It is important to note that the forward swap is sometimes positive and sometimes negative. As we shall see, this depends on which of the two currencies involved has higher interest rates. As with spot prices and outright prices, swap prices are quoted as two-way prices.

Example 4

Spot USD/CHF: 1.7166/1.7171
Forward swap: 0.0150/0.0155

spot + swap = forward outright

In this case: $1.7166 + 0.0150 = 1.7316$
                     $1.7171 + 0.0155 = 1.7326$

Therefore the two-sided outright price is 1.7316/1.7326

As before, it is possible to give a formula for what the forward swap theoretically should be:

Forward swap

$$= \text{spot} \times \frac{\left(\left(\text{variable currency interest rate} \times \frac{\text{days}}{\text{variable year}}\right) - \left(\text{base currency interest rate} \times \frac{\text{days}}{\text{base year}}\right)\right)}{\left(1 + \left(\text{base currency interest rate} \times \frac{\text{days}}{\text{base year}}\right)\right)}$$

As before, the length of each year may be 360 or 365 days.

Example 5

What two-sided price can be constructed for the GBP/USD 3-month forward swap, given the following? The 6-month period is 183 days.

GBP/USD spot: 1.4120/26
GBP 6-month interest rate: 5.10/5.20%
USD 6-month interest rate: 4.30/4.40%

For the left side:

$$1.4123 \times \frac{\left(\left(0.0430 \times \frac{183}{360}\right) - \left(0.0520 \times \frac{183}{365}\right)\right)}{\left(1 + \left(0.0520 \times \frac{183}{365}\right)\right)} = -0.0058$$

For the right side:

$$1.4123 \times \frac{\left(\left(0.0440 \times \frac{183}{360}\right) - \left(0.0510 \times \frac{183}{365}\right)\right)}{\left(1 + \left(0.0510 \times \frac{183}{365}\right)\right)} = -0.0044$$

The swap price is therefore −0.0058/−0.0044

Note that in Example 5, we used the same spot rate to calculate each side, and that the spot rate we used was a middle rate. Using either the bid or offer spot rate would make only an extremely small difference.

As expected, the swap calculated in Example 5, when combined with the spot rate, gives the same outright as Example 3:

Spot:	1.4120/ 1.4126
6-month swap:	−0.0058/−0.0044
6-month outright:	1.4062/ 1.4082

If the year basis is the same for the two currencies and the number of days is sufficiently small, the following is a good approximation:

Approximation

$$\text{Forward swap} \approx \text{spot} \times \text{interest rate differential} \times \frac{\text{days}}{\text{year}}$$

Example 6

USD/CHF spot:	1.7100
92-day USD interest rate:	5%
92-day CHF interest rate:	2%

Using the precise formula:

$$1.7100 \times \frac{\left(\left(0.02 \times \frac{92}{360}\right) - \left(0.05 \times \frac{92}{360}\right)\right)}{\left(1 + \left(0.05 \times \frac{92}{360}\right)\right)} = -0.0129$$

Using the approximate formula:

$$1.7100 \times (-0.03) \times \frac{92}{360} = -0.0131$$

USD/CHF spot: 1.7100
365-day USD interest rate: 5%
365-day CHF interest rate: 2%

Using the precise formula:

$$1.7100 \times \frac{\left(\left(0.02 \times \frac{365}{360}\right) - \left(0.05 \times \frac{365}{360}\right)\right)}{\left(1 + \left(0.05 \times \frac{365}{360}\right)\right)} = -0.0495$$

Using the approximate formula:

$$1.7100 \times (-0.03) \times \frac{365}{360} = -0.0520$$

Example 6 shows that the approximation is generally rather good for short periods but rather inaccurate for longer periods. It also becomes less accurate if the base currency interest rate is large.

Discounts and premiums

When the base currency interest rate is lower than the variable currency rate, the forward outright exchange rate is always greater than the spot rate. That is, the base currency is worth more units of the variable currency for delivery forward than it is for delivery spot. This can be seen as compensating for the lower interest rate: if I deposit money in the variable currency rather than the base currency, I will receive more interest. However, if I sell forward the maturing deposit amount, in an attempt to lock in this advantage, the forward exchange rate is correspondingly worse so I lose the advantage. In this case, the base currency is said to be at a *premium* to the variable currency, and the forward swap price must be positive. At the same time, the variable currency is said to be at a *discount* to the base currency.

The reverse also follows. In general, given two currencies, the currency with the higher interest rate is at a discount (worth fewer units of the other currency forward than spot) and the currency with the lower interest rate is at a premium (worth more units of the other currency forward than spot). When the base currency is at a premium to the variable currency (and the variable currency is at a discount to the base currency), the forward swap price is positive; when the base currency is at a discount (and the variable currency is at a premium), the forward swap price is negative.

When the swap price is positive, and the forward dealer applies a bid/offer spread to make a two-way swap price, the left price is smaller than the right price as usual. When the swap price is negative, he must similarly quote a more negative number on the left and a more positive number on the right in order to make a profit. This can be seen in Example 5 above, where the swap price was $-0.0058/-0.0044$.

However, the minus sign '$-$' is generally not shown. The result is that, when the swap price is negative, the larger number appears to be on the left. As a result, whenever the swap price appears larger on the left than the right, it is in fact negative, and must be subtracted from the swap rate rather than added.

Swap prices are generally quoted as points, in such a way that the last digit of the swap points coincides with the same decimal place as the last digit of the spot price. For example, if the spot price is quoted to 4 decimal places – say 1.716<u>6</u> – and the swap price is 12<u>0</u> points, this means a swap price of 0.012<u>0</u>. If the spot price is quoted to 2 decimal places – say 171.6<u>6</u> – and the swap price is 12<u>0</u> points, this means a swap price of 1.2<u>0</u>.

The currency with the higher interest rate is at a discount and the currency with the lower interest rate is at a premium.

When the base currency is at a premium and the variable currency is at a discount, the forward swap points are positive and the left price appears smaller than the right price. When the base currency is at a discount and the variable currency is at a premium, the forward swap points are negative and the left price appears bigger than the right price.

Example 7

euro interest rate: 4%
dollar interest rate: 5%
yen interest rate: 1%

The euro is at a premium to the dollar
The dollar is at a discount to the euro
The forward swap points for EUR/USD are positive

The dollar is at a discount to the yen
The yen is at a premium to the dollar
The forward swap points for USD/JPY are negative

Example 8

EUR/USD spot is 0.8723/28 and the 3-month swap rate is quoted as 20/22.

Spot EUR/USD:	0.8723/	28
3-month swap:	20/	22
3-month outright	0.8743/0.8750	

USD/JPY spot is 127.23/28 and the 3-month swap rate is quoted as 20/22.

Spot USD/JPY:	127.23/	28
3-month swap:	20/	22
3-month outright	127.43/127.50	

USD/CHF spot is 1.7723/28 and the 3-month swap rate is quoted as 22/20.

Spot USD/CHF:	1.7723/	28
3-month swap:	− 22/−	20
3-month outright	1.7701/1.7708	

If a forward swap price includes the word *par* it means that the spot rate and the forward outright rate are the same: par in this case represents zero. *A/P* is *around par*, meaning that the left-hand side of the swap must be subtracted from spot and the right-hand side added. This happens when the two interest rates are the same or very similar.

Example 9

USD/CAD spot is 1.4723/28 and the 3-month swap rate is quoted as 6/4 A/P.

Spot USD/CAD:	1.4723/	28
3-month swap:	− 6/+	4
3-month outright	1.4717/1.4732	

The swap price in Example 9 would often be written as −6/+4, which means the same as 6/4 A/P but indicates the price more clearly.

It is important to be careful about the terminology regarding premiums and discounts. The clearest terminology, for example, is to say that "the euro is at a premium to the dollar" or that "the dollar is at a discount to the euro"; there is then no ambiguity. If, however, a London dealer says that "the EUR/USD is at a discount", he generally means that the <u>variable</u> currency, the dollar, is at a discount and that the swap points are to be added to the spot. Similarly, if he says that "the GBP/JPY is at a premium", he means that the <u>variable</u> currency, the yen, is at a premium and that the points are to be subtracted from the spot. If there is no qualification, he is generally referring to the variable currency, not the base currency. This is <u>not</u> the same in all countries, however, so beware! It is better to avoid this terminology and always explain which of the two currencies is meant when referring to premiums and discounts.

What is a forward swap deal?

In order to see why a bank trades in forward swaps rather than forward outrights, consider how the following swap and outright rates change as the spot rate and interest rates move:

spot rate	USD interest rate	CHF interest rate	92-day forward outright	92-day forward swap
1.7100	5.0%	2.0%	1.6971	−0.0129
1.7200	5.0%	2.0%	1.7070	−0.0130
1.7200	4.5%	2.0%	1.7091	−0.0109

A movement of 100 points in the exchange rate from 1.7100 to 1.7200 has affected the forward swap price only slightly (by 1 point). A change in the interest rate differential from 3.0% to 2.5%, however, has changed it significantly. Essentially, a forward swap is an interest rate instrument rather than a currency instrument: when a bank takes a forward swap position, it is taking an interest rate view rather than a currency view. If bank dealers traded outrights, they would be combining two related but different markets in one deal, which is less satisfactory.

So far, we have seen what the swap price is only as a number to be added to or subtracted from the spot rate in order to achieve the outright rate. However, the forward swap is also an instrument in its own right. The swap deal itself is an exchange of one currency for another currency on one date, to be reversed on a given future date. A swap deal is therefore always a deal to 'sell and buy' or 'buy and sell' a currency – i.e., to sell it for settlement spot <u>and</u> buy it back for settlement forward, or vice versa. The following example shows how this fits into the construction of a forward outright. Then we consider what the swap is on its own.

Example 10

A bank sells dollars 3 months forward outright to a counterparty, against Swiss francs. The bank can be seen as creating the outright in the following way:

Spot deal:	bank's spot dealer sells dollars spot
Forward swap deal: $\left\{ \rule{0pt}{40pt}\right.$	bank's forward dealer buys dollars spot <u>and</u> bank's forward dealer sells dollars 3 months
Net effect:	bank sells dollars 3 months forward outright

The customer in the example above thinks of the deal as a single deal, with a single price, for a single settlement and receives only one confirmation, for the forward outright settlement. However, internally, the deal is split between the spot dealer's trading book and the forward dealer's trading book.

When a bank quotes a swap rate, it quotes in a similar manner to a spot rate: the bank's <u>forward</u> dealer buys the base currency <u>forward</u> on the left (at the same time as selling it spot), and sells the base currency <u>forward</u> on the right (at the same time as buying it spot). For example, on a USD/CHF 3-month forward swap quote of 22/20, the bank quoting the price does the following:

−22	/	−20
sell dollars spot		buy dollars spot
<u>and</u> buy dollars forward		<u>and</u> sell dollars forward

---

The quoting bank <u>always</u> 'sells and buys' (in that order) the base currency on the left and 'buys and sells' the base currency on the right.

A forward foreign exchange swap viewed on its own, rather than as part of an outright, is therefore a temporary purchase or sale of one currency against another. An equivalent effect could be achieved by borrowing one currency for a given period, while lending the other currency for the same period. This is why the approximate formula shown earlier for the swap points reflects the interest rate differential (generally based on Eurocurrency interest rates rather than domestic interest rates) between the two currencies, converted into foreign exchange terms.

Suppose that a forward dealer has undertaken a similar deal to the one above – bought and sold dollars (in that order) – but as a speculative position, rather than in order to provide an outright to a customer. In this case, what interest rate view has he taken? He has effectively borrowed dollars and lent Swiss francs for the period. He probably expects US interest rates to rise (so that he can relend them at a higher rate) and/or Swiss rates to fall (so that he can reborrow them at a lower rate). In fact the important point is that the interest differential should move in the dollar's favour. For example, even if US interest rates fall rather than rise, the dealer will still make a profit as long as Swiss rates fall even more than dollar rates.

Although only one single price is dealt (the swap price), the swap transaction has two separate settlements:

(i)   A settlement on the spot value date
(ii) A settlement on the forward value date

There is no net outright position taken, and the spot dealer's spread will therefore not be involved, but some benchmark spot rate will nevertheless be needed in order to arrive at the settlement rates. As the swap is a representation of the interest rate differential between the two currencies quoted, as long as the near and far sides of the swap settlement preserve this differential, it does not generally make a significant difference which exact spot rate is used as a base for adding or subtracting the swap points. The rate must, however, generally be a current rate. This is discussed further below – see the section on 'Historic rate rollovers' and also Chapter 10.

Example 11

At the moment, 3-month dollar interest rates are higher than 3-month sterling rates. You expect this difference to narrow. Rates are quoted to you as follows:

GBP/USD spot: 1.4752/58
3-month swap: 80/86.

You 'buy and sell' GBP 5 million (which is also selling and buying dollars), spot against 3 months. This is equivalent to borrowing sterling and at the same time lending dollars. This will make you a profit if rates move as you expect: for example, if sterling rates rise, you could lend out the sterling at a higher rate, or if dollar rates fall, you could borrow the dollars at a lower rate.

You therefore deal at 80 points because the bank quoting the price 'sells and buys' the base currency on the left. You agree a settlement rate for spot as say 1.4755 (the mid-rate). Therefore the two legs of the swap are settled at 1.4755 and 1.4835 (=1.4755 + 0.0080):

Value spot, you buy GBP 5 million against dollars at 1.4755
   and
Value 3 months, you sell GBP 5 million against dollars at
   1.4835

Later in the same day, the rates have moved as follows. The differential has narrowed as you expected, and the spot rate has also moved:

GBP/USD spot: 1.4910/20
3-month swap: 70/76.

You now close out your position to take your profit, by selling and buying GBP 5 million at 76 points. You agree settlement rates of 1.4915 and 1.4991 (=1.4915 + 0.0076):

Value spot, you sell GBP 5 million against dollars at 1.4915
   and
Value 3 months, you buy GBP 5 million against dollars at
   1.4991

Your cashflows are therefore as follows:

	Spot	3 months
Original deal:	+ GBP 5,000,000	− GBP 5,000,000
Original deal:	− USD 7,377,500	+ USD 7,417,500
Close out:	− GBP 5,000,000	+ GBP 5,000,000
Close out:	+ USD 7,457,500	− USD 7,495,500
Net cashflows:	+ USD 80,000	− USD 78,000

You could therefore be said to have a profit of USD 2,000 (= + USD 80,000 − USD 78,000).

However, this does not take account of the time value of money (see Chapter 2). Assuming that there are 91 days in the 3-month period and that the 3-month dollar interest rate is 5%, the NPV of the net cashflows is USD 2,973.53:

$$+ \text{USD } 80{,}000 - \frac{\text{USD } 78{,}000}{\left(1 + \left(0.05 \times \dfrac{91}{360}\right)\right)} = +\text{USD } 2{,}973.53$$

A dealer expecting the interest rate differential to move in favour of the base currency (for example, base currency interest rates to rise or variable currency interest rates to fall) will 'buy and sell' the base currency. This is equivalent to borrowing the base currency and depositing in the variable currency. And vice versa.

Valuation of a swap book

In Example 11, we valued the result of two swaps, where the second swap neatly offset the first. In practice, a dealer will have many swaps on his book, resulting in many cashflows in different currencies on different dates. The entire book can be valued by calculating the present value of each cashflow separately and then adding up all the present values – some positive and some negative – including those of the cashflows in the dealer's home currency, to calculate a *net present value (NPV)*.

Historic rate rollovers

We have mentioned above that the settlement rates (spot and forward) for a forward swap deal must generally be based on a current market spot rate. This is because many central banks require that banks under their supervision use only current rates, except in occasional and well-documented circumstances. The following example illustrates why a corporate customer might wish to use a historic rate rather than a current rate, and the effect.

Example 12

In June, a US company sells USD 1 million forward outright for value 15 August against Swiss francs, at a forward outright rate of 1.7250. This deal is done to cover the cost the company expects to pay for Swiss imports. On 13 August, the company realizes that it will not need to pay the Swiss francs to its supplier until a month later. It therefore rolls over the foreign exchange cover by using a forward swap – buying and selling dollars, spot against one month.

On 13 August, the exchange rates are as follows:

USD/CHF spot: 1.8166/71
31-day swap: 20/22

The company therefore buys and sells dollars at 1.8168 (spot) and 1.8168 + 0.0020 = 1.8188 (forward).

The company's cashflows will then be:

15 August	15 September
sell USD 1,000,000	
buy CHF 1,725,000	
buy USD 1,000,000	sell USD 1,000,000
sell CHF 1,816.800	buy CHF 1,818,800
Net:	sell USD 1,000,000
sell CHF 91,800	buy CHF 1,818,800

The overall net result is that the company sells USD 1 million against CHF 1,727,000 (=CHF 1,818,800 – CHF 91,800) – an all-in rate of 1.7270, which is effectively the original rate dealt of 1.7250 adjusted by the swap price of 20 points. The company might, however, have a cashflow problem on 15 August, because there is a cash outflow then of CHF 91,800.

The company might therefore prefer to request the bank to base the swap on the historic rate of 1.7250 – dealing instead at 1.7250 spot and 1.7270 forward. The cashflows would then be:

15 August	15 September
sell USD 1,000,000	
buy CHF 1,725,000	
buy USD 1,000,000	sell USD 1,000,000
sell CHF 1,725,000	buy CHF 1,727,000
Net:	sell USD 1,000,000
	buy CHF 1,727,000

The overall net result is the same as before, but there is no cashflow problem.

Underlying this arrangement, however, is an effective loan from the bank to the company of CHF 91,800 for 31 days. If the bank is, exceptionally, prepared to base the swap on a historic

> rate in this way, it needs to charge the company interest on this hidden loan. This interest would normally be incorporated into a less favourable swap price.

The reason many central banks discourage historic rate rollovers is that they might help a bank's customer to conceal foreign exchange losses. If a customer has taken a speculative position which has made a loss, a historic rate rollover enables it to roll the loss over to a later date rather than realize it.

As a result, if a bank does agree to a historic rate rollover, it must generally insist that the reasons be agreed between senior management of the customer and the bank, with appropriate documentary evidence of this.

Short dates

For convenience, we have repeated here a short part of the introductory chapter. Value dates earlier than 1 month are referred to as *short dates*. There are certain regular dates usually quoted, and the terminology used is the same as in the deposit market, as follows:

Overnight (O/N): a deposit or foreign exchange swap from today until tomorrow

Tom-next (T/N): a deposit or foreign exchange swap from tomorrow until the next day (spot)

Spot-next (S/N): a deposit or foreign exchange swap from spot until the next day

Spot-a-week (S/W): a deposit or foreign exchange swap from spot until a week later

'Tomorrow' means the next working day after today and 'next' means the next working day following (i.e. spot).

Outright deals (as opposed to swaps) are referred to as 'value today', 'value tomorrow', etc.

Deals cannot always be done for value today. For example, when London and European markets are open, Japanese banks have generally closed their books for today, so deals in yen can only be done for value tomorrow. Similarly in London, most European currencies can only be dealt early in the morning for value today, because of the time difference and the mechanical difficulties of ensuring good value. For many currencies, even the market for value tomorrow generally closes during the morning.

In considering swaps and outrights for short dates later than the spot date, exactly the same rules apply as in calculating longer dates. However, confusion can arise in considering outrights for dates earlier than spot – i.e., outright value today and outright value tomorrow. The rules are still the same in that the bank always 'sells and buys' (in that order) the base currency on the left and 'buys and sells' the base currency on the right – regardless of whether it is before or after spot. The confusion can arise because the spot value date – effectively the baseline date for calculation of the outright rate – is the near date when calculating most forward prices. For value today and tomorrow, however, the spot date becomes the far date and the outright date is the near date.

Example 13

A bank sells dollars for outright value tomorrow to a counter-party, against Swiss francs. The bank can be seen as creating the outright in the following way:

tom-next deal:	bank's forward dealer sells dollars tomorrow <u>and</u> bank's forward dealer buys dollars spot
spot deal:	bank's spot dealer sells dollars spot
net effect:	bank sells dollars outright tomorrow

It is useful to compare this with Example 10. Importantly, notice that, because tomorrow is earlier than spot, the tom-next deal in Example 13 is 'sell and buy', whereas in Example 10 the swap deal was 'buy and sell'. In Example 10, the spot dealer and the forward dealer both dealt on the right side of the quote. In Example 13, however, the spot dealer still deals on the right side of the price but the forward dealer deals on the left side of the price. For example, on a USD/CHF tom-next quote of 2/1, the bank quoting the price does the following (this is the same way round as for all swaps):

-2	/	-1
sells dollars tomorrow		buys dollars tomorrow
and buys dollars spot		and sells dollars spot

Swap prices for very short periods like O/N, T/N and S/N are very small numbers. The forward points are therefore often less than 1 point and it is important to line them up correctly when they are being added to or subtracted from the spot. Sometimes they are quoted as fractions – for example, a price of "$1\frac{1}{2}/1\frac{1}{4}$" means "one and a half points/one and a quarter points" – and sometimes as decimals – for example, a price of "1.5/1.25" again means "1.5 points/1.25 points". In this case, that part of the price which is immediately before the decimal point should be lined up with the final digit of the spot price. If, for example, USD/JPY spot is 125.67/72 and the S/N price is 1.5/1.25, they would be combined as follows:

	↓	↓
Spot:	125.6**7**	/125.7**2**
S/N:	0.0**1**5/	0.0**1**25
Outright:	125.6**6**5/	125.7**0**75
	↑	↑

Example 14

Spot USD/CHF:	1.7505/10
Overnight swap:	1/ $\frac{3}{4}$
Tom-next swap:	$\frac{1}{2}$/ $\frac{1}{4}$
1-week swap:	7/ 5

(i) Suppose a customer wishes to sell dollars for outright value one week after spot. The bank spot dealer buys dollars for value spot on the left at 1.7505. The bank forward dealer 'sells and buys' dollars also on the left at a swap difference of 7 points. Therefore the bank buys dollars outright one week after spot at $1.7505 - 0.0007 = 1.7498$. The other side of the one week outright price is $1.7510 - 0.0005 = 1.7505$.

(ii) Suppose the customer wishes to sell dollars for outright value tomorrow. This is equivalent to selling dollars for value spot and, at the same time, undertaking a swap to sell dollars for value tomorrow and buy dollars back for value spot.

Again, the bank spot dealer buys dollars for value spot on the left at 1.7505. However, the bank forward dealer 'buys and sells' dollars tomorrow against spot on the right at a swap difference of $\frac{1}{4}$ point. Furthermore (because Swiss interest rates are lower than dollar rates), the dollar is at a discount to the Swiss franc: the 'bigger number' $\frac{1}{2}$ is on the left. The dollar is therefore worth less on the far date (i.e. spot) and more on the near date (i.e. tomorrow). The swap difference is therefore added to the spot rate, rather than subtracted, to give an outright value tomorrow price of $1.7505 + \frac{1}{4} = 1.750525$. The other side of the value tomorrow outright price is $1.7510 + \frac{1}{2} = 1.75105$.

A simple rule to remember for the calculation of dates earlier than spot is 'reverse the swap points and proceed exactly as for a forward later than spot'. In the above example, this would mean reversing '$\frac{1}{2}/\frac{1}{4}$' to '$\frac{1}{4}/\frac{1}{2}$'. The outright value tomorrow price is then $(1.7505 + \frac{1}{4})/(1.7510 + \frac{1}{2})$, obtained by adding the swap points to the spot rate because the 'bigger' swap number is now on the right. **However, it is important always to remember to make this reversal in your head only! Never actually quote the price in reverse!**

O/N prices are the only regular swap prices not involving the spot value date – i.e., the O/N swap is from today until tomorrow, not from today until spot. To calculate an outright value today price, it is therefore necessary to combine the spot with both the overnight price and the tom-next price:

(iii) Suppose the customer wishes to sell dollars for outright value today. This is equivalent to three separate transactions: selling dollars for value spot, undertaking a swap to sell dollars for value tomorrow and buy dollars back for value spot (tom-next swap) and undertaking another swap to sell dollars for value today and buy dollars back for value tomorrow (overnight swap). The price is therefore $1.7505 + \frac{1}{4} + \frac{3}{4} = 1.7506$.

The rules can be thought of in terms of premiums and discounts, which apply in the same way as with forwards after spot. The swaps in the previous example show a dollar discount because Swiss franc interest rates are lower than dollar interest rates. Consequently, if the customer sells dollars value today and not value spot, he will receive the currency with the lower interest rate two days early. The extra point which he receives from the bank reflects this.

Example 15

The following are rates for EUR/USD:

Spot: 0.8763/58
O/N: 1.30/1.80
T/N: 1.60/2.10
S/N: 1.70/2.20

spot: 0.8763 /0.8768
S/N   0.00017/0.00022
outright day after spot: 0.87647/0.87702

spot:	0.8763 /0.8768
T/N	0.00016/0.00021
outright tomorrow:	0.87609/0.87664

spot:	0.8763 /0.8768
T/N	0.00016/0.00021
O/N	0.00013/0.00018
outright today:	0.87591/0.87651

Forward-forwards

A *forward-forward* swap is a swap deal between two forward dates rather than from spot to a forward date – for example, to sell US dollars 1 month forward and buy them back 3 months forward. In this case, the swap is for the 2-month period between the 1-month date and the 3-month date. A company might undertake such a swap because it has previously bought dollars forward but wishes now to defer the transaction by a further two months, as it will not need the dollars as soon as it thought.

As with forward-forward interest rates, FX forward-forwards are referred to by the beginning and end dates of the forward period, compared with the spot value date. Thus the forward-forward described here is a '1v3', meaning that the forward period starts 1 month from now and ends 3 months from now.

From the bank's point of view, a forward-forward swap can be seen as constructed from two separate swaps, each based on spot.

Example 16

USD/CHF spot rate:	1.7325/ 35
1-month swap:	65/ 61
3-month swap:	160/155

If our bank's counterparty wishes to sell dollars 1 month forward, and buy them back 3 months forward, this is the same as undertaking one swap to buy dollars spot and sell dollars 1 month forward, and another swap to sell dollars spot and buy dollars 3 months forward.

As swaps are always quoted as how the quoting bank 'sells and buys' the base currency on the left, and 'buys and sells' the base currency on the right, the counterparty can 'buy and sell' dollars spot against 1 month at a swap price of −65, with settlement rates of spot and (spot − 0.0065). He can simultaneously 'sell and buy' dollars spot against 3 months at a swap price of − 155 with settlement rates of spot and (spot − 0.0155). He can therefore do both – 'sell and buy' dollars 1 month against 3 months – at settlement rates of (spot − 0.0065) and (spot − 0.0155), which implies a difference between the two forward settlement rates of (−155) − (−65) = −90 points.

Conversely, the counterparty can 'buy and sell' dollars 1 month against 3 months at a swap price of (−160) − (−61) = −99 points. The two-way price is therefore −99/−90, quoted as usual without the '−' signs, as 99/90.

As with a swap from spot to a forward date, the two settlement prices in a forward-forward must be based on a current market rate. In the above example, using the middle spot rate, for example, the settlement rates could be 1.7265 (= 1.7330 − 0.0065) for 1 month forward and 1.7175 (= 1.7330 − 0.0155) for 3 months forward.

These settlement rates would enable our forward dealer to cover his position exactly with another bank. We could, for example, ask another bank for a 1-month swap price to cover the first leg of the forward-forward. Assuming prices have not moved, we could deal at −65 points with settlement rates of 1.7330 (spot) and 1.7265 (1 month). We could then cover the second leg with a 3-month swap at another bank's price of − 155, with settlement rates of 1.7330 (spot) and 1.7175 (3 months). The spot settlements would offset each other and the forward settlements would exactly offset the settlements with our own counterparty.

In practice, however, forward dealers often base the settlement rate for the first leg on a middle rate for spot and also a middle rate for the near forward date. In the example above, this would give a settlement rate of 1.7330 (middle) − 0.0063 (middle) = 1.7267. The settlement rate for the second leg would then be 1.7267 − 0.0090 = 1.7177. The difference between the two settlement rates is still the −90 points agreed, but the settlement rates are slightly different.

If the yield curves of the two currencies cross over at some point between the two forward dates, the forward points will show a premium for one period but a discount for the other. In this case, it is important to make sure that the '+' and '−' signs are correctly shown before constructing the forward-forward price, and also to remember that two negatives make a positive.

Forward-forward price after spot

First, insert '−' signs where necessary. Then:

left side = (left side of far-date swap)

 − (right side of near-date swap)

right side = (right side of far-date swap)

 − (left side of near-date swap)

The bid–offer spread of the resulting price is the sum of the two separate bid–offer spreads.

Example 17

Given the following prices, you need to 'sell and buy' sterling against euros forward-forward 2v5.

EUR/GBP spot: 0.6235/45
2-month swap: 17/13
5-month swap: 25/31

The 2-month price is −17/−13 (a euro discount) but the 5-month price is +25/+31 (a euro premium). The 2v5 price is therefore:

$$25 - (-13) = 38 \text{ on the left}$$

and $\qquad 31 - (-17) = 48$ on the right

On this forward-forward price of 38/48, you deal at 38 (the quoting bank always 'sells and buys' the base currency on the left).

The middle rate for 2 months forward is 0.6225 (=0.6240 − 0.0015). You therefore agree to settlement rates of 0.6225 for 2 months and 0.6263 (=0.6225 + 0.0038) for 5 months.

Care needs to be taken with swaps from before spot until after spot.

Example 18

USD/CHF spot rate	1.7325/35
T/N swap:	3/2
3-month swap:	160/155

If a counterparty requests a price to 'sell and buy' dollars tomorrow against 3 months after spot, this can be seen as a price to sell tomorrow and buy spot at (−2) points with settlement rates of (spot + 0.0002) and spot, and a price to sell spot and buy 3 months later at (−155) points, with settlement rates of spot and (spot − 0.0155). The total price is therefore the difference between (spot − 0.0155) and (spot + 0.0002), which is (−155) − (+2) = −157. The other side of the price is (−160) − (+3) = −163. The 2-sided price is therefore 163/157.

Forward-forward price from before spot until after spot

First, insert '−' signs where necessary. Then:

left side = (left side of far-date swap)

+ (left side of T/N or T/N <u>and</u> O/N)

right side = (right side of far-date swap)

+ (right side of T/N or T/N <u>and</u> O/N)

The bid–offer spread of the resulting price is the sum of the separate bid–offer spreads.

A forward-forward from before spot might be for a regular period from the start date, rather than until a regular date after spot. For example, a swap for '3 months out of today' would mean that the end date is not 3 months after the spot date but 3 months after today. The regular 3-month price is therefore too long a period to use, and the correct period must be interpolated (see Chapter 2) from the 2-month price and the 3-month price.

Example 19

Today is 15 April, spot is 17 April, 2 months from spot is 17 June and 3 months from spot is 17 July. You need to quote to customer a swap price for 3 months out of today which is from 15 April to 15 July.

GBP/USD spot rate	1.4325/35
O/N swap:	4/3
T/N swap:	3/2
2-month swap (61 days):	100/95
3-month swap (91 days):	160/155

The period from spot until 17 June is 61 days.
The period from spot until 15 July is 89 days.
The period from spot until 17 July is 91 days.

Interpolating, the left side of the swap price from spot until 15 July is:

$$-100 + \left((-160 - -100) \times \frac{(89-61)}{(91-61)}\right) = -156$$

Similarly, the right side is:

$$-95 + \left((-155 - -95) \times \frac{(89-61)}{(91-61)}\right) = -151$$

To calculate the swap we need, we therefore add the following prices:

O/N swap:	$-4/$	-3
T/N swap:	$-3/$	-2
swap from spot to 15 July:	$-156/$	-151
	$-163/$	-156

Calculation summary

It might be helpful to collect together here the various rules which apply to calculating forwards:

The currency with higher interest rate (=the currency at a discount) is worth less in the future. If this is the base currency, the points are negative.
The currency with lower interest rate (=the currency at a premium) is worth more in the future. If this is the base currency, the points are positive.

The bank quoting the price <u>always</u> 'sells and buys' the base currency on the left and 'buys and sells' the base currency on the right.

If the swap price appears larger on the right than the left, it is positive.

If the swap price appears larger on the left than the right, it is negative.

For outright forwards later than spot:

The left swap price is added to (or subtracted from) the left spot price.

The right swap price is added to (or subtracted from) the right spot price.

For outright deals earlier than spot:

Calculate as if the swap price were reversed.

Forward-forwards:

First, insert '−' signs where necessary. Then:

<u>after spot:</u>

left side = (left side of far-date swap)

− (right side of near-date swap)

right side = (right side of far-date swap)

− (left side of near-date swap)

<u>from before spot until after spot:</u>

left side = (left side of far-date swap)

+ (left side of T/N or T/N <u>and</u> O/N)

right side = (right side of far-date swap)

+ (right side of T/N or T/N <u>and</u> O/N)

In general:

Of the two prices available, the customer gets the worse one. Thus if the swap price is 3/2 and the customer knows that the points are in his favour (the outright will be better than the spot), the price will be 2. If he knows that the points are against him (the outright will be worse than the spot), the price will be 3.

The bid–offer spread of the resulting price is the sum of the separate bid–offer spreads.

Cross-rate calculations

A forward cross-rate is calculated in a similar way to a spot cross-rate as explained in the previous chapter, but using outrights. The same is true for any outright calculated from two other outrights and is true for short dates as well as any other outrights:

- To calculate an outright from two exchange rates with the same base currency (for example, the dollar), divide opposite sides of the individual outrights.
- To calculate an outright from two exchange rates with the same variable currency, again divide opposite sides of the individual outrights.
- To calculate an outright from two rates where the common currency is the base for one but the variable for the other, multiply the same sides of the individual outrights.

To calculate cross-rate forward swaps, the process above must be taken a step further:

(i)   calculate the spot cross-rate as usual
(ii) calculate the two individual forward outrights as above
(iii) from (ii) calculate the forward outright cross-rate
(iv) subtract (i) from (iii) to give the cross-rate swap

Example 20

Based on the following prices, what is the EUR/GBP 6-month swap?

EUR/USD spot:	0.8734/39
6 months:	23/19
GBP/USD spot:	1.4237/42
6 months:	63/67

EUR/USD spot:	0.8734/ 0.8739
6 months:	−0.0023/−0.0019
outright:	0.8711/ 0.8720

GBP/USD spot:	1.4237/ 1.4242
6 months:	0.0063/ 0.0067
outright:	1.4300/ 1.4309

$$0.8734 \div 1.4242 = 0.6133 \qquad 0.8739 \div 1.4237 = 0.6138$$

$$0.8711 \div 1.4309 = 0.6088 \qquad 0.8720 \div 1.4300 = 0.6098$$

EUR/GBP 6-month outright:	0.6088/ 0.6098
EUR/GBP spot:	0.6133/ 0.6138
EUR/GBP 6-month swap:	−0.0045/−0.0040 i.e. 45/40

The same approach can be used for calculating a USD-based rate from two cross-rates, and also for calculating short-date swaps.

Example 21

Based on the following prices, what is the USD/SEK O/N swap?

EUR/USD spot:	0.8734/39
O/N:	0.6/0.4
T/N:	0.7/0.5
EUR/SEK spot:	8.3975/95
O/N:	2.4/2.6
T/N:	2.3/2.5

EUR/USD spot:	0.8734 / 0.8739
T/N:	−0.00007/−0.00005
outright tomorrow:	0.87345/ 0.87397
O/N	−0.00006/−0.00004
outright today:	0.87349/ 0.87403

EUR/SEK spot:	8.3975 / 8.3995
T/N:	0.00023/ 0.00025
outright tomorrow:	8.39725/ 8.39927
O/N:	0.00024/ 0.00026
outright today:	8.39699/ 8.39903

$$8.39699 \div 0.87403 = 9.607210 \qquad 8.39903 \div 0.87349 = 9.615485$$

$$8.39725 \div 0.87397 = 9.608167 \qquad 8.39927 \div 0.87345 = 9.616200$$

USD/SEK outright tomorrow:	9.608167/9.616200
USD/SEK outright today:	9.607210/9.615485
USD/SEK O/N swap:	0.000715/0.000957 i.e. 7.1/9.6

Remember that in calculating the outright today and outright tomorrow rates above for EUR/USD and EUR/SEK, each spot price is combined with the opposite side of the swap price and the sign is 'reversed'. Similarly, in the final calculation of the O/N swap price for USD/SEK, the swap price appears to be 'reversed' for the same reason.

In order to calculate a cross-rate forward-forward, extend the process: calculate the cross-rate swap for the near date of the forward-forward and also the cross-rate swap for the far date, and then combine them as usual.

It might be possible to use cross-rates to construct an outright in a more cost-efficient way if prices are out of line, as in the following example.

Example 22

Based on the following prices available to you in the market, what is best price at which you can buy euros against sterling, 6 months forward outright?

EUR/GBP spot:	0.6132/37
6 months:	44/39
EUR/USD spot:	0.8734/39
6 months:	23/19
GBP/USD spot:	1.4237/42
6 months:	63/67

The outright EUR/GBP must be constructed from a spot and a swap. We are dealing on the right-hand side.

For the spot, the straightforward EUR/GBP price of 0.6137 is better than the price of 0.6138 which can be constructed via the cross-rate calculation (see Example 20, which is based on the same market prices).

For the swap, the price of −40 points which can be constructed via the cross-rate calculation (again see Example 20, which is based on the same market prices) is better than the straightforward EUR/GBP price of −39 points.

Therefore an outright price of 0.6097 (=0.6137 − 0.0040) can be achieved by:

> buying euros against sterling directly at 0.6137
> and   selling and buying euros against dollars at −19 points
> and   buying and selling sterling against dollars at +63 points

Non-deliverable forwards (NDFs)

A *non-deliverable forward (NDF)* is a forward outright where, instead of settling the outright amounts at maturity, the two parties agree at the outset that they will settle only the change in value between the forward rate dealt and the spot rate two working days before maturity. The economic effect is the same as if a normal forward outright had been dealt and then closed out two days before maturity by an offsetting spot deal.

One advantage of an NDF is that it can be used to trade non-convertible currencies. In this case, the settlement at maturity of the NDF is necessarily made in a convertible currency – generally one of the pair of currencies being traded. An NDF also reduces the counterparty credit risk, as the risk is limited to the settlement amount and does not involve the usual settlement risk of the whole principal amount of the deal.

An NDF is a contract for differences, analogous to an FRA for interest rates.

Example 23

It is now 15 April. A company needs to buy TWD 100 million against sterling for settlement in 3 months (17 July). It buys this amount 3 months forward using an NDF, at a rate of 49.06.

On 15 July, the company and the bank agree a GBP/TWD spot rate of 48.43 for settlement.

$$\frac{100,000,000}{49.06} = 2,038,320.42$$

$$\frac{100,000,000}{48.43} = 2,064,835.85$$

The profit or loss is settled as if the company had bought TWD 100 million at 49.06 and then sold again at 48.43. As this is an NDF, there is no need to transact an actual spot deal on 15 July.

buy TWD 100,000,000, sell GBP 2,038,320.42
sell TWD 100,000,000, buy GBP 2,064,835.85
profit GBP   26,515.42

The company therefore receives a settlement of GBP 26,515.42 from the bank on 17 July.

If this were a speculative transaction, nothing further would be required. However, the company physically needs the TWD 100 million. Therefore, it buys TWD 100 million spot on 15 July for value 17 July at 48.43 in the normal way. This will cost GBP 2,064,835.85. The net effect for the company is therefore a cost of GBP 2,038,320.42 (=GBP 2,064,835.85 − GBP 26,515.42), leaving the company in the same position as if it had been able to buy the TWD 100 million 3 months forward in the first place.

In practice, the net effect might be slightly worse than this because the NDF would be settled against a middle reference rate but the spot deal would be at bid rate. However, if the company had been able to transact a normal forward outright in the first place, that also would have involved the bid side of the spot rate.

A source must be agreed for the reference spot rate to be used for calculating the settlement amount if the NDF is left open until maturity. The conventional source will vary from currency to currency and could, for example, be a central bank fixing rate or a rate published on Reuters or Telerate.

If the NDF is used speculatively, an alternative is for the NDF to be closed out early and for the settlement amount to be based on the difference between the two rates dealt. In this case, the settlement can be paid at maturity date of the two NDFs or discounted to a present value and settled early.

Example 24

It is now 15 April. A dealer takes a speculative 3-month position by buying TWD 100 million against sterling for value 17 July, using an NDF, at a rate of 49.06.

On 22 April, the dealer closes out the position with another NDF for value 17 July at 48.43.

As in the last example, the dealer is due a profit of GBP 26,515.42 for settlement on 17 July:

buy TWD 100,000,000, sell GBP 2,038,320.42
sell TWD 100,000,000, buy GBP 2,064,835.85
                    profit GBP   26,515.42

There are 84 days from 24 April to 17 July. Assuming that the sterling interest rate for the period is say 5%, the present value of this amount could be settled instead on 24 April as GBP 26,213.78:

$$\frac{GBP\ 26,515.42}{\left(1 + \left(0.05 \times \frac{84}{365}\right)\right)} = GBP\ 26,213.78$$

Time options

When a bank makes a forward outright deal with a company, it quotes a rate for a fixed date, which means the company must deliver one currency and receive another on that date.

If the company has a commitment in the future but does not know the exact delivery date required, it has an alternative means of covering this exposure in the traditional foreign exchange market, using a *time option* (also known as an *option forward*). This allows the company to deal now, but to choose the maturity date later within a specified period. There is, however, no choice about whether to deliver – delivery must take place at some point during the agreed period, for the amount and rate agreed.

It is important not to confuse time options in this sense with currency options. A currency options entails the up-front payment of an 'insurance premium', in return for which the customer has the right to choose whether or not to deal at all.

In pricing a time option, the bank will always assume that the company will take delivery of the currency at the worst possible time for the bank. Therefore the company will always be charged the worst possible forward rate within the period of the time option.

Example 25

The bank's customer wishes to transact a forward deal in dollars against Swiss francs, with a flexible delivery date of between 2 and 3 months. Given the following market prices, what rate does the bank quote?

USD/CHF spot rate: 1.7325/ 35
2-month swap: 130/125
3-month swap: 160/155

The 2-month outright would be 1.7195/1.7210:

$$\frac{\begin{array}{cc} 1.7325/1.7335 \\ 130/ \quad 125 \end{array}}{1.7195/1.7210}$$

The 3-month outright would be 1.7165/1.7180:

$$\frac{\begin{array}{cc} 1.7325/1.7335 \\ 160/ \quad 155 \end{array}}{1.7165/1.7180}$$

If the customer is selling dollars, the worse price is the 3-month price of 1.7165. If the customer is buying dollars, the worse price is the 2-month price of 1.7210. Therefore the time option price is a swap price of 160/125, or an outright price of 1.7165/1.7210.

The advantage to a company of a time option is its flexibility. The company can lock in a fixed exchange rate at which it knows it can deal. There is no exposure to interest rate changes which would affect it if commitments were covered with a forward outright which subsequently needed to be adjusted by means of forward swaps. The disadvantage is the cost, given the wide bid/offer spread involved, particularly if the time period of the option is a long one.

> A time option price is the best for the bank/worst for the customer over the time option period

Long-dated forwards

The formulas we have already seen for a forward outright less than 1 year are:

Forward outright

$$= \text{spot} \times \frac{\left(1 + \left(\text{variable currency interest rate} \times \dfrac{\text{days}}{\text{variable year}}\right)\right)}{\left(1 + \left(\text{base currency interest rate} \times \dfrac{\text{days}}{\text{base year}}\right)\right)}$$

forward swap

$$= \text{spot} \times \frac{\left(\left(\text{variable currency interest rate} \times \dfrac{\text{days}}{\text{variable year}}\right) - \left(\text{base currency interest rate} \times \dfrac{\text{days}}{\text{base year}}\right)\right)}{\left(1 + \left(\text{base currency interest rate} \times \dfrac{\text{days}}{\text{base year}}\right)\right)}$$

These were derived from the assumption that the interest on a deposit or loan is paid on a simple basis as described in Chapter 2. For deposits and loans over 1 year, the interest must be compounded because interest is normally paid at the end of each year. In this case, the corresponding theoretical formulas for a forward outright and a forward swap are as follows:

For long-dated forwards:

Forward outright

$$= \text{spot} \times \left(\left(\frac{(1 + \text{variable interest rate})}{(1 + \text{base interest rate})}\right)^{\text{number of years}}\right)$$

Forward swap

$$= \text{spot} \times \left(\left(\frac{(1 + \text{variable interest rate})}{(1 + \text{base interest rate})}\right)^{\text{number of years}} - 1\right)$$

The interest rates in this case are bond basis rates – quoted on the basis of a true calendar year rather than a 360-day year. These theoretical formulas are not precise in practice for two reasons. Firstly, this compounding does not take account of reinvestment risk. This problem is overcome by using zero-coupon yields for the interest rates. More importantly, the market in long-dated forwards is not very liquid and spreads are very wide. The prices available in practice therefore depend partly on banks' individual positions and hence their interest in quoting a price.

Example 26

What are the theoretical GBP/USD 3-year outright and forward swap, based on the following?

GBP/USD spot: 1.4123
GBP 3-year interest rate: 5.15%
USD 3-year interest rate: 4.35%

$$\text{Forward outright} = 1.4123 \times \left(\left(\frac{1.0435}{1.0515} \right)^{3} \right) = 1.3803$$

$$\text{Forward swap} = 1.4123 \times \left(\left(\frac{1.0435}{1.0515} \right)^{3} - 1 \right)$$

$$= -0.0320 = -320 \text{ points}$$

Synthetic agreements for forward exchange (SAFEs)

SAFES are used very little now, but we have included them here for completeness. A SAFE is an off-balance sheet forward-forward foreign exchange swap. There are two versions of a SAFE – an *FXA* and an *ERA*.

An FXA (*forward exchange agreement*) exactly replicates the economic effect of a forward-forward in the cash market which is reversed at the first settlement date of the forward-forward in order to take a profit or loss. A price for an FXA is quoted in the same way as a forward-forward price, and is dealt in the same way. A forward-forward swap results in two cash settlements, each for the whole amount of the deal. An FXA, however, is settled in a manner analogous to the way an FRA is settled. On the nearer of the two forward dates, a settlement amount is paid from one party to the other to reflect the movement in rates between dealing and settlement, using an agreed settlement rate.

The settlement formula ensures that the result is economically the same as the profit or loss would be with a cash forward-forward. To do so, it takes account of the movement in the spot rate from dealing to settlement, as well as the movement in the forward swap points. This is because, although a forward dealer takes a position on the basis of his expectations of swap movements, his profit or loss is also affected to some extent by spot rate movements. The reason for this is discussed in Chapter 10. As with an FRA, the settlement formula involves an element of discounting, because the settlement is made at the beginning of the forward-forward period.

An FXA can have equal or unequal notional base currency amounts at each end of the swap.

An ERA (*exchange rate agreement*) price is exactly the same as an FXA price, and allows for a discounted settlement to be made at the beginning of the forward-forward period in the same way as an FXA.

The ERA settlement, however, deliberately takes no account of the movement in the spot rate, and the settlement formula is correspondingly simpler. The settlement amount is simply the notional amount of the contract multiplied by the change in the swap rate. With an ERA, only one notional base currency amount is involved.

The two instruments can therefore be compared as follows:

> An FXA replicates exactly the economic effect of a cash forward-forward. In a trading strategy that requires a forward-forward, an FXA is an alternative.
>
> An ERA may be used to trade movements in forward swap prices when the trader specifically wishes the result to be unaffected by movements in the spot rate. This does not exactly replicate a forward-forward.

Advantages of SAFEs

The advantages of a SAFE lie in the problems which arise on credit lines and balance sheet utilization. In the absence of an appropriate netting agreement, when a bank deals forward-forward, its credit lines to and from the counterparty are generally utilized to the extent of twice the notional credit amount applied to the deal – once for each leg of the forward-forward. Between dealing date and the first settlement date, however, the real risk might be far less than this, because the two legs of the deal largely offset each other. The credit exposure allocated to a SAFE, as a contract for differences, will be far less. The capital utilization requirements (see Chapter 12) are similarly reduced. Rather than having two deals on the balance sheet, there are none.

A further advantage of an ERA arises if a forward trader wishes to trade the forward swap points without needing to hedge the effect of potential spot rate movements (although this does not avoid the effect that a significant spot rate movement has on the swap price itself).

The FXA settlement amount
(as an amount of the variable currency)

Settlement amount = first amount

$$\times \left(\frac{\begin{array}{c}\text{(outright exchange rate} - \text{settlement spot rate)} \\ + \text{(swap price dealt} - \text{settlement swap price)}\end{array}}{\left(1 + \left(\text{variable currency LIBOR} \times \dfrac{\text{days in swap period}}{\text{variable year}}\right)\right)} \right)$$

$$- \text{ second amount} \times \text{(outright exchange rate} \\ - \text{spot price used for settlement)}$$

> ### The ERA settlement amount
> #### (as an amount of the variable currency):
>
> Settlement amount = base currency amount
>
> $$\times \frac{(\text{swap price dealt} - \text{settlement swap price})}{\left(1 + \left(\text{variable currency LIBOR} \times \dfrac{\text{days in swap period}}{\text{variable year}}\right)\right)}$$
>
> The settlement amount is paid by the seller of the FXA or ERA to the buyer (or vice versa if it is a negative amount), where the buyer is the party which 'buys and sells' the base currency.

In the above settlement formulas:

- 'First amount' is the base currency amount transacted at the beginning of the swap.
- 'Second amount' is the base currency amount transacted at the end of the swap.
  (These amounts can be the same but do not need to be.)
- 'Outright exchange rate' is the outright, to the near date of the forward-forward period, when the FXA is transacted.
- 'Settlement spot rate' is the reference spot agreed 2 working days before the swap period.
- 'Settlement swap price' is the reference swap price agreed 2 working days before the swap period.
- 'LIBOR' is for the swap period, agreed 2 working days before the swap period.

Example 27

At the moment, dollar interest rates are lower than sterling rates. You expect this difference to narrow and therefore decide to sell a 1v3 SAFE for GBP 5 million. The 1v3 month period is 61 days. Rates are quoted to you as follows:

GBP/USD 1-month outright: 1.4675
1v3 swap: 86/80.

You sell the SAFE at −80 points. Two business days before the 1-month settlement date, rates are as follows:

GBP/USD spot: 1.4915
2-month swap: −76.
USD 2-month LIBOR: 4.23%.

If you have used an FXA, the settlement amount will be a profit of USD 1131.79 (the settlement formula gives a negative amount so it is payable by the buyer to the seller):

$$5{,}000{,}000 \times \left(\frac{\substack{(1.4675 - 1.4915) \\ + (-0.0080 - -0.0076)}}{\left(1 + \left(0.0423 \times \dfrac{61}{360}\right)\right)} \right)$$

$$- 5{,}000{,}000 \times (1.4675 - 1.4915) = -1{,}131.79$$

If you have used an ERA, the settlement amount will be a profit of USD 1,985.77:

$$5{,}000{,}000 \times \frac{(-0.0080 - -0.0076)}{\left(1 + \left(0.0423 \times \dfrac{61}{360}\right)\right)} = -1{,}985.77$$

Summary of uses of forward FX instruments

Hedging

A company which expects to pay or receive foreign currency at a future date can lock in the exchange rate for doing this with a forward outright. If the currency requirement is earlier than spot then, depending on the currency and provided the deal is done early enough, the company can deal for outright value today or tomorrow.

If a company has already transacted a forward deal but wishes to delay settlement because the commercial requirement has not arisen as early as originally anticipated, it can roll the maturing deal forward with a swap. If the requirement is earlier than expected, it can roll it nearer with a swap the other way round. If the need to adjust the date in this way is seen ahead of time, the company can use a forward-forward in the same way.

Time options, while generally rather cost-inefficient, provide flexibility to a hedger. NDFs provide a mechanism for hedging currencies which are not fully convertible.

A bank dealer can use forwards to hedge his existing positions. A trading bank which needs to provide an outright for a customer will construct it from a spot and a swap. However, a dealer in a small bank covering a customer position might himself ask another bank, more active in foreign exchange, for a forward outright price.

Speculation

A dealer wishing to take a strategic (i.e. medium-term) speculative position in a currency, will use a forward outright, rather than a spot deal which would continually require rolling over with swaps.

Forward swaps are essentially interest rate instruments. A dealer wishing to speculate on the interest rate differential between two currencies will 'buy and sell' or 'sell and buy'. Frequently, a dealer will establish forward-forward positions, either directly for this purpose, or as a result of two or more swap deals he has transacted with customers in different maturities.

Arbitrage

The relationship between interest rates and swap prices allows for the possibility of arbitrage. This is considered in Chapter 9.

Exercises

1 Which of the following are true?

   (a) If the 6-month USD/CHF forward swap points change from 125/120 to 135/130, USD interest rates might have fallen.
   (b) If the 3-month forward swap points are greater on the left than the right, then the variable currency has a higher interest rate than the base currency.
   (c) The 2-month GBP/USD swap points are 67/72. If dollar interest rates then rise but nothing else changes, the swap points will get bigger.
   (d) If the 1-month forward points for AUD/CAD are 123/118, the Canadian dollar is at a forward discount against the Australian dollar.
   (e) If the 3-month EUR/GBP swap is par and the 3-month GBP interest rate is 5.0%, then the 3-month euro interest rate is also 5.0%.
   (f) An FX spot trader who went home last night leaving an open position will adjust his position at the start of today using O/N and T/N swaps.

2 What should the mid-rate theoretically be for the USD/CHF 3-month outright, given the following? The 3-month period is 92 days.

USD/CHF spot: 1.7120/26,
USD 3-month interest rate: 5.10/5.20%
CHF 3-month interest rate: 2.70/2.80%

3 What is the two-way 3-month swap price for USD/CHF, based on the following borrowing and lending rates? The 3-month period is 91 days.

USD/CHF spot: 1.7120/26,
USD 3-month interest rate: 5.10/5.20%
CHF 3-month interest rate: 2.70/2.80%

4 You wish to take a particular speculative position and ask a bank for a 3-month USD/CHF swap price. It is quoted to you as 127/122 and you deal at 127. What is your expectation for market movements?

5 EUR/USD forward swaps are as follows. What can you say about the euro and dollar yield curves?

6 months: 10/5
12 months: 5/10

6 You are a dealer and quote a customer 56/61 for a EUR/GBP 6-month swap (182 days). The customer buys and sells GBP 10 million and you base the spot on 0.6215.
   You immediately ask another bank for a 6-month price because you wish to cover this position. You deal on the price quoted to you of 58/62 and you base the spot on 0.6205.
   What is your resulting profit or loss? Euro interest rates are 4% and sterling interest rates are 6%.

7 Given the following prices:

USD/CAD   spot: 1.5671/77   6-month swap 30/33
USD/SEK   spot: 10.3458/68   6-month swap 70/67

(a) What is the two-way 6-month forward outright price for CAD/SEK and at what price can a customer sell Canadian dollars?
(b) What is the two-way 6-month swap price for CAD/SEK, and at what price can a customer sell and buy Canadian dollars?

8 You are a dealer and quote a 6-month GBP/JPY swap to a customer as 435/425. The customer buys and sells GBP 1,000,000, based on a spot of 178.10. You cover this position using two 6-month swaps quoted to you as follows:

73/69 for GBP/USD (the deal is for GBP 1,000,000 and the spot is set at 1.4260)
240/235 for USD/JPY (the deal is for USD 1,426,000 and the spot is set at 124.85).

What are your net cashflows spot and forward?

9 You are quoted all the following rates. What is the best rate at which you can sell sterling against yen 6 months forward outright, and how do you achieve it?

GBP/JPY spot: 178.05/15 6-month swap: 435/425
GBP/USD spot: 1.4255/65 6-month swap: 73/69
USD/JPY spot: 124.80/90 6-month swap: 240/235

10 Given the following rates for GBP/USD:

Spot: 1.4253/58
O/N: 1.80/1.30
T/N: 2.10/1.60
S/N: 2.20/1.70
3 months: 183/178

(a) At what rate can a customer buy sterling for outright value the day after spot?
(b) At what rate can a customer sell dollars for outright value tomorrow?
(c) At what rate can a customer sell sterling for outright value today?
(d) What is a two-way forward-forward swap from the day after spot until 3 months after spot?
(e) What is a two-way swap from today until 3 months after spot?

11 Today is Monday 27 October 2003. What are the spot and 1 month value dates?

12 Today is Wednesday 25 February 2004. What are the spot and 1-month value dates?

13 You need to sell and buy dollars against sterling forward-forward 2v5, given the following:

GBP/USD spot: 1.4235/45
2-month swap: 15/11
3-month swap: 8/3
5-month swap: 12/18

(a) What two-way forward-forward swap price do you expect to be quoted to you?
(b) At what price do you deal?
(c) What settlement rates might be set for the two legs of the deal?

14 What is the two-way time option outright price for delivery between 3 and 5 months, given the following prices?

GBP/USD spot: 1.4235/45
3-month swap: 8/3
5-month swap: 12/18

15 You transact an NDF to buy HUF 1,000 million against USD at 301.55, for value 17 August. On 15 August, the spot rate for settlement of the NDF is 295.71. What is your profit or loss in US dollars?

Hedging swaps with deposits, FRAs and futures, covered interest arbitrage and creating synthetic FRAs

The link between interest rates and forward swaps explained in the previous chapter allows dealers and end-users of the market to take advantage of opportunities in different markets, in two ways. Firstly, it enables a dealer with a forward swap position to hedge this position by using money market borrowings and deposits, if it turns out to be cheaper or easier to do so.

Secondly, it enables a borrower or investor to borrow or invest in a different currency from that in which he originally intended to deal, and then to convert this transaction to the intended currency by using a swap. Again, he would do so if the result were a better all-in rate, or if it were easier to arrange.

These two strategies are in fact essentially the same idea, viewed from different angles; the second strategy is known as *covered interest arbitrage*. Both depend on the fact that an FX swap is broadly equivalent to a borrowing plus a deposit.

Both these ideas can be extended from forwards to forward-forwards. This means that a forward-forward swap position can be hedged by using FRAs and futures, and an FRA in one currency can be created from, or arbitraged against, an FRA in another currency by using forward-forward swaps.

Hedging FX forwards using borrowings and deposits

Hedging a forward swap

When a dealer buys and sells one currency against another, he is taking a position economically very similar to borrowing the first currency and lending the second. Therefore, he can hedge the swap position by doing the opposite – i.e. lending the first currency and borrowing the second.

Example 1

A dealer buys and sells USD 10 million against yen, spot against 3 months (91 days) at 118.50 and 117.25.

He hedges the position by lending USD 10 million for 3 months at 4.8% and borrowing JPY 1,185,000,000 for three months at 0.5%. The total proceeds due back from the lending, and the repayment amount on the borrowing, are as follows:

$$\text{Interest} = \text{USD } 10,000,000 \times 0.048 \times \frac{91}{360} = \text{USD } 121,333$$

$$\text{Principal} + \text{interest} = \text{USD } 10,000,000 + \text{USD } 121,333$$

$$= \text{USD } 10,121,333$$

$$\text{Interest} = \text{JPY } 1,185,000,000 \times 0.005 \times \frac{91}{360} = \text{JPY } 1,497,708$$

$$\text{Principal} + \text{interest} = \text{JPY } 1,185,000,000 + \text{JPY } 1,497,708$$

$$= \text{JPY } 1,186,497,708$$

The cashflows from the deal and the cover are therefore as follows:

	spot		3 months	
original deal:	+ USD	10,000,000	− USD	10,000,000
	− JPY	1,185,000,000	+ JPY	1,172,500,000
lend dollars:	− USD	10,000,000	+ USD	10,121,333
borrow yen:	+ JPY	1,185,000,000	− JPY	1,186,497,708
net cashflows:			+ USD	121,333
			− JPY	13,997,708

If the dealer is dollar-based, for example, he could then remove the remaining small risk by buying JPY 13,997,708 3 months forward outright. If the rate for this forward outright is 117.25, this would give additional cashflows as follows:

forward outright hedge:	− USD	119,383
	+ JPY	13,997,708
net profit:	+ USD	1,950

This gives the dealer a net profit of USD 1,950 after 3 months.

The dealer is now hedged, as the result measured in dollars is unaffected by any subsequent change in rates. The result is a small profit, rather than zero, because the rate of the original swap deal (−125 points) is not exactly the same as the rate implied by the borrowing and lending interest rates – see 'Why bother?' below.

The small forward outright purchase of JPY 13,997,708 in the previous example is intended to 'tidy up' the position by removing any residual currency risk. In practice, this amount might be left unhedged. For completeness however, we will continue to assume in our examples here that the bank does want to hedge this completely.

If this amount is to be hedged, using a forward outright as a hedge is rather messy. An alternative would be to use a small spot hedge rather than a small forward outright hedge. In this case, however, in order to hedge completely, the amounts of the borrowing and lending would need to be slightly different. It would be necessary to calculate the amount of dollars it is necessary to lend at the beginning, in order to achieve proceeds of exactly USD 10,000,000 after 3 months. Similarly, it would be necessary to calculate the amount of yen it is necessary to borrow at the beginning, in order to achieve a repayment of exactly JPY 1,172,500,000 after 3 months. This is effectively the same as calculating present values (see Chapter 2) and can be seen in the following example.

Example 2

With the same original deal as in the previous example, the dealer hedges by matching the 3-month FX cashflows exactly with a borrowing and a deposit, and then doing a spot hedge for the small unmatched amount of yen, which can be seen to be JPY 13,980,039.

$$\text{Amount of dollars to lend} = \frac{\text{USD } 10,000,000}{\left(1 + \left(0.048 \times \frac{91}{360}\right)\right)}$$

$$= \text{USD } 9,880,121$$

$$\text{Amount of yen to borrow} = \frac{\text{JPY } 1,172,500,000}{\left(1 + \left(0.005 \times \frac{91}{360}\right)\right)}$$

$$= \text{JPY } 1,171,019,961$$

The cashflows from the deal and the cover are then as follows:

	spot		3 months	
original deal:	+ USD	10,000,000	– USD	10,000,000
	– JPY	1,185,000,000	+ JPY	1,172,500,000
lend dollars:	– USD	9,880,121	+ USD	10,000,000
borrow yen:	+ JPY	1,171,019,961	– JPY	1,172,500,000
spot hedge:	– USD	117,975		
	+ JPY	13,980,039		
net profit:	+ USD	1,904		

This second example gives the dealer a net profit of USD 1,904, rather than the USD 1,950 in the first example. The difference arises in two ways. Firstly, the USD 1,904 profit is value spot, whereas the USD 1,950 profit is in 3 months' time. The present value of the USD 1,950 (i.e. the worth of that cashflow now – see Chapter 2) is in fact USD 1,927, as follows:

$$\frac{\text{USD } 1,950}{\left(1 + \left(0.048 \times \frac{91}{360}\right)\right)} = \text{USD } 1,927$$

Secondly, the forward swap price and interest rates in the examples are slightly out of line. That is, the dollar rate of 4.8% and the yen rate of 0.5% do not correspond exactly to the swap price of −125 points (the difference between 118.50 and 117.25). Indeed, this might be the reason why the dealer is using the borrowing and deposit (rather than a swap) to hedge the position in the first place. The sizes of the borrowing and deposit are slightly greater in the first example than in the second example, so that slightly greater advantage is taken of this discrepancy, leading to a slightly greater profit.

Why bother?

The dealer could have hedged his original forward swap position by using another swap. How did he know that he would benefit by using a borrowing and deposit instead? He could calculate the effective swap price achieved via the borrowing and deposit by using exactly the same formula as in the previous chapter for deriving swap points from interest rates:

Forward swap

$$= \text{spot} \times \frac{\left(\left(\begin{array}{c}\text{variable}\\\text{currency}\\\text{interest}\\\text{rate}\end{array} \times \dfrac{\text{days}}{\text{year}}\right) - \left(\begin{array}{c}\text{base}\\\text{currency}\\\text{interest}\\\text{rate}\end{array} \times \dfrac{\text{days}}{\text{year}}\right)\right)}{\left(1 + \left(\text{base currency interest rate} \times \dfrac{\text{days}}{\text{year}}\right)\right)}$$

This gives:

Forward swap effectively achieved

$$= 118.50 \times \frac{\left(\left(0.005 \times \dfrac{91}{360}\right) - \left(0.048 \times \dfrac{91}{360}\right)\right)}{\left(1 + \left(0.048 \times \dfrac{91}{360}\right)\right)} = -1.2726$$

The forward swap achieved synthetically is therefore −1.2726, which is −127.26 points. Presumably, therefore, the dealer has chosen to hedge via the borrowing and deposit because the straightforward swap price available for hedging is not as good as −127.26 points. In practice, a bank would need to take account also of the balance sheet and capital adequacy implications of hedging by using deposits in this way – see Chapter 12.

The original deal was transacted at −125 points. If the borrowing and deposit hedge is used, the dealer expects a profit after 3 months of 2.26 points (the difference between −125 points and −127.26 points).

This is JPY 226,000, which has a present value of JPY 225,715, which is worth USD 1,904 as expected:

$$10,000,000 \times JPY\ 0.0226 = JPY\ 226,000$$

$$\frac{JPY\ 226,000}{\left(1 + \left(0.005 \times \frac{91}{360}\right)\right)} = JPY\ 225,715$$

$$\frac{225,715}{118.50} = 1,904$$

> A foreign exchange swap position to buy and sell one currency against another can be hedged by lending the first currency and borrowing the second currency, plus small spot or outright hedges to bring net foreign currency cashflows to zero.

Hedging a forward outright

A forward outright can be hedged in the same way. A forward outright is constructed from – and normally hedged by – a spot deal and a swap deal. The swap hedge can be replaced by a borrowing and a deposit as above.

Example 3

A foreign exchange dealer sells USD 10 million 3 months outright to a customer, against yen at 117.25. The US dollar deposit dealer in his own bank is short of dollars and is prepared to pay the foreign exchange dealer 4.8% to borrow dollars from him. The foreign exchange dealer therefore covers his forward outright position by buying dollars spot in the market at 118.50, lending dollars to his colleague, and borrowing yen from the market at 0.5%. His cashflows are as follows:

	spot		3 months	
original deal:			– USD	10,000,000
			+ JPY	1,172,500,000
spot hedge:	+ USD	10,000,000		
	– JPY	1,185,000,000		
lend dollars:	– USD	10,000,000	+ USD	10,121,333
borrow yen:	+ JPY	1,185,000,000	– JPY	1,186,497,708
net cashflows:			+ USD	121,333
			– JPY	13,997,708

> Exactly as in Examples 1 and 2, the remaining USD/JPY risk can be hedged by a spot or forward deal.

A forward outright position to sell one currency against another can be hedged by buying the first currency spot, lending the first currency and borrowing the second currency, plus small spot or outright hedges to bring net foreign currency cashflows to zero.

Hedging FX forward-forwards with FRAs or futures

In running a forward book, a dealer will normally have forward-forward positions. Suppose, for example, that a dealer does only two deals, each in response to a customer. In the first deal, he buys and sells USD 10 million against yen, spot against 1 month. In the second deal, he sells and buys USD 10 million against yen, spot against 4 months. The dealer now has a net forward-forward position in USD 10 million, 1 month against 4 months. Alternatively, the dealer might have established the same forward-forward position without any customer-related business, purely as a speculative position.

If the dealer wishes to hedge this position, he could do so simply by buying and selling USD 10 million, 1 month against 4 months. Alternatively, he could hedge the position by borrowing and lending, as in the examples above. Because it is a forward-forward position rather than a spot-to-forward position, however, the borrowing and lending must also be forward-forward, to match the cashflow timings.

Another approach, which uses the balance sheet less, is to use FRAs or futures, because these are exactly off-balance sheet equivalents of cash forward-forward borrowings. These instruments are covered in Chapter 6.

The following example is parallel to Example 2, with the same exchange rates, but with the cashflows in the future rather than based on spot.

Example 4

A dealer buys and sells USD 10 million against yen, 1 month against 4 months (91 days) at 118.50 and 117.25.

He hedges the position by selling a 1v4 FRA for USD 9,880,121 at 4.8% and buying a 1v4 FRA for JPY 1,171,019,961 at 0.5%.

As in Example 2, there is another small FX risk to be hedged. Consider what the cashflows would be if, instead of using a yen FRA, the dealer used a cash forward-forward yen borrowing. There would be a cash inflow of 1,171,019,961 after 1 month and a cash outflow of JPY 1,172,500,000 after 4 months, similar to the flows in Example 2. The dealer therefore also buys JPY 13,980,039 (the difference between JPY 1,171,019,961 and JPY 1,185,000,000) 1-month forward outright. This is the amount which would make the yen cashflows net to zero if we were using cash forward-forward borrowings.

Also, as the FRAs are in fact contracts for differences rather than cash instruments, the dealer will still need to reverse the swap cashflows when the first leg of the forward-forward swap settles after one month. This can be done using either a 3-month swap again, or a borrowing and a deposit. We will assume here that the dealer simply uses a swap.

After 1 month, US dollar LIBOR is set at 4.95% and yen LIBOR is set at 0.6%, and the USD/JPY spot rate is 125.00. Assuming that the USD/JPY 3-month FX swap at the same time is exactly in line with these interest rates, the 3-month outright rate is 123.6425 (this is unrealistically precise, but helps to clarify the figures in this example).

The settlements on the FRAs are a payment of USD 3,700 and a receipt of JPY 295,560, as follows:

$$\frac{9,880,121 \times (0.048 - 0.0495) \times \dfrac{91}{360}}{\left(1 + \left(0.0495 \times \dfrac{91}{360}\right)\right)} = -3,700$$

$$\frac{1,171,019,961 \times (0.005 - 0.006) \times \dfrac{91}{360}}{\left(1 + \left(0.006 \times \dfrac{91}{360}\right)\right)} = -295,560$$

The cashflows from the deal and the cover are therefore as follows:

	1 month	4 months
original deal:	+ USD 10,000,000	– USD 10,000,000
	– JPY 1,185,000,000	+ JPY 1,172,500,000
1-month hedge:	– USD 117,975	
	+ JPY 13,980,039	
dollar FRA settlement:	– USD 3,700	
yen FRA settlement:	+ JPY 295,560	
reverse deal:	– USD 10,000,000	+ USD 10,000,000
	+ JPY 1,250,000,000	– JPY 1,236,425,000
net cashflows:	– USD 121,675	
	+ JPY 79,275,599	– JPY 63,925,000

At the 1-month date, the final net 4-month cashflow of – JPY 63,925,000 can be converted to – USD 517,015 (using the 3-month forward outright rate then prevailing of 123.6425). This dollar cashflow has a present value on the 1-month date of –USD 510,626:

$$\frac{-517,015}{\left(1 + \left(0.0495 \times \dfrac{91}{360}\right)\right)} = -510,626$$

Also, the cashflow of +JPY 79,275,599 can be converted to +USD 634,205 (using the spot rate of 125.00 then prevailing).

The 3 resulting cashflows of – USD 121,675, +JPY 79,275,599 and – JPY 63,925,000 therefore represent a net profit after one month of:

$$-USD\ 121,675 + USD\ 634,205 - USD\ 510,626 = +USD\ 1,904$$

This net profit of USD 1,904 is, as expected, exactly the same as in Example 2.

In the last example, the dealer must in practice also take account of the fact that the swap ultimately used to reverse the flows may not be exactly in line with the LIBORs. Also, even if it is, he will presumably be taking the price from someone else and therefore losing the bid/offer spread.

Apart from these problems, the swap formula used previously can be applied to calculate the forward-forward swap rate created synthetically from FRAs:

Forward-forward swap rate created synthetically

$$= \text{outright to near date} \times \frac{\left(\left(\substack{\text{variable} \\ \text{currency FRA}} \times \frac{\text{days}}{\text{variable year}}\right) - \left(\text{base currency FRA} \times \frac{\text{days}}{\text{base year}}\right)\right)}{\left(1 + \left(\substack{\text{base currency} \\ \text{FRA}} \times \frac{\text{days}}{\text{base year}}\right)\right)}$$

As covered briefly in Chapter 6, futures are the exchange-traded equivalent of FRAs. The last example could therefore have used futures as a hedge, instead of FRAs. In major currencies at least, futures have the advantage of being liquid and finely priced. The drawbacks for hedging, however, include the mechanical complexity of margin calls and the inflexibility regarding periods and dates. The following example is parallel to the last one, using futures instead of FRAs.

Example 5

Today is 5 March, spot is 7 March, the 1-month date is 7 April and the 4-month date is 7 July. A dealer buys and sells USD 10 million against yen, 1 month against 4 months (91 days) at 118.50 and 117.25.

He hedges the position by buying 10 March dollar futures contracts at 95.30 (representing USD 10 million at 4.70%) and selling 12 March yen futures contracts at 99.55 (representing JPY 1,200 million at 0.45%).

As in Example 4, there is another small FX risk to be hedged. Again, consider what the cashflows would be if, instead of using yen futures, the dealer used a cash forward-forward yen borrowing for 90 days at 0.45%. There would be a cash inflow of 1,200,000,000 after 1 month and a cash outflow of JPY 1,201,350,000 after 4 months. The dealer therefore also sells JPY 15,000,000 (the difference between JPY 1,200,000,000 and JPY 1,185,000,000) 1 month forward outright and also buys JPY 28,850,0000 (the difference between JPY 1,201,350,000 and JPY 1,172,500,000) 4 months forward outright.

On 17 March (the last trading day for March futures), the futures positions are closed out and rolled into June futures – i.e. the March futures are reversed and replaced by new June futures positions. The closing prices for the March futures are 95.25 for dollars (representing a dollar interest rate of 4.75%) and 99.52 for yen (representing a yen interest rate of 0.48%). The June futures prices at the same time are 94.90 for dollars and 99.40 for yen.

On 5 April, the dealer closes out the June futures contracts. The futures prices are then 94.80 for dollars and 99.35 for yen. As in Example 4, the USD/JPY spot rate is 125.00 and the 3-month outright rate is 123.6425.

The profits and losses on the futures contracts are as follows:

March contracts:

$$\text{USD } 10,000,000 \times \left(\frac{-95.30 + 95.25}{100} \right) \times \frac{3}{12} = -\text{USD } 1,250$$

$$\text{JPY } 1,200,000,000 \times \left(\frac{+99.55 - 99.52}{100} \right) \times \frac{3}{12} = +\text{JPY } 90,000$$

June contracts:

$$\text{USD } 10,000,000 \times \left(\frac{-94.90 + 94.80}{100} \right) \times \frac{3}{12} = -\text{USD } 2,500$$

$$\text{JPY } 1,200,000,000 \times \left(\frac{+99.40 - 99.35}{100} \right) \times \frac{3}{12} = +\text{JPY } 150,000$$

The cashflows from the deal and the cover are therefore as follows:

		1 month		4 months
original deal:	+ USD	10,000,000	– USD	10,000,000
	– JPY	1,185,000,000	+ JPY	1,172,500,000
outright hedges:	+ USD	126,582	– USD	246,055
	– JPY	15,000,000	+ JPY	28,850,000
dollar futures:	– USD	3,750		
yen futures:	+ JPY	240,000		
reverse deal:	– USD	10,000,000	+ USD	10,000,000
	+ JPY	1,250,000,000	– JPY	1,236,425,000
net cashflows:	+ USD	122,832	– USD	246,055
	+ JPY	50,240,000	– JPY	35,075,000

At the 1-month date, the final 4-month cashflow of – JPY 35,075,000 can be converted to – USD 283,681 (using the 3-month forward outright rate then prevailing of 123.6425). This gives a total dollar cashflow at 4 months of – USD 529,736

(= −USD 246, 055 − USD 283, 681). This dollar cashflow has a present value on the 1-month date of − USD 523,190:

$$\frac{-529,736}{\left(1 + \left(0.0495 \times \dfrac{91}{360}\right)\right)} = -523,190$$

Also, the cashflow of +JPY 50,240,000 can be converted to +USD 401,920 (using the spot rate of 125.00 then prevailing).

The four resulting cashflows of +USD 122,832, +JPY 50,240,000, −USD 246,055 and −JPY 35,075,000 therefore represent a net profit after 1 month of:

+USD 122, 832 + USD 401, 920 − USD 523, 190 = +USD 1, 562

The net profit of USD 1,562 in the above example is a little different from the USD 1,904 in the previous example, because futures are a less exact hedge. In particular:

- The amount of the hedge is restricted to a round number – USD 10 million and JPY 1,200 million in this case.
- The futures contract period does not coincide exactly with the swap period. In this case, it was also necessary to roll over the futures when they expired in March.
- The profit and loss on these futures contracts is calculated using a 90-day period, whereas there are in fact 91 days in this particular 3-month period.
- There is a basis risk. That is, the movements in the futures prices do not necessarily match exactly the movement in the interest rates underlying the swap price. In this example, there was a total gain on the yen futures contract of 8 basis points (3 basis points gained on the March contract from 99.55 to 99.52, plus 5 basis points gained on the June contract, from 99.40 to 99.35) However, the movement in the forward interest rate underlying the swap was 10 basis points, from 0.5% to 0.6%. It is possible to improve slightly the hedge against this basis risk, but the detailed use of futures strategies is really outside the scope of this book.
- The timing of the cashflows on the futures also affects the result, because part of the loss on the dollar futures and the profit on the yen futures arose in March – although we did not take account of this timing complication above, assuming instead that all the profit and loss on the futures arose in April.

A forward-forward FX position to buy and sell one currency against another can be hedged by selling an FRA (or buying futures) in the first currency and buying an FRA (or selling futures) in the second currency, plus small spot or outright hedges to bring the notional net foreign currency cashflows to zero.

Covered interest arbitrage

Borrowing or investing via a different currency

Suppose that an organization needs to fund itself in one currency but can borrow relatively more cheaply in another; it can choose deliberately to borrow in that second currency and use a forward swap to convert the borrowing to the first currency. This might be done, for example, if the resulting all-in cost of borrowing were slightly less than the cost of borrowing the first currency directly. It might also be done if borrowing in the original currency of choice were for some reason unavailable.

Even if it does not need to borrow, a bank can still borrow in the second currency, use a forward swap to convert the borrowing to the first currency and then make a deposit directly in the first currency; a reason for doing this would be that a profit can be locked in because the swap price is slightly out of line with the interest rates.

Taking advantage of such a strategy is known as covered interest arbitrage.

Covered interest arbitrage is synthetically creating a loan (or deposit) in one currency by combining a loan (or deposit) in another currency with a forward foreign exchange swap.

Example 6

A dealer needs to produce (i.e. borrow) GBP 1 million for 6 months (183 days) from spot. The following rates are quoted to him:

GBP/USD	spot:	1.4250/56
	6 months:	133/131
GBP	6 months:	6.0/6.1%
USD	6 months:	4.0/4.1%

The simplest approach would be to borrow sterling directly at 6.1%. An alternative is to borrow dollars at 4.1% and swap them to sterling as follows.

The dealer borrows enough dollars so that when converted to sterling for value spot, he receives exactly GBP 1 million. Based on a spot rate of 1.4250 (see below for why we have chosen the left side of the spot rate), the amount to borrow is USD 1,425,000.

He calculates the amount of dollars to be repaid after six months:

$$\text{interest} = 1,425,000 \times 0.041 \times \frac{183}{360} = 29,699.38$$

$$\text{principal} + \text{interest} = 1,425,000.00 + 29,699.38 = 1,454,699.38$$

He transacts a foreign exchange swap to buy and sell sterling against dollars, spot against 6 months. The dollar amount transacted for value spot is the amount of dollars borrowed (USD 1,425,000); the dollar amount transacted for value 6 months is the amount of dollars repaid (USD 1,454,699.38). The swap deal is transacted on the left side of the price (because the market-maker who has quoted the price is selling and buying the base currency) at −133 points. Therefore if the settlement rate for spot is set at 1.4250, the settlement rate for 6 months must be set at 1.4117 (= 1.4250 − 0.0133).

Applying these settlement rates, the cashflows are as follows:

	spot	6 months
dollar borrowing:	+ USD 1,425,000	− USD 1,454,699.38
swap:	− USD 1,425,000	+ USD 1,454,699.38
	+ GBP 1,000,000	− GBP 1,030,459.29
net cashflows:	+ GBP 1,000,000	− GBP 1,030,459.29

The net result is effectively a borrowing of GBP 1,000,000 with a total repayment after six months of GBP 1,030,459.29 – i.e. an effective interest cost of GBP 30,459.29.

This cash interest cost is for a period of 183 days. It can be expressed as an interest rate per annum of 6.075%:

$$\frac{30,459.29}{1,000,000} \times \frac{365}{183} = 0.06075 = 6.075\%$$

This rate achieved of 6.075% is slightly cheaper than the 6.1% cost of borrowing sterling directly. It is therefore worthwhile to create a synthetic sterling borrowing via dollars in this way.

Three points to notice in the above Example are:

- The Example assumes that the dealer is taking another bank's rates to borrow dollars at 4.1% and another bank's rates to swap at −133 points. If he were able to trade on his own prices, the result would be even better.
- When a swap is dealt, the amount of the deal (for example, GBP 1,000,000) is usually the same at both ends of the deal, spot and forward. In the example above, however, the amounts are mismatched, with GBP 1,030,459.29 at the far end in order to match the swap cashflows exactly with the underlying flows arising from the borrowing. It is generally acceptable in the market to use mismatched amounts in this way as long as the mismatch is not great.
- When dealing a forward swap rather than a forward outright, it is the swap price that is dealt rather than the spot price; the spot price is needed only for settlement. The spot dealer is not involved and the spot spread is not involved. In general, therefore, the spot and forward settlement prices could be 1.4250 (the bid side of the spot price, as used in the example above) and 1.4117, or 1.4256 (the offer side of the spot price) and 1.4123, or something between such as 1.4253 and 1.4120. The important point is that the spot rate must be a current market rate and the difference between the spot and forward settlement prices must be the correct swap price of −133 points.

Conventionally for a swap, an approximate mid-price is taken for the spot. In an example such as this where the amounts are mismatched, however, it is common to use, for the whole deal, whichever side of the spot price would normally be used for the mismatch amount. The mismatch in this example is a forward purchase of GBP 30,459.29 $(= 1,030,459.29 - 1,000,000)$. For an outright alone, the quoting bank would wish to deal on the left for this, based on a spot of 1.4250, so that the settlement rates would be 1.4250 and 1.4117; commonly therefore, it would choose to deal on these same rates for the whole mismatched swap.

Although this approach is common, it does not necessarily benefit the quoting bank. In the example above, the quoting bank does indeed benefit by using a spot of 1.4250, as we have done. In general, however, this depends on whether the forward points are positive or negative. Specifically in the case of a mismatched swap for covered interest arbitrage, it is usually the case that:

– if the points are negative, the quoting bank benefits slightly by using the spot rate on the same side as the swap: if the left swap price is used (as in the example above), the quoting bank benefits by using the left side of the spot price; if the right swap price is used, the quoting bank benefits by using the right side of the spot price.

– if the points are positive, the quoting bank benefits slightly by using the spot rate on the opposite side from the swap: if the left swap price is used, the quoting bank benefits by using the right side of the spot price; if the right swap price is used, the quoting bank benefits by using the left side of the spot price.

The effect is in any case generally not great, as can be seen in Example 7 below.

The formula we saw in the previous chapter for calculating a forward outright from interest rates was:

Forward outright

$$= \text{spot} \times \frac{\left(1 + \left(\text{variable currency interest rate} \times \dfrac{\text{days}}{\text{year}}\right)\right)}{\left(1 + \left(\text{base currency interest rate} \times \dfrac{\text{days}}{\text{year}}\right)\right)}$$

This formula can be turned round to give the result of the covered interest arbitrage from the swap price:

Covered interest arbitrage

Creating the variable currency interest rate synthetically by using a borrowing or deposit in the base currency:

Variable currency interest rate created synthetically

$$= \left(\left(1 + \left(\begin{array}{c}\text{base currency}\\\text{rate}\end{array} \times \frac{\text{days}}{\text{base year}}\right)\right) \times \frac{\begin{array}{c}\text{exchange rate}\\\text{for far date}\end{array}}{\begin{array}{c}\text{exchange rate}\\\text{for near date}\end{array}} - 1\right)$$

$$\times \frac{\text{variable year}}{\text{days}}$$

---

or:

Creating the base currency interest rate synthetically by using a borrowing or deposit in the variable currency:

Base currency interest rate created synthetically

$$= \left(\left(1 + \left(\begin{array}{c} \text{variable} \\ \text{currency rate} \end{array} \times \frac{\text{days}}{\text{variable year}} \right) \right) \times \frac{\begin{array}{c} \text{exchange} \\ \text{rate for} \\ \text{near date} \end{array}}{\begin{array}{c} \text{exchange} \\ \text{rate for} \\ \text{far date} \end{array}} - 1 \right)$$

$$\times \frac{\text{base year}}{\text{days}}$$

Note that the formulas are very similar – be careful about which way round the two exchange rates are!

Example 7

Using the same information as in the last example, the effective interest cost in sterling can be calculated as follows:

Sterling interest rate created synthetically

$$= \left(\left(1 + \left(\begin{array}{c} \text{USD} \\ \text{rate} \end{array} \times \frac{\text{days}}{\text{USD year}} \right) \right) \times \frac{\begin{array}{c} \text{GBP/USD rate} \\ \text{for near date} \end{array}}{\begin{array}{c} \text{GBP/USD rate} \\ \text{for far date} \end{array}} - 1 \right)$$

$$\times \frac{\text{GBP year}}{\text{days}}$$

$$= \left(\left(1 + \left(0.041 \times \frac{183}{360} \right) \right) \times \frac{1.4250}{1.4117} - 1 \right) \times \frac{365}{183}$$

$$= 0.060752 = 6.0752\%$$

Using slightly different settlement rates, as discussed above, would produce only a slightly different synthetic sterling cost. The result based on a spot of 1.4253 would be 6.0748%:

Sterling interest rate created synthetically

$$= \left(\left(1 + \left(0.041 \times \frac{183}{360} \right) \right) \times \frac{1.4253}{1.4120} - 1 \right) \times \frac{365}{183}$$

$$= 0.060748 = 6.0748\%$$

The result based on a spot of 1.4256 would be 6.0744%:

Sterling interest rate created synthetically

$$= \left(\left(1 + \left(0.041 \times \frac{183}{360}\right)\right) \times \frac{1.4256}{1.4123} - 1\right) \times \frac{365}{183}$$

$$= 0.060744 = 6.0744\%$$

The following Example shows how covered interest arbitrage can be used in the same way by an investor, rather than a depositor. The Example also shows the use of the formula with a tom/next swap. As mentioned above, when using the formula to calculate the effective rate achieved, be careful about which is the exchange rate for the near date and which is the exchange rate for the far date.

Example 8

An investor has SEK 5 million to invest tom/next. He can either invest directly in kronor at 5.3%, or invest in euros at 4.5% and swap them to kronor. The following exchange rates are quoted to him:

EUR/SEK   spot: 11.2360/70
            T/N: 3/4

Investing via euros would be as follows.

Sell SEK 5 million and buy euros, value tomorrow.
Invest the euros tom/next at 4.5%.
Sell forward the maturing euro deposit amount back into kronor.

The swap involves buying and selling the euros tom/next, at +3 points. If the quoting bank determines 11.2370 as the spot rate, the settlement rates are 11.2367 (tomorrow) and 11.2370 (spot).
    The amount of the euro deposit is:

$$\frac{5,000,000}{11.2367} = 444,970.50$$

The maturing amount of the deposit is then:

$$\text{Interest} = 444,970.50 \times 0.045 \times \frac{1}{360} = 55.62$$

Principal + interest = $444,970.50 + 55.62 = 445,026.12$

The cashflows are as follows:

	spot	6 months
euro deposit:	− EUR 444,970.50	+ EUR 445,026.12
swap:	+ EUR 444,970.50	− EUR 445,026.12
	− SEK 5,000,000.00	+ SEK 5,000,758.51
net cashflows:	− SEK 5,000,000.00	+ SEK 5,000,758.51

The net result is effectively a tom/next deposit of SEK 5,000,000 with total proceeds of SEK 5,000,758.51 – i.e. effective interest received of SEK 758.51.

This interest earned is for a period of 1 day. It can be expressed as an interest rate per annum of 5.46%:

$$\frac{758.51}{5,000,000} \times \frac{360}{1} = 0.0546 = 5.46\%$$

This yield of 5.46% is higher than the 5.3% quoted for kronor. It is therefore worth while to create a synthetic krona deposit via euros in this way.

This synthetic yield can be calculated using the formula as follows:

Krona interest rate created synthetically

$$= \left(\left(1 + \left(\text{EUR rate} \times \frac{\text{days}}{\text{EUR year}} \right) \right) \times \frac{\text{EUR/SEK rate for far date}}{\text{EUR/SEK rate for near date}} - 1 \right)$$

$$\times \frac{\text{SEK year}}{\text{days}}$$

$$= \left(\left(1 + \left(0.045 \times \frac{1}{360} \right) \right) \times \frac{11.2370}{11.2367} - 1 \right) \times \frac{360}{1}$$

$$= 0.0546 = 5.46\%$$

A borrowing (or lending) in one currency can be created by borrowing (or lending) a second currency and buying and selling (or selling and buying) the first currency against the second currency.

Creating an FRA in one currency from an FRA in another currency

The concept of covered interest arbitrage can be used for any period, including one that starts in the future. For example, a borrowing in sterling from 1 month forward to 7 months forward can be created synthetically from a forward-forward borrowing in dollars combined with a forward-forward FX swap. This is exactly the same structure as used in Example 7, with the difference that the start date is in 1 month's time, rather than spot. Because an FRA is the off-balance sheet equivalent of a cash forward-forward borrowing or deposit, the same structure can be used to create a synthetic FRA in one currency from an FRA in another currency. The following example is parallel to Example 6, using the same rates but based on a forward start date. The result is a synthetic sterling FRA at exactly the same rate as the synthetic sterling borrowing rate achieved in Example 6.

Example 9

A dealer wishes to create a synthetic long FRA position in GBP 1 million for 1 month against 7 months (183 days). The following rates are quoted to him:

GBP/USD	1-month outright:	1.4250
	1 v 7:	133/131
GBP FRA	1 v 7:	6.0/6.1%
USD FRA	1 v 7:	4.0/4.1%

The dealer buys a dollar FRA at 4.1% for the 1-month forward dollar equivalent of GBP 1 million. Based on 1.4250, this is USD 1,425,000.

He calculates the amount of dollars which would be repaid 6 months later, on a borrowing of USD 1,425,000 at 4.1%:

$$\text{Interest} = 1,425,000 \times 0.041 \times \frac{183}{360} = 29,699$$

$$\text{Principal} + \text{interest} = 1,425,000 + 29,699 = 1,454,699$$

He transacts a forward-forward FX swap to buy and sell sterling against dollars, 1 month against 7 months. The dollar amount transacted for value 1 month is the amount of the dollar FRA (USD 1,425,000); the dollar amount transacted for value 7 months is the amount of dollars which would have been repaid on a cash borrowing (USD 1,454,699). The swap deal is transacted on the left side of the price at −133 points. Therefore if the settlement rate for 1 month is set at 1.4250, the settlement rate for 6 months must be set at 1.4117 (= 1.4250 − 0.0133).

After 1 month, GBP/USD spot is 1.4560, sterling 6-month LIBOR is 6.5% and dollar 6-month LIBOR is 3.9%. The dollar FRA settlement is a loss of USD 1,421:

$$\frac{1,425,000 \times (0.041 - 0.039) \times \dfrac{183}{360}}{\left(1 + \left(0.039 \times \dfrac{183}{360}\right)\right)} = 1,421$$

At the same time as the FRA is settled, the dealer reverses the original swap. The dollar amount of this reverse swap can be calculated to include also the dollar FRA settlement amount. Assuming that the current swap rate is exactly in line with the current sterling and dollar LIBORs of 6.5% and 3.9%, based on a spot of 1.4560, the swap rate would be −180 points.

The resulting cashflows are as follows:

	1 month	7 months
swap:	− USD 1,425,000	+ USD 1,454,699
	+ GBP 1,000,000	− GBP 1,030,459
FRA settlement:	− USD 1,421	
reverse swap:	+ USD 1,426,421	− USD 1,454,699
	− GBP 979,685	+ GBP 1,011,613
net cashflows:	+ GBP 20,315	− GBP 18,846

The amount of − GBP 18,846 has a present value of − GBP 18,251:

$$\frac{-18,846}{\left(1 + \left(0.065 \times \dfrac{183}{365}\right)\right)} = -18,251$$

The two net sterling cashflows therefore have a net present value of + GBP 2,064 (= +GBP 20, 315 − GBP 18, 251).

This net sterling settlement amount implies a sterling FRA rate of 6.075%. This can be seen because a sterling FRA at

6.075% on GBP 1,000,000 would have resulted in exactly the same sterling settlement amount (allowing for rounding differences):

$$\frac{1{,}000{,}000 \times (0.06075 - 0.065) \times \dfrac{183}{365}}{\left(1 + \left(0.065 \times \dfrac{183}{365}\right)\right)} = 2{,}064$$

The effective sterling FRA rate achieved could have been calculated more simply by using exactly the same covered interest arbitrage formula as before:

Sterling interest rate created synthetically

$$= \left(\left(1 + \left(\frac{\text{USD}}{\text{rate}} \times \frac{\text{days}}{\text{USD year}}\right)\right) \times \frac{\substack{\text{GBP/USD rate} \\ \text{for near date}}}{\substack{\text{GBP/USD rate} \\ \text{for far date}}} - 1\right)$$

$$\times \frac{\text{GBP year}}{\text{days}}$$

$$= \left(\left(1 + \left(0.041 \times \frac{183}{360}\right)\right) \times \frac{1.4250}{1.4117} - 1\right) \times \frac{365}{183}$$

$$= 0.060752 = 6.075\%$$

A long (or short) position in an FRA in one currency can be created from a long (or short) position in an FRA in a second currency by buying and selling (or selling and buying) the first currency against the second currency forward-forward.

Creating the variable currency FRA rate synthetically by using an FRA in the base currency

Variable currency FRA rate created synthetically

$$= \left(\left(1 + \left(\frac{\text{base currency}}{\text{FRA rate}} \times \frac{\text{days}}{\text{base year}}\right)\right)\right.$$

$$\left. \times \frac{\text{exchange rate for far date}}{\text{exchange rate for near date}} - 1\right) \times \frac{\text{variable year}}{\text{days}}$$

or

> ### Creating the base currency FRA rate synthetically by using an FRA in the variable currency
>
> Base currency FRA rate created synthetically
>
> $$= \left(\left(1 + \left(\text{variable currency FRA rate} \times \frac{\text{days}}{\text{variable year}}\right)\right)\right.$$
>
> $$\left.\times \frac{\text{exchange rate for near date}}{\text{exchange rate for far date}} - 1\right) \times \frac{\text{base year}}{\text{days}}$$

Exercises

1 You are a dealer and a customer has just sold you GBP 5 million against EUR for value 3 months forward outright. Which of the following are possible ways of hedging your risk, either mostly or completely?

 (a) Buy EUR against GBP for value 3 months forward outright.

 (b) Buy EUR spot, and also buy and sell EUR against GBP in a 3-month swap.

 (c) Buy EUR spot, and also borrow GBP for 3 months, and also lend EUR for 3 months.

2 You have just bought and sold EUR 10 million against USD, spot against 3 months (91 days) at 0.9120 and 0.9163. You hedge the position approximately by lending EUR 10 million at 3.0% and borrowing USD 9.12 million at 5%. If you are based in EUR, what additional small transaction could you undertake to completely hedge any remaining risk?

3 It is now the middle of April. You have bought and sold EUR 10 million against Swiss francs, 2 months against 5 months (a 91-day period), with settlement rates of 1.6000 and 1.5910. You wish to hedge the position. Given the following rates, what is the cheapest way of hedging, and approximately what profit or loss do you expect on doing so?

EUR/CHF	spot:	1.6038/48
	2 months:	69/65
	5 months:	168/162
EUR	2v5 FRA:	4.0/4.1%
CHF	2v5 FRA:	1.5/1.6%
EUR	June futures:	95.95/95.96
CHF	June futures:	98.39/98.40

4   An investor has EUR 3 million to invest for one week from spot. He can either invest directly in euros at 4.9%, or he can invest in dollars at 4.5%. The following exchange rates are quoted to him:

EUR/USD   spot: 0.9125/29
1 week: 1.2/1.1

What yield can he achieve if he invests via dollars?

5   A dealer needs to produce overnight sterling on Friday (i.e. for a 3-day run from Friday to Monday). He decides that he can do it most cheaply via euros. If the following rates are quoted to him, what is his effective borrowing cost in sterling?

EUR/GBP   spot: 0.6250/55
               O/N: 1.1/1.2
               T/N: 1.5/1.6
EUR   O/N: 3.2/3.3%
GBP   O/N: 6.3/6.4%

6   You wish to buy a Swiss franc 2v5 FRA (a 92-day period). Given the following market prices, at what rate can you create one synthetically via sterling?

GBP/CHF   spot: 2.4038/48
               2 months: 124/120
               5 months: 298/292
GBP   2v5 FRA: 6.0/6.1%

Managing the spot risk on a forward FX position

It may be helpful to explain why we have included this chapter here, rather than including it within the 'Bank risk management' chapter later in the book. Although it is important for dealers to understand the wide range of risks faced by a bank, most of these risks fall to be controlled largely by someone other than the dealer. The particular risk discussed in this chapter, however, requires continual positive action by the dealer which forms an essential part of his day-to-day trading activity.

When a forward dealer takes a position, he is taking a risk deliberately because he is hoping to make a profit out of changes in the forward swap price, which depends essentially on interest rates as discussed in an earlier chapter. However, also as mentioned earlier, for each forward foreign exchange position, there is another risk, which arises out of potential spot exchange rate movements. This risk is known as the *tail* of the forward position.

Hedging a forward swap position

The valuations, and calculations of profit and loss, in this chapter, as well as the calculation of the hedge required, depend on the concept of *present value*. This is covered in Chapter 2.

Example 1

A forward dealer in a euro-based bank buys and sells USD 10 million against Norwegian kroner, spot against 6 months when rates are as follows:

USD/NOK	spot:	10.9530
	6-month swap:	+2171 points
EUR/USD	spot:	0.9000
EUR/NOK	spot:	9.8577
USD 6-month interest rate:		4.0%
NOK 6-month interest rate:		8.0%

The settlement rates on the deal are set as 10.9530 and 11.1701. The 6-month period is 182 days.

Later the same day, the dollar interest rate rises to 4.15%, NOK interest rates rise to 8.07%, and the forward swap points move in line to +2126. The spot rate does not change. The dealer now closes out his position, in order to take his profit. He therefore sells and buys USD 10 million against kroner at 10.9530 and 11.1656.

The cashflows arising from the two deals are as follows:

	Spot	6 months
Original deal:	+ USD 10,000,000	− USD 10,000,000
	− NOK 109,530,000	+ NOK 111,701,000
Close deal:	− USD 10,000,000	+ USD 10,000,000
	+ NOK 109,530,000	− NOK 111,656,000
Net result:		+ NOK 45,000

The profit of NOK 45,000 arising after 6 months has a present value of NOK 43,236:

$$\frac{\text{NOK } 45,000}{\left(1 + \left(0.0807 \times \dfrac{182}{360}\right)\right)} = \text{NOK } 43,236$$

This profit can be valued in euros by converting at the spot rate of 9.8577, to give a profit of EUR 4,386.

Example 2

Now suppose that, having made the original transaction exactly as in Example 1, the USD/NOK spot rate also changes, at the same time as the dollar interest rate, to 10.6800. As a result, the forward swap points become +2073 rather than +2126 and the settlement rates on the closing deal are set as 10.6800 and 10.8873.

The cashflows from the two deals are now as follows:

	Spot	6 months
Original deal:	+ USD 10,000,000	– USD 10,000,000
	– NOK 109,530,000	+ NOK 111,701,000
Close deal:	– USD 10,000,000	+ USD 10,000,000
	+ NOK 106,800,000	– NOK 108,873,000
Net result:	– NOK 2,730,000	+ NOK 2,828,000

Suppose that the euro exchange rates also change as follows:

EUR/USD   spot: 0.9100
EUR/NOK   spot: 9.7188

Overall, the dealer still appears to show a profit, which is now NOK 98,000 (=–NOK 2,730,000 + NOK 2,828,000). However, there is now a cashflow problem. The cash outflow of NOK 2,730,000 arises 6 months earlier than the cash inflow of NOK 2,828,000 and must therefore be funded for this period. The bank therefore has a funding cost of:

$$\text{NOK } 2,828,000 \times 0.0807 \times \frac{182}{360} = \text{NOK } 115,378$$

This funding cost is greater than the apparent profit of NOK 98,000. As a result, the bank actually makes a real loss.

As before, the net result can be calculated as a present value in euros by first calculating the present value of the NOK 2,828,00 future cashflow, combining this with the NOK 2,730,000 spot cashflow, and finally converting to euros at the spot rate of 9.7188, to give a net loss of EUR 1,323:

$$\frac{+\text{NOK } 2,828,000}{\left(1 + \left(0.0807 \times \frac{182}{360}\right)\right)} = +\text{NOK } 2,717,145$$

$$- \text{NOK } 2,730,000 + \text{NOK } 2,717,145 = -\text{NOK } 12,855$$

$$\frac{-12,855}{9.7188} = -1,323$$

The spot rate movement used in this example might be rather large for a movement during 1 day, although certainly possible. Over several days, it might not be unusual. The important point is that a forward dealer might anticipate correctly the relative change in interest rates and hence the direction of change in the forward swap points, but have his profit significantly reduced, or even completely offset, by a change in the spot rate.

Clearly, the forward dealer would like to be able to hedge against this effect. To a large extent, this is possible to do, by hedging the net present value of the cashflows:

Example 3

With all the same rates as in the previous example, the cashflows arising from the original deal are as follows:

	Spot	6 months
Original deal:	+ USD 10,000,000	– USD 10,000,000
	– NOK 109,530,000	+ NOK 111,701,000

The present value of the 6-month krone cashflow is as follows:

$$\frac{+\text{NOK } 111,701,000}{\left(1 + \left(0.08 \times \dfrac{182}{360}\right)\right)} = +\text{NOK } 107,358,928$$

Therefore the net present value of the spot and forward krone cashflows together is:

$$-\text{NOK } 109,530,000 + \text{NOK } 107,358,928 = -\text{NOK } 2,171,072$$

Similarly, the net present value of the spot and forward dollar cashflows is:

$$+\text{USD } 10,000,000 - \frac{\text{USD } 10,000,000}{\left(1 + \left(0.04 \times \dfrac{182}{360}\right)\right)} = +\text{USD } 198,214$$

Suppose that the dealer hedges both these present value positions (net short NOK 2,171,072 and net long USD 198,214) against euros at the spot rates of 9.8577 and 0.9000. When he closes his original position, he also closes out the hedges at the new spot rates of 9.7188 and 0.9100. The cashflows are then as follows:

		Spot		6 months
Original deal:	+ USD	10,000,000	− USD	10,000,000
	− NOK	109,530,000	+ NOK	111,701,000
Hedges:	+ NOK	2,171,072		
	− EUR	220,241		
	− USD	198,214		
	+ EUR	220,238		
Close deal:	− USD	10,000,000	+ USD	10,000,000
	+ NOK	106,800,000	− NOK	108,873,000
Close hedges:	− NOK	2,171,072		
	+ EUR	223,389		
	+ USD	198,214		
	− EUR	217,818		
Net result:	− NOK	2,730,000	+ NOK	2,828,000
	+ EUR	5,568		

In addition to the actual overall net present value loss of EUR 1,323 as calculated in Example 2. there is now also a profit on the hedges of EUR 5,568. The net result is therefore:

−EUR 1,323 + EUR 5,568 = +EUR 4,245

Because of the hedges, this is close to the result in Example 1, where there was no change in the spot rate.

The result of Example 3 (where changes in the spot rates were offset by the result of the spot hedge) is not exactly the same as the result of Example 1 (where there were no changes in the spot rates).

The main reason for this difference is that the hedge protects against the effect of spot rate changes on the net present value of the original deal, but cannot hedge against the effect of spot rate changes on the size of the profit itself. If there had been no profit – because there were no interest rate changes – then the hedge would have been complete. This can be seen by analyzing the values of the cashflows as follows:

Originally:

- Spot cashflow of +USD 10,000,000 is worth (at 0.9000): +EUR 11,111,111
- 6-month cashflow of −USD 10,000,000 has a present value at 4.0% of −USD 9,801,786
  This is worth (at 0.9000): −EUR 10,890,873

- Spot cashflow of −NOK 109,530,000 is worth
  (at 9.8577):   −EUR 11,111,111
- 6-month cashflow of +NOK 111,701,000 has
  a present value at 8.0% of +NOK 107,358,928
                      This is worth (at 9.8577): +EUR 10,890,870

After the rate changes:

- Spot cashflow of +USD 10,000,000 is worth
  (at 0.9100):   +EUR 10,989,011
- 6-month cashflow of −USD 10,000,000 has a
  present value at 4.15% of −USD 9,794,506
                      This is worth (at 0.9100): −EUR 10,763,193
- Spot cashflow of −NOK 109,530,000 is worth
  (at 9.7188):   −EUR 11,269,910
- 6-month cashflow of +NOK 111,701,000 has a
  present value at 8.07% of +NOK 107,322,424
                      This is worth (at 9.7188): +EUR 11,042,765

The spot hedges protect all the original dollar and krone present values (+USD 10,000,000, −USD 9,801,786, −NOK 109,530,000 and +NOK 107,358,928) against changes in the euro spot exchange rates. After the interest rates change, however, these present values themselves change slightly: −USD 9,801,786 becomes −USD 9,794,506 and +NOK 107,358,928 becomes +NOK 107,322,424. These differences represent the expected profit or loss arising from having taken the position in the first place. The spot hedges cannot protect the euro value of these differences, because it is impossible to know what the size of any such profits or losses will be.

After the interest rates change, therefore, the present value of the dollar cashflows has increased by USD 7,280 (the difference between −USD 9,801,786 and −USD 9,794,506). The euro value of this USD 7,280 profit is therefore not protected. As the EUR/USD rate has moved from 0.9000 to 0.9100, the euro value of this profit is diminished in by EUR 89.

Similarly, the present value of the krone cashflows has fallen by NOK 36,504 (the difference between +NOK 107,358,928 and +NOK 107,322,424). Again, the euro value of this NOK 36,504 loss is not protected and the exchange rate change from 9.8577 to 9.7188 increases this loss by EUR 53.

The dealer's profit is therefore diminished by EUR 142 (= EUR 89 + EUR 53). In normal circumstances, this consideration is a relatively minor one.

A hedged position will therefore not remain completely hedged, so that the required amounts of the hedges change as interest rates change. In the example, once the interest rates have changed, the amount of the dollar hedge should be increased by USD 7,280 and the amount of the krone hedge should be increased by NOK 36,504.

This approach applies not just to a single position, but to a portfolio of positions. In order to hedge his book, a forward dealer needs to calculate the net present value of all spot and future cashflows of all his positions in a particular currency – including any spot hedge he already has in place. This net position can then be hedged spot against his own reporting currency. After rehedging, the net present value of all his cashflows in each foreign currency, including his spot hedges, should have been brought back to zero.

> After hedging, the net present value of all cashflows in each foreign currency, including the spot hedges themselves, should be zero.

Two further points are worth mentioning. Firstly, the hedge will also only be exact to the extent that the interest rates used to discount the cashflows reflect the interest rates implicit in the forward exchange rates.

Secondly, there is a further, less important, reason for the discrepancy between the results in Examples 1 and 3 above. The forward points used in the examples are consistent with the theoretical rates derived from the interest rates used. However, because the forwards are only quoted to four decimal places, there is a certain amount of rounding involved which makes a small difference.

Measuring the spot risk on a forward outright position

So far, we have considered a forward swap position. The same considerations apply to a forward outright position. If a bank wants to measure the risk, valued at the spot date, of a particular open forward outright position, this risk can, as above, be measured as the present value of the outright position.

Example 4

A euro-based bank buys USD 10 million 6 months forward outright (182 days) at 11.1701 against NOK 111,701,000 when rates are as follows:

USD/NOK	spot:	10.9530
	6-month swap:	+2171 points
EUR/USD	spot:	0.9000
EUR/NOK	spot:	9.8577
USD 6-month interest rate:		4.0%
NOK 6-month interest rate:		8.0%

Later the same day, the spot rates change as follows:

USD/NOK	spot:	10.6800
EUR/USD	spot:	0.9100
EUR/NOK	spot:	9.7188

and the forward swap points move in line to +2117. The dealer now closes out his position by selling USD 10 million 6 months forward at 10.8917 against NOK 108,917,000.

The dealer has made a loss of NOK 2,784,000, value 6 months forward. The present value of this loss is EUR 275,320:

$$\frac{-\text{NOK } 2,784,000}{\left(1 + \left(0.08 \times \frac{182}{360}\right)\right)} = -\text{NOK } 2,675,780$$

$$-2,675,780 \div 9.7188 = -275,320$$

The risk of the position could have been measured originally as the present value of the forward outright position, which is long USD 9,801,786 and short NOK 107,358,928:

$$\frac{\text{USD } 10,000,000}{\left(1 + \left(0.04 \times \frac{182}{360}\right)\right)} = \text{USD } 9,801,786$$

$$\frac{\text{NOK } 111,701,000}{\left(1 + \left(0.08 \times \frac{182}{360}\right)\right)} = \text{NOK } 107,358,928$$

The effect on this position, of the changes in exchange rates would be EUR 275,331:

$$\frac{9,801,786}{0.9100} - \frac{9,801,786}{0.9000} = -119,680$$

$$\frac{-107,358,928}{9.7188} + \frac{107,358,928}{9.8577} = -155,651$$

$$-119,680 - 155,651 = -275,331$$

Apart from rounding, this is the same as above, illustrating that the forward outright position of USD 10 million dollars against NOK can be seen as having the same spot risk as a spot position of the present values of the outright position.

Exercise

1 You are a forward dealer in a sterling-based bank. You have taken a position by selling and buying EUR 5 million against Swiss francs, 2 months against 6 months, at a swap rate of − 100 points. The rates are set at 1.5950 and 1.5850. What would be an appropriate hedge to put in place against the spot risk? Current rates are as follows:

EUR/GBP spot:		0.6250
GBP/CHF spot:		2.5600
EUR	2 months (61 days):	4.1%
	6 months (183 days):	4.3%
CHF	2 months (61 days):	2.2%
	6 months (183 days):	2.4%

11

Currency relationships

Overview

In considering exchange rate movements, both historical and prospective, it is useful to see different currencies within some structure. This is not an exact science, but broadly speaking there are at least two major currency blocs – the US dollar bloc and the euro bloc – and several major currency pairs which are traded in great volume and around which other relationships revolve – USD/EUR, USD/JPY and EUR/JPY. For many exchange rates other than these, it is often helpful to consider these few rates as central and other rates as satellites around them.

Consider, for example, the exchange rate between the Canadian dollar and the Danish krone. In practice, the market tends to think in terms of the Canadian dollar relative to the US dollar. This does not imply that the USD/CAD rate is, or is expected to be, stable but rather just that dealers tend to focus on changes in the USD/CAD rate when they think about the Canadian dollar. This is not surprising, given the close historical and economic relationship between the USA and Canada. Similarly, when considering the Danish krone, the market tends to focus on its rate against the euro, rather than against the dollar. Therefore in analysing the CAD/DKK rate, one would tend to analyse separately 3 rates – USD/CAD, EUR/DKK and EUR/USD. The movement in the CAD/DKK rate is in practice a combination of these three.

In the same way, the dollar generally serves as a convenient benchmark for considering currencies in Latin America, the Middle East, Africa and the Far East, such as the Brazilian real, the Saudi Arabian riyal, the Somalian shilling and the Singapore dollar. As with the Canadian dollar, this does not imply stability against the dollar – often quite the contrary – but merely gives a starting point. The euro bloc is composed not only of the other currencies in the EU (Danish krone, Swedish krona and to some extent sterling) but also of such other European currencies as the Swiss franc and Norwegian krone.

The yen, the most important currency outside these 2 groupings, is likely to become increasingly the centre of a third major bloc (Figure 11.1).

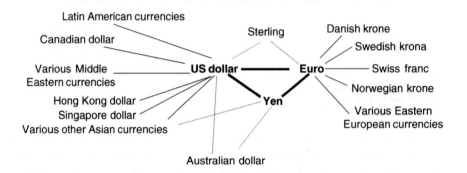

Figure 11.1   The three major currency blocs.

Exchange rate regimes

Government policy with regard to how it chooses to manage or not manage the exchange rate of its currency, is clearly important to exchange rate movements. Again, distinctions between the following categories are in practice generally not clear-cut, but they neverthe-less offer a helpful framework:

- **Fixed-rate regime**   Under a fixed-rate system, the exchange rate of a currency is fixed by the government for the foreseeable future with respect to some other currency.

    The Hong Kong dollar, for example, is fixed against the US dollar at 7.80, although in practice it generally trades slightly stronger than this. The monetary authorities try to correct it if it moves significantly away from this level. The Saudi Arabian riyal is fixed very tightly to the dollar at 3.75. The CFA franc is fixed against the euro, following its former link to the French franc.
- **Floating-rate regime**   Under a freely floating system, the value of a currency is determined by the market, with no government intervention. Exchange rates are determined entirely by forces of

supply and demand. The three major currencies, the US dollar, euro and yen, for example, essentially float freely against one another. Although there is occasionally intervention by central banks to put a limit to, or even reverse, very large changes in these rates, this is comparatively rare.

A problem with such a regime is that the free-market exchange rate at any moment might not be consistent with longer-term equilibrium. In practice therefore, governments sometimes intervene to smooth movements in the foreign exchange market. This is a *dirty floating* or *managed floating* system. Although there is no official rate between the Swiss franc and euro, for example, the exchange rate has in practice remained within a range of 1.40 to 1.80 (or the previous equivalent against the Deutschemark) for very many years.

- **Crawling peg/adjustable peg**   Under a crawling peg system, the par value of a currency relative to some other currency is adjusted regularly – often monthly. The par value and rate of adjustment are determined with reference to some measure of the external strength of a currency such as inflation differentials with other countries. The policy on exchange rate adjustments is announced in advance, so that it provides some measure of certainty.

  An adjustable peg is similar to a crawling peg, except that the adjustments are on more of an *ad hoc* basis, rather than predetermined. The Egyptian pound is managed on an adjustable peg against the US dollar.

  The European ERM (see below) has been in practice a hybrid between a dirty floating system and an adjustable peg, whereby the exchange rates have been maintained by the governments within limits around par values value with respect to each other.

- **Basket arrangements**   Some currencies are managed under a fixed regime or on a crawling peg, but against an average basket of currencies rather than against a single currency, where the currencies in the basket are weighted according to their importance in the country's international transactions.

  The *SDR* (*special drawing right*) – the artificial accounting currency of the IMF – is itself a basket currency, composed of fixed amounts of US dollars, euro, sterling and yen.

- **Dual rates**   One means of controlling speculation against a currency is a system of multiple exchange rates, whereby the rate for the currency is differentiated according to the type of transaction.

European Monetary Union

The European monetary system

The *European monetary system* (*EMS*), launched on 13 March 1979, grouped together the currencies of eight European countries. The EMS included a mechanism for enabling currency adjustments to take place in an orderly way – the *exchange rate mechanism* (*ERM*). This was built around the *ECU*, a basket currency composed of different weightings of the national currencies.

The EMS also represented the initial phase of European monetary and economic integration. The system's original goals were:

- To facilitate exchange rate stability in order to foster monetary and price stability as well as intra-European trade and thereby to promote economic integration within the European Union (EU).
- To put the responsibility for correcting policies on governments asking for changes in exchange rate parities. For example, a government seeking a devaluation of its currency was obliged to tighten monetary and/or fiscal policies to reduce economic imbalances.
- To facilitate the eventual creation of a European currency – now the euro.

In line with these aims, each member country had to reduce pressure on its currency when it became apparent that its economic pattern was diverging from other members' economies and creating problems in the foreign exchange market. The action might be increased intervention in the foreign exchange market, a change in economic policies, or a devaluation or revaluation of the currency.

From January 1987 to 1992, there were no revaluations or devaluations of any member currencies except for devaluations of the lira. This was essentially because no government wished to be seen as having a weak economy and currency. There were nevertheless significant economic divergences between the economies and pressures therefore built on the ERM. By September 1992, market speculation was sufficient to force the lira and sterling to leave the ERM (the alternative would have been to devalue massively) – although the lira rejoined in November 1996. By August 1993, speculation forced a more general readjustment of the currencies. The governments concerned still did not wish to be seen as giving in to the markets, however. The EU chose to avoid the issue by widening the ERM bands from ±2.25% as they then were for most currencies (±6% for ESP and PTE) to ±15% for all currencies. The result was bands so wide that there was little incentive for the market to speculate against any member currency. This begged the question of whether a system with such tolerant limits was in fact a system at all, and remained the situation until *European Monetary Union (EMU)* in 1999.

EMU and the euro

The Maastricht Treaty of 1991 set out a three-stage path towards monetary union. The first stage, already begun in mid-1990, involved the easing of restrictions on capital movements and closer economic policy co-ordination. The second stage, started at the beginning of 1994, established a European Monetary Institute (EMI) in Frankfurt to pave the way for transition to the final stage through closer alignment or convergence of the economic policies and the economies of the member states. The EMI was replaced in July 1998 by the establishment of a European Central Bank (ECB).

The third and final stage was the introduction of a single currency, the euro, at the beginning of 1999. In order to provide benchmarks for economic soundness, there were five convergence criteria which should have been met or approached in 1997 by countries intending to participate:

(i)   The country's general government budget deficit should be no more than 3% of GDP.
(ii) The country's total general government debt outstanding should be no more than 60% of GDP, or approaching that level satisfactorily.
(iii) Consumer price inflation should be no more than 1.5% higher than the average of the inflation in the three countries with the lowest inflation.
(iv) Long-term government bond yields should be no more than 2.0% higher than the average of the long-term interest rates of the same three countries as in (iii).
(v)   The country's exchange rate must have been maintained within the 'normal fluctuation bands' for 2 years prior to joining.

The 12 EMU currencies

Following this process, it was determined on 2 May 1998 which eleven currencies would join the euro on 1 January 1999, and at what fixed exchange rates against each other. These rates were in fact the same central ERM cross-rate parities then prevailing. On 31 December 1998, the rates were announced at which each of these currencies was then fixed irrevocably against the euro. This rate depended partly on the 2 non-EMU components of the ECU – sterling and the Danish krone (the drachma and the Swedish krona were not in the ECU basket).

The Greek drachma joined the euro subsequently, on 1 January 2001.

The 12 *national currency units* or *legacy currencies* continued to exist, but only as units of the euro, until early 2002.

The irrevocably fixed rates of the legacy currencies against the euro were set at the following:

	Fixed rate against the euro
Austrian Schilling	13.7603
Belgian franc	40.3399
Finnish markka	5.94573
French franc	6.55957
Deutschemark	1.95583
Irish pound	0.787584
Italian lira	1936.27
Luxembourg franc	40.3399
Dutch guilder	2.20371
Portuguese escudo	200.482
Spanish peseta	166.386
Greek drachma	340.750

ERMII

The EU countries not joining EMU in 1999 were Denmark, Greece, Sweden and the UK. Of these currencies, the Danish krone and the Greek drachma transferred from the former ERM to a new ERMII.

Under the rules of ERMII, the member currencies (now only the krone) must be kept within an agreed band around an agreed central rate against the euro. In the case of the krone, the band is ±2.25%.

As with the original ERM, once a currency is in danger of breaching its bands, the government concerned is obliged to do one of the following:

- Intervene directly in the foreign exchange market to strengthen or weaken the currency. All governments may support the intervention, but the onus is on the government of the currency involved.
- Adjust economic policy to affect currency market perceptions. For example, the government of a weak currency might raise interest rates to make the currency more attractive.
- Revalue or devalue the central rate against the euro.

Analysing currency movements

Overview

This book does not attempt to provide a recipe for forecasting exchange rates. Rather, this is a very brief look at the framework in which forecasts are developed. There are essentially 2 very different approaches.

Technical analysis

One approach is *technical analysis* or *charting*. In its purest form, this depends entirely on examining past price movements and ignoring any outside factors which the forecaster may anticipate. An important principle of technical analysis is that the current price already reflects all known factors, as they have been absorbed into past price movements by market participants. There is no value in superimposing further factors and the chartist's forecast is therefore generated entirely from past price patterns.

By careful observation of price, volume and open interest and mathematical analysis of patterns in the price movement, the chartist constructs a picture that reflects existing investor sentiment and psychology and hence how investors view the market. On this basis, future price movements are forecast.

Fundamental analysis

The second approach is to assume that the forecaster can validly anticipate changes in outside factors and that he should do so and base his forecast on these. This is termed *fundamental* or *judgmental* forecasting. The forecaster must use his judgement in assessing which factors are important, how these factors will develop, and what effect they will have on the price being forecast. For example: are world political developments likely to have an effect on the EUR/USD exchange rate? If so, what are these developments expected to be? Will these developments have a positive or negative effect on the exchange rate? The answers to these questions can all change over time. Rising US interest rates, for example, have, at different times in the past, had a strongly negative effect on the US dollar, a strongly positive effect, and no effect at all. The fundamental approach can be considered in several stages – long-term, medium-term and short-term.

> Technical analysis assumes that the current price already reflects all known factors and that future price movements can be forecast on the basis of past price patterns.

> Fundamental analysis assumes that the forecaster can validly anticipate changes in outside factors and that future price movements can be forecast on the basis of these changes.

The long-term view – purchasing power parity

Fundamentally, in a free market, an exchange rate is the mechanism by which prices of goods in different countries are equated. Assume that identical goods, freely tradeable, are obtainable from either country A or country B. If I am in country C, I am concerned only with the price to me in my own currency of buying from either A or B. If the prices are the same when converted into my own currency, then the exchange rate between A and B is at a fair level in relation to these goods. Suppose that over the next ten years, inflation in country A is much higher than in country B, so that the price of the goods rises much faster in A than in B. If the A/B exchange rate does not change, I will buy only from B, not from A. To overcome this lack of competitiveness in country A, the exchange rate must move over the ten years in such a way as to take account of the inflation differential. This is the *purchasing power parity* (*PPP*) concept.

> PPP is the idea that a currency's exchange rate must move, in the long term, to adjust for inflation differentials against other countries.

This theory can sometimes be seen to function reasonably well in the very long run. In the short and medium term, however, it is generally a poor indicator of currency movements. There are several difficulties with it:

- Many goods are not internationally tradeable. The prices of a haircut, a mortgage or local fresh food may be important parts of inflation as measured, but have no bearing on international trade. Ideally, a measure of inflation is needed which only measures internationally traded goods.
- In practice, most goods are not identical in different countries. Even when they are, other factors such as product quality, delivery time, credit terms, prestige, after-sales service, reliability, prejudice etc. may affect the extent to which one country can sell its goods more easily than another.
- Price differentials may be maintained by tariff and trade controls, transportation costs, different national resources, or technological innovations.

- Price equalization cannot, in practice, hold for individual goods. One test is to compare a country's domestic prices for a range of goods with a weighted average of prices for similar imported products.
- Once a country has a balance of payments deficit, its exchange rate may need to be even weaker than implied by purchasing power parity in order to redress the balance. This gives rise to the concept of a *Fundamental Equilibrium Exchange Rate* (*FEER*). This is the rate which is necessary in order to achieve a sustainable balance in the country's external current account.

Figures 11.2 and 11.3 show two examples. In both cases, the inflation differential used is based on producer price indexes (German PPI ÷ US PPI and German PPI ÷ UK PPI respectively). The GBP/DEM demonstrates a reasonably good long-term correlation between the curves. The USD/DEM is reasonable in the very long term but dramatically wrong in the short term. In the case of Germany, the exchange rate has been expressed against the Deutschemark rather than the euro, as the Deutschemark was the currency for most of the period. From 1999 onwards, the euro rate has been converted at the fixed EUR/DEM parity.

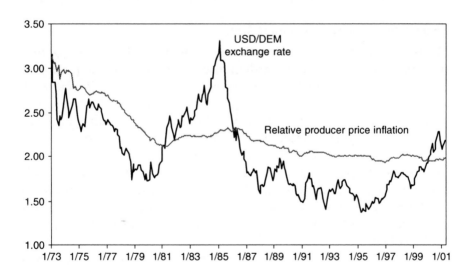

Figure 11.2   Purchasing power parity for USD/DEM.

The medium-term view

There are very many factors which can affect an exchange rate in the medium term including, for example, economic growth, monetary

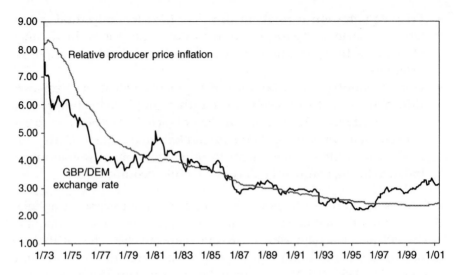

Figure 11.3 Purchasing power parity for GBP/DEM.

policy, fiscal policy, political developments, natural disasters and changes in sentiment, as well as the balance of payments and inflation. The forecaster's skill arises in selecting the appropriate factors from time to time, as well as in forecasting those factors themselves.

Short-term influences – market forces

Attitudes towards the foreign exchange market shift strongly from time to time, as different participants place different emphasis on particular factors which influence market behaviour. In the early and mid-1970s, relative monetary growth became fashionable as a currency indicator. In 1980, it was the turn of nominal and real interest rates. During much of 1987/88, the focus was more on trade imbalances. In 1988/89 attention turned more to interest rates again. In 1995, the biggest single emphasis was possibly on economic growth expectations. From the introduction of the euro in 1999 onwards, the EUR/USD rate has been dominated by a rather intangible disenchantment with the strength and direction of European Central Bank (ECB) policy.

No matter how irrelevant a factor may appear, potential changes in market focus makes that factor an essential element in exchange rate forecasting. The market is therefore often characterized by sudden shifts of sentiment which may violently distort supply and demand relationships.

Expectations also have a crucial role in exchange rate determination. A discrepancy between a previous expectation of a particular economic event and the actual outcome of that event may well move an exchange rate. For example, a currency may strengthen in anticipation of a good economic announcement but then weaken perversely when the announcement is made, even if it is as good as expected. Hence, there is a market saying: "Buy the rumour; sell the fact".

It is not possible to suggest a recipe for forecasting. The essence of fundamental forecasting is that it is judgemental and the forecaster's judgement may call for widely differing ingredients from time to time.

The forward rate

The forward outright exchange rate is, in one sense, strictly the mathematical result of combining the spot rate with interest rates, as we have seen in Chapter 2. In this sense, it cannot be a forecast of anything. Assuming free financial markets, however, this is a circular argument. If the current forward rate differs from the average expectation of market participants, then those participants will tend to move the forward rate towards that expectation by buying or selling the currency. This will move the spot rate and/or the two interest rates involved. The result will be that the forward rate will tend to reflect this average market expectation; in this sense, it is a forecast.

Effective exchange rates

An *effective exchange rate* measures a currency's average experience against other currencies which are important to that country for trade purposes. This average measure serves as a summary indicator of the currency's performance and is therefore a useful basis for foreign exchange market intervention by the government.

A *real effective exchange rate* measures the effective exchange rate, after adjustment for inflation differences between countries. This is useful for judging the country's competitive position in international markets.

An effective exchange rate measures a currency's average experience against other currencies.

A real effective exchange rate adjusts this for inflation.

Part 4

Risk Management

12

Bank risk management

Overview

In this chapter, we focus mostly on the risks arising from the instruments discussed in this book. We do not, for example, consider the risks arising specifically from trading options.

There are different ways of categorizing risks. The risks we describe here might therefore be grouped together slightly differently in another book. This is unimportant to the understanding of the risks and their management. The list is also not exhaustive – the reader will no doubt come across other examples.

The first two categories – market risk and credit risk – are risks which the bank often takes deliberately, in return for potential reward, in the normal course of its business – although it will be selective in this, choosing to hedge against some of the risks from time to time. The remaining risks – operational risk, fraud, systemic risk, legal and regulatory risk and business risk – are risks which arise because of the mechanics of doing business, but which the bank seeks to avoid, or at least minimize.

Many risks have a knock-on effect and affect more than 1 category. For example, failure to send a deal confirmation (an operational risk) can lead to both market risk and credit risk. We have given examples below of such knock-on effects.

Market risk

The risks

Market risk is the risk that the value of a position falls due to changes in market rates or prices. This is generally a major source of risk for the bank.

As mentioned, this is a risk which the bank might take on deliberately, to the extent that it seeks to make a profit by taking a position in a particular market. However, there are also situations where a market risk arises either unintentionally or unknowingly, possibly as a result of a credit or operational failure.

Movements in any market can be relevant. In general, there are four broad categories of market prices which are usually considered – FX, interest rates, equities and commodities.

Foreign exchange

A currency movement affects a spot dealer's position in an obvious way. However, it also affects a forward swap dealer's position; it is possible for a forward dealer to take a position which correctly anticipates a market move in the forward swap rates, but which causes the bank a loss because of spot rate movements. This risk (the *tail* of the position) might not be correctly recognized by the dealer or correctly hedged. This is covered fully in Chapter 10.

Example 1

A dealer buys USD 10 million against CHF. For each 1 point fall in the exchange rate, the bank would lose CHF 1,000.

Currency risks might in fact be less significant than they appear when measured against the base or reporting currency, because of cross-rate implications. For example, a yen-based organization might report two positions, the first long EUR 10 million against yen and the second short DKK 75 million against yen. The net exposure of long euros against kroner is likely to be a much less significant one than the two JPY exposures viewed separately, because of the relationship between the euro and the krone.

Interest rates

The value of many securities traded, including the ones discussed earlier in this book, is dependent on interest rates. If the bank holds a short-term security to maturity, the cashflows are not vulnerable to interest rate movements because there are no interim cashflows to be reinvested. However, the bank is still vulnerable because it cannot assume that the security will be held to maturity. Although that might be the intention, changing circumstances might force an early sale of the security at a time of high interest rates (and hence low prices).

A bank which buys or sells an FRA is also exposed to interest rates, as the settlement amount depends directly on the change in the rate between transaction and settlement.

Example 2

A dealer buys a 182-day US Treasury bill with face value USD 10 million, at a discount rate of 5.00%, for which he pays USD 9,747,222.22. He funds the position at a day-to-day cost of 5.20%.

$$10,000,000 \times \left(1 - \left(0.05 \times \frac{182}{360}\right)\right) = 9,747,222.22$$

The next day, if the discount rate is still the same, the bill would be worth USD 9,748,611.11, so that he has a mark-to-market profit of USD 1,388.89.

$$10,000,000 \times \left(1 - \left(0.05 \times \frac{181}{360}\right)\right) = 9,748,611.11$$

His funding cost so far is USD 1,407.93

$$9,747,222.22 \times 0.052 \times \frac{1}{360} = 1,407.93$$

He is therefore running a loss of USD 19.04 per day.

Other market risks

There are clearly markets other than currency and interest rates which can affect the bank's position. Positions held in securities related to commodity markets or equities will clearly be affected by movements in those markets. The risks might also be interrelated. For example, a rise in interest rates might weaken the equity market, so that a long position in interest rate securities might possibly be partly relieved by a short position in equities. Currency movements similarly might affect some commodity prices, and commodity price movements might affect some equity prices.

Market movements can also affect the value of collateral which the bank is holding against credit extended to its customers and counterparties. This collateral is not part of the bank's positions but, if the collateral value falls sharply, the bank becomes vulnerable to a credit risk which was previously secured.

Basis risk

Basis risk is the risk that two instruments do not move exactly in line as anticipated. Suppose, for example, that the bank has an FRA position which is matched by a futures position. The net position should be invulnerable to interest rate movements. There is, however, a basis risk, as the two markets might in fact not move exactly together. A similar basis risk might arise in any position, so that the actual price change is less favorable than the expected change.

Example 3

On 15 February 2002, the bank sells a 3v6 FRA to a customer for USD 10 million at 4.90%. The bank hedges this by selling 10 June futures contracts at 95.10. On 15 May, LIBOR is set at 5.20% and therefore on 17 May the bank pays a FRA settlement of USD 7,566.12.

$$10,000,000 \times \frac{(0.052 - 0.049) \times \dfrac{92}{360}}{\left(1 + \left(0.052 \times \dfrac{92}{360}\right)\right)} = 7,566.12$$

Also on 15 May, the bank closes out the hedge by buying back the 10 futures contracts. The price at that time is 94.85. The profit on the futures is USD 6,250.

$$10,000,000 \times (0.9510 - 0.9485) \times \frac{3}{12} = 6,250$$

The hedge has not matched the original exposure, because the June futures price has not moved to the same extent as the difference between the original FRA price and the LIBOR fixing on 17 May.

Liquidity risk

Liquidity risk is related to market risk. It is the risk of being unable to find a liquid market for a particular instrument, when the time comes to close out a position. An extreme example of lack of liquidity occurred following 11 September 2001 when the New York stock exchange was closed for several days, making it impossible to liquidate positions. A less extreme example is the common problem of a particular stock or bond in which there is very little trading.

Example 4

A dealer sells an FRA to a customer in a minor currency, intending to hedge this using futures. He then finds that the

futures market is not liquid enough to provide the hedge required, so that he must keep the risk uncovered for the moment.

Model risk

Model risk is the risk that a computer model used by a dealer to price
and value an instrument is wrong. This can also be considered as
forming a part of operational risk rather than market risk.

Risk measurement and controls

Measurement

Risks are measured in various ways, some of which are appropriate
to different instruments and in different situations.

- Firstly, positions are netted for market risk. For example, if a
  US dollar-based bank has only two deals, one of which is a spot
  purchase of JPY 1 billion and the other of which is a spot sale of
  JPY 1 billion, then there is zero market risk – although there is
  likely to be credit risk.
- Banks continually *mark-to-market* trading positions. This means
  that the position is revalued by calculating the profit or loss which
  would be realized if the position were closed out at current rates.
  This unrealized profit or loss is taken into the accounts daily.
- Risk on positions in interest rate instruments can be estimated
  using *modified duration*. This is a factor measuring the sensitivity
  of a position to changes in interest rates. For example, if a particular long position in a security has a modified duration of 4, then
  an immediate increase of 0.01% in all interest rates would cause
  an immediate loss of approximately 0.04% of the value of the
  position.
- *Gap analysis* – see below – is also used to measure risk on interest
  rate positions and forward FX positions.
- Increasingly, banks use *value at risk (VaR)* to measure risk over
  all their positions. This is considered later in the chapter.

Limits

An essential control is to set maximum limits on the size of positions
and the extent of market risk which dealers are allowed to take, and
to ensure that management procedures are in place to keep positions
strictly within these limits. Limits are set in various ways:

- Position limits are set for each trading position, depending on both
  the instrument concerned and the experience and expertise of the
  dealer.

- Limits might be set on the maximum size of a single transaction.
- Limits are set for the maximum size of a forward dealer's or deposit dealer's gap exposure.
- Limits are set for both intra-day positions (*daylight limit*) and positions left open overnight (*overnight limit*).
- *Stop loss* and *take profit* levels are set. These are prices or rates which, if touched in the market, will trigger the closing of a position, in order to avoid any further loss or to ensure that an existing profit is captured.
- Limits are set for overall risk across various positions in different securities or currencies.
- Limits are set for overall risk across the bank's worldwide operations, as well as in each center.
- Limits are set on the level of VaR.

Gap analysis

Gap analysis is a measure of the difference in exposures to interest rates in different periods. Clearly a portfolio consisting of a USD 1 million asset and a USD 1 million liability both of exactly 1 year maturity, and a USD 2 million asset and a USD 2 million liability both of exactly 2 years' maturity is not at risk to interest rate changes in general, although it might of course involve basis risk.

If, however, the portfolio consists of the following net positions:

1 year maturity:	short USD 3 million
10 years' maturity:	long USD 3 million

then there is a risk to general changes along the yield curve, even if there is no basis risk.

Suppose, for example, that interest rates rise by 0.5% for 1-year yields and 0.8% for 10-year yields (a steepening positive yield curve, or a flattening negative one). Broadly speaking, the effect will be a gain of USD 15,000 per annum for 1 year on the assets but a much greater loss of USD 24,000 per annum for 10 years on the liabilities. In order to control this risk, gap analysis considers a portfolio broken down by period. In a major portfolio, this cannot conveniently be done in great detail, so that periods will be grouped, with more subdivision of shorter time periods, where yield curve changes are likely to be more pronounced. Thus, for example, maturities might be split as follows:

0–7 days 7–30 days 1–3 months 3–6 months 6–12 months 1–2 years 2–5 years 5–10 years

Analysis in this way forces consideration of maturity imbalances, and of potential liquidity problems, but has several weaknesses, as follows:

- Because the groupings are discrete, the position can appear to change sharply from one day to the next. For example, a loan of 5 years plus one day would shift from one period to another a day later, given the schedule suggested above.
- For the same reason, if gap analysis shows a particular exposure which the bank wishes to cover, it is likely that the cover taken will create a new risk later: the cover might reduce the gap now, but re-create another one in due course.
- Most importantly, gap analysis does not take account of the time-value of money on the assets and liabilities, or the reinvestment risks. A 5-year zero-coupon asset appears to match a 5-year liability with semi-annual interest, whereas in fact the cashflow profiles are of course very different.

Other controls

There are other elements of control which should be in place, including the following:

- All deals should be input immediately to the bank's systems for both settlement processing and risk measurement.
- It is important that, for risk and accounting purposes, any transaction intended to be a hedge is linked to the underlying deal it is intended to cover.
- There must be rigorous testing of computer valuation models before they are used.

Credit risk

The risks

Credit risk is the risk that a counterparty might default on a transaction by failing to pay amounts due or failing to deliver a security or failing in some other way (*counterparty risk*), or that the issuer of a security defaults on coupon or interest payments.

In the case of a loan made to a counterparty, the whole principal amount of the loan is potentially at risk. The same is true of a long position in a security if the issuer defaults.

In many cases, however, counterparty risk is rather smaller. For example, if the counterparty is bankrupted before a forward foreign exchange outright matures, our bank knows that it will not receive anything from the counterparty and therefore deliberately does not deliver its side of the deal either. In this case, how much will our bank lose? If the deal is showing a loss from our point of view, we will not lose anything. In practice, in this case the administrators of the bankrupt counterparty should insist on consummation of the deal anyway, so that there would be no effect on our bank.

Suppose, however, that the deal is showing a mark-to-market profit to our bank. That is, the deal would show a loss to the counterparty if it were closed out now. In this case, the deal will simply not be consummated. Our loss is therefore limited to the profit on the deal. This loss can be seen as how much it will cost our bank to replace the deal with a similar deal with another counterparty. The risk is therefore called *replacement risk*.

For a short period during the settlement cycle when a FX deal is delivered, the risk does involve the entire principal amount of the deal. After our bank has already committed itself to making payment on its part, but before it can be certain that its counterparty has done the same, the whole amount of the trade is at risk. This is known as *settlement risk* (also *Herstatt risk* in the case of foreign exchange after Bank Herstatt, which defaulted in 1974). This risk is removed when securities are delivered against payment through a clearing organization.

Example 5

On 15 August, the bank sells USD 10 million against CHF to a counterparty for value 17 September at 1.7324. By 22 August, the forward rate has moved to 1.7188. The bank has a potential profit of CHF 136,000 on 17 September, which it would lose if the counterparty goes bankrupt. The size of the replacement risk is therefore the present value of CHF 136,000.

$$10,000,000 \times (1.7324 - 1.7188) = 136,000$$

Settlement risk in foreign exchange should be rather short-term because payment instructions should be revocable (able to be cancelled) until settlement date. In practice, however, the cut-off time for irrevocable instructions is sometimes earlier.

The clearing houses for futures exchanges are generally considered to be free of credit risk because of their arrangements for *margin*. This is a combination of collateral placed with the clearing house in case of default (*initial margin*) and the requirement to pay losses as they arise daily (*variation margin*) rather than on final settlement.

Exchanges do not all have the same rules, however, and, in extreme circumstances, could possibly still fail.

Credit risk can increase during the life of a deal for two reasons. Firstly, the credit rating of a counterparty, or of the issuer of a security in the bank's portfolio, might weaken after a deal has been transacted or a security purchased. Secondly, credit risk will change as the market moves. For example, the bank has no counterparty risk when a forward foreign exchange deal is first transacted. If the counterparty goes bankrupt immediately, there is no mark-to-market profit or loss, so that our bank can replace the deal with another counterparty at the same rate. If the market then moves so that our bank is in profit however, this creates a replacement risk. Credit risk and market risk are in this way interlinked.

Credit risk includes both issuer default risk and counter-party risk.

Counterparty risk is credit risk arising from default of a counterparty at any time.

Where a deal can be replaced, counterparty risk is called replacement risk and is limited to the cost of replacement – i.e. any mark-to-market profit.

After irrevocable payment instructions have been given, counterparty risk is called settlement risk and is potentially the entire amount of the deal.

Controls

The essential first step in reducing credit risk is rigorous credit assessment of counterparties and issuers. If there are no defaults, there is no credit risk. In practice, however, there will always be credit risk.

- As with market risk, there must be limits set on the size of outstanding transactions with any one counterparty together with the value of securities held which have been issued by that counterparty. Within the limit, the amount of business allowed will depend on the nature of the transaction. A USD 1 million loan to a counterparty is much riskier (because the whole principal amount is at risk) than a USD 1 million FRA transacted with the same counterparty.
- Limits are set not only on individual counterparties, but also, for example, on each sector of industry and each country.
- Monitoring of credit risk must take account of the fact that credit risk can depend on market movements, as described earlier.

- The value of any collateral taken from counterparties must be carefully monitored and additional collateral called for when appropriate.
- All settlements expected from counterparties must be reconciled promptly, as a warning system for potential default.
- Operations staff should be trained in what constitutes a default.
- The bank should negotiate the latest possible cut-off times for making payments.
- Wherever possible, the bank should set up legally enforceable documentation with each counterparty which incorporates *obligation netting* and *close-out netting*. The bank should also use netting systems, and *DvP* and *PvP* systems where possible. These various areas are outlined in the next section.

Netting

Netting cash payments means transferring net amounts rather than gross amounts between parties. Transfers of a particular security can be netted in the same way.

Example 6

Bank A is due to make a payment of USD 5 million to Bank B on 15 June in settlement of one transaction and Bank B is due to make a payment of USD 4 million to Bank A on the same date in settlement of a different transaction. Instead of making both these payments gross, Banks A and B could agree that Bank A pays Bank B an amount of USD 1 million (=USD 5 million – USD 4 million) as full net settlement of the two transactions.

The purposes of netting are to reduce credit risk, improve liquidity and reduce operational risks and costs. In the above Example, if the two gross payments are made separately, Bank A must normally give irrevocable instructions to pay away USD 5 million before it knows whether it has received the USD 4 million from Bank B. If Bank B subsequently proves unable to pay the USD 4 million, Bank A might have a USD 4 million loss. Bank B is similarly exposed to the credit risk of Bank A. This risk reduction also enables an increase in the volume of business transactions between the two parties, because of the reduction in capital requirements allowed by supervisors where there is appropriate netting – see 'Capital adequacy requirements' later in this chapter. The bank's credit risk monitoring system should accurately reflect the effect of netting.

In the same Example, the net settlement improves liquidity. If Bank A only has to pay the net USD 1 million, its available funds are reduced by that amount. If, however, it must pay USD 5 million, its available funds are reduced by USD 5 million until it has finally received the USD 4 million from Bank B. The net settlement in the example should also reduce the operational cost and risk of error, as there is only one payment rather than two.

An arrangement to net should always be supported by a written master agreement between the parties to that effect. A master agreement is one which covers all deals of a particular type between the two parties, except those which are specifically agreed at the time of the deal to be treated separately. There are two netting aspects to a master agreement. The first is netting of settlements in the normal course of business as described in the example above; this is known as obligation netting. The second is close-out netting, which occurs when one of the parties is in default of the agreement for any reason; close-out netting allows the non-defaulting party to close-out all existing transactions – i.e., terminate them early. Agreement to close-out netting provides that, in these circumstances, a single net settlement is made for all outstanding transactions. This removes the possibility of *cherry-picking*, a term used to describe the way in which an administrator for a counterparty in liquidation might be able to insist on consummating profitable deals with a particular counterparty, while defaulting on unprofitable ones.

Netting in a master agreement is effective only if it will prove to be legally binding in the event of dispute. Whether this is so might depend on the various legal jurisdictions of the agreement itself, the parties and any correspondent banks or custodians involved in the settlements. It is therefore always important for legal opinions to be sought. Legal opinions in the UK and USA, for example, support the use of netting domestically, but there are still concerns over the enforceability of cross-border netting.

Netting in master agreements is often netting by novation. This involves legally substituting a new single contract between the two parties to combine and replace all existing similar contracts between them for a given settlement date. The major master agreements used internationally which cover the instruments described in this book are:

- IFEMA (International Foreign Exchange Master Agreement) for foreign exchange spot and forward deals.
- ISDA (International Swaps and Derivatives Association) master agreement for FRAs (also used for swaps, options and other

transactions). FRABBA (The BBA's documentation for FRAs) is also used, but less frequently.
- GMRA (Global Master Repo Agreement) for repos and buy/sell-backs.
- SAFEBBA (The BBA's documentation for SAFEs)

Netting systems

The example above involves bilateral netting – netting between two parties. It is possible to organize such netting through a third-party bilateral netting system. FXNET is such an organization, which runs a bilateral netting system for banks involved in foreign exchange deals.

A multilateral netting system nets payments between more than two banks. Transactions between all the banks involved are netted so that, in each currency, each bank only receives one net amount or pays one net amount or does neither.

Example 7

Suppose the following gross amounts are due, all on the same date:

Bank A owes Bank B USD 5 million
Bank B owes Bank A USD 4 million
Bank A owes Bank C USD 3 million
Bank C owes Bank A USD 5 million
Bank B owes Bank C USD 10 million
Bank C owes Bank B USD 8 million

The net result for Bank A is that it is owed USD 1 million (=–USD 5 million + USD 4 million – USD 3 million + USD 5 million). The net result for Bank B is that it owes USD 1 million (=–USD 5 million + USD 4 million + USD 10 million – USD 8 million). The net result for Bank C is zero (= –USD 3 million + USD 5 million – USD 10 million + USD 8 million). In this case, multilateral settlement could be achieved by a simple payment of USD 1 million from Bank B to Bank A, instead of six gross bilateral payments.

PvP and DvP

Bilateral and multilateral netting systems operate by netting and settling the payments due on a particular date at certain times on that day – often at the end of the day. An alternative is a *payment versus payment (PvP)* system. In this, a payment from Bank A to

Bank B is made only if, and at the same time as, the corresponding payment from Bank B to Bank A is made. The payments are made during the day on a real-time basis and, once made, are final. Such a system – *continuous real-time linked settlement (CLS)* – has been developed for FX settlements by CLS Bank, starting in 2002 with settlements for USD, CAD, EUR, GBP, CHF, AUD and JPY, and extending to SEK, NOK, DKK and SGD in 2003. Settlement is available during a 5-hour window from 07:00 to 12:00 Central European Time. Members of CLS need to maintain collateral in the system to cover the net risk they represent to other members. A danger of PvP is that there can be non-credit-related reasons for non-payment, such as systems failures, strikes, severe weather problems, human error etc. Non-settlement could cause the whole system to fail, causing a liquidity crisis. A systemic failure in one country, for example, could bring the system down.

Delivery versus payment (DvP) is the corresponding settlement mechanism, used widely both domestically and internationally, for settlement of securities transactions. In this, a payment from Bank A to Bank B is made only if, and at the same time as, the corresponding security is delivered from Bank B to Bank A.

Contracts for differences

A contract for differences is a transaction where only the net difference between two amounts is settled, and the principal amount involved is not transferred. This reduces credit risk very significantly. Generally the settlement is the difference between the rate or price dealt at the outset and a reference rate or price at maturity, calculated on a notional principal amount.

FRAs, Futures and SAFEs, covered earlier in this book, are contracts for differences.

Forward outrights are available as non-deliverable forwards (NDFs), also covered earlier. These contracts for differences are largely used in emerging currencies for exchange control reasons rather than risk control, but the concept can be extended to major currencies.

Operational risk

The risks

Operational risk is a wide term, covering the risk of losses due to failures in the bank's operations generally. This includes the activities of the operations department itself (deal input, confirmation, netting, payments and reconciliation) but also covers other areas such as the bank's computer systems (*system risk*), accounting, personnel problems and even third-party organizations such as custodians and correspondent banks. The problems might arise from staff mistakes, management weaknesses or system errors. Many of the risks can have knock-on effects on market risk or credit risk.

Example 8

Operational risk can arise in many ways. The following are just some examples:

A deal ticket for the purchase of USD 10 million from Bank A against CHF at 1.7324 is entered incorrectly in the bank's system as a sale of USD 10 million. A dealer covers the short USD exposure which the system is showing, by buying USD 10 million from Bank B. In fact this has doubled the size of the long position, rather than reducing the exposure to zero. The dollar now falls to 1.7188 and the bank makes a loss of CHF 272,000.

If in fact the dollar had risen instead, there would have been a profit on the original deal with bank A, giving rise to a credit risk from bank A. The system, however, would show no such credit risk because the deal would appear to show a loss.

The error could thus give rise to market risk or credit risk, by mis-stating the position in both.

A deal confirmation sent to a counterparty is incorrect, or an incorrect incoming confirmation is not checked properly. This could similarly give rise to market and/or credit risk, as well as harm the bank's reputation (reputational risk).

The payment in settlement of a deal is sent incorrectly, so that the counterparty, which does not receive the funds on time, makes a claim for interest.

A power cut causes the computer systems to crash and there is no adequate back-up power system.

The bank relies on a few key staff members for processing certain complex transactions and this whole team of staff leaves the bank to join a competitor. Errors are made as further deals of this type are processed, leading to market risk, credit risk and reputational risk.

A bomb or a natural disaster makes it impossible for the bank to carry on its business at its usual premises and there are no adequate back-up facilities. This could lead to the loss of a considerable volume of business, as well as creating market, credit and reputational risks.

Controls

The task of controlling operational risk is as broad as operational risk itself. It is paramount that staff are competent and well trained and that systems are thoroughly tested. An approach to reducing human error is the introduction of *straight-through processing (STP)*. This is a general term for the computerization of tasks in such a way that each process feeds automatically to the next. Other points include:

- No deal should be undertaken unless operations staff, risk managers, accounting staff and IT staff all understand the mechanics of the transaction. Existing systems might not be adequate, or input might be required to several incompatible systems for position recording, risk management, settlement etc.
- It is important that confirmations are sent, and incoming confirmations checked, as quickly as possible. Speed is particularly important in areas where a loss could increase very quickly.
- It is important to have a team approach, as the individual processes relating to a trade are completed by different people. Each person should know how his role fits into the whole process.

Other risks

Fraud

It is possible for the bank to try to address the risks mentioned so far – even though risk is rarely reduced to zero. The perpetrator of a fraud, however, is presumably circumventing exactly those controls which have been put in place to protect the bank. This could perhaps be seen as yet another type of operational risk. For example, it could be difficult to prevent fraud if there were sufficient collusion between dealers and operations staff in two counterparty banks.

Segregation of responsibilities

An important principle – particularly in seeking to avoid fraud but also to help control operational risks – is the segregation of responsibilities between the *front office* (the dealers) and the *back office* (the operational staff). It is essential that the two areas be totally separate in terms of both staff and management reporting. Ideally, they should be physically separate also, although this might not always be practicable. It is important also that computer access by dealing staff to the back-office systems is not possible. Operational errors or oddities are less likely to be noticed – or remedial action taken – if the same person is responsible for more than one of these areas. The internal audit function should also be totally separate.

Systemic risk

This is the risk of failure in the entire system of which the bank itself is only a part – for example, a failure of the entire payment clearing system or the entire banking system. This could, for example, be because of mechanical difficulties (a computer failure) or because a major payment default by another bank, which might be one with whom our bank has no dealings, has caused a chain reaction of defaults, seizing up the payment clearing.

Legal and regulatory risk

This is the risk that the bank's business is affected by changes in laws and regulations, or by existing laws and regulations which it had not properly taken into account. Again, this may be seen as a type of operational risk, but some of the risks here arise from changes outside the bank's control and which it might not reasonably be likely to anticipate.

Example 9

The bank expects to receive an FRA settlement from a counterparty. Although financially healthy, the counterparty refuses to pay the settlement and the bank is unable to enforce settlement because the counterparty is in a legal jurisdiction which does not support the transaction. Alternatively, the counterparty did not have the authorization for the transaction, which is then considered legally void.

A corporate customer refuses to consummate a particular transaction, because it claims that it was misadvised by the bank in undertaking it, and the courts support the customer.

Some of the bank's outstanding transactions are adversely affected by changes in taxation or changes in the requirements for capital adequacy (see later in this chapter).

The bank permits transactions, knowingly or unknowingly, which involve money laundering, and the bank is subsequently penalized by the authorities for doing so.

Business risk

The bank is at risk to general business conditions in the same way as any other business, although this can possibly be magnified. A severe recession, for example, as well as possibly reducing demand for the bank's services, could result in a fall in creditworthiness of the bank's existing business across the board. The bank also faces other commercial risks, such as the commercial value of its buildings.

A fall in the bank's own credit rating for any reason will also result in higher funding costs compared with its competitors.

Value at risk (VaR)

A full treatment of VaR is mathematically complex and outside the scope of this book. This is therefore an overview only, aimed at giving the reader an understanding of the process. The details of the first section on basic statistics are not essential to understanding the VaR section which follows it, but they might be helpful if you are interested.

Basic statistics

Mean, variance and standard deviation

The arithmetic *mean* of a series of numbers is the average of the numbers as we normally understand it. If we have the following five numbers:

52, 53, 57, 58, 60

then their mean is:

$$\frac{(52 + 53 + 57 + 58 + 60)}{5} = 56$$

The mean is useful, because it gives us an idea of the how big the numbers are – about 56. However, if we knew only this mean, 56, it would not give us any idea of how spread out all the numbers are around 56; perhaps they are all very close to 56, or perhaps they are very spread out.

The standard deviation of the same numbers is a measure of how spread out the numbers are around this mean. If all the numbers were exactly the same, the standard deviation would be zero. If the numbers were very spread out, the standard deviation would be very high. Effectively, the standard deviation gives an idea of the answer to the question: On average, how far away are the numbers from their mean?

The mean is the average of a set of numbers.

Standard deviation is a measure of how spread out the numbers are around the mean.

The standard deviation is defined as the square root of the *variance*. The variance in turn is defined as the average of the squared difference between each number and their average.

Consider the two sets of numbers in Figures 12.1 and 12.2. They also each have a mean of 56, but in Figure 12.1 the first set is closely packed together and the second set in Figure 12.2 is very spread out. In fact, the first set has a standard deviation of 1.4 and the second set has a standard deviation of 4.3. If the standard deviation or variance is lower, the histogram is compressed horizontally – it looks taller and thinner – and there is a lower probability that any particular number is a long way from the mean. If the standard deviation or variance is greater, the histogram is more stretched out horizontally – it looks lower and fatter – and more numbers are further from the mean.

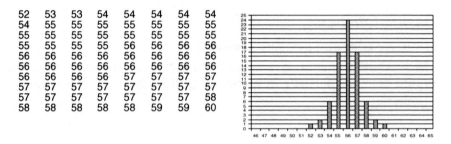

Figure 12.1   The set of numbers is closely packed together.

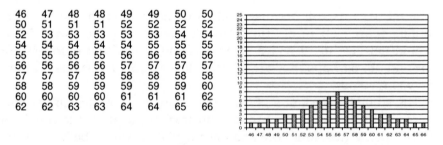

Figure 12.2   Here the set of numbers is very spread out.

Mean (μ) = sum of all the values divided by the number of values

Variance (σ^2) = mean of (difference from mean)^2

$$= \frac{\text{sum of all the (difference from the mean})^2}{\text{the number of values}}$$

This gives the variance of a set of numbers, given that all the numbers are known. Very often, however, a sample only of the numbers is used. For example, a representative sample of prices for a particular instrument might be the daily closing prices over a period of only one year, rather than over the entire history of that instrument since it began trading. In this case, a better estimate of the variance of all the numbers is:

$$\text{Estimated variance} = \frac{\text{sum of all the (difference from the mean)}^2}{\text{(the number of values} - 1)}$$

Whichever formula is used,

$$\text{Standard deviation} = \sqrt{\text{variance}}$$

Example 10

What are the variance and standard deviation of the following numbers?

52, 53, 57, 58, 60

As above, their mean is:

$$\frac{(52 + 53 + 57 + 58 + 60)}{5} = 56$$

Numbers	Difference between the numbers and 56	(Difference)^2
52	−4	16
53	−3	9
57	+1	1
58	+2	4
60	+4	16
Mean = 56		Total = 46

The variance is therefore $\frac{46}{5} = 9.2$ and the standard deviation is $\sqrt{9.2} = 3.03$.

Correlation and covariance

Correlation and covariance are measures of the extent to which two things do, or do not, move together. The precise mathematical definitions are given below.

Consider, for example, the USD/DKK exchange rate and the USD/EUR exchange rate. Generally, one rate will rise and fall in line with the other. The two rates are therefore very closely correlated. On the other hand, the USD/DKK exchange rate will fall as the EUR/USD exchange rate rises, so that there is a close negative correlation between these two rates. There is probably very little relationship at all between Mexican interest rates and the HUF/JPY exchange rate, so these 2 numbers have no correlation – the price of one moving up or down suggests no information about whether the other is moving up or down.

A correlation coefficient lies between +1 and −1. If two series of numbers are perfectly correlated – they move exactly in line – their correlation coefficient is +1. if they move exactly in line but in opposite directions, their correlation coefficient is −1. If there is no link at all between the two series, their correlation coefficient is 0.

A correlation coefficient lies between −1 and +1 and measures the extent to which two things do, or do not, move together.

Covariance quantifies this in terms of the magnitudes of the two things.

Example 11

First series	Second series	Correlation coefficient	First series	Second series	Correlation coefficient	First series	Second series	Correlation coefficient
1	2		1	−2		1	10	
2	4		2	−4		2	2	
3	6	+1	3	−6	−1	3	4	0
4	8		4	−8		4	6	
5	10		5	−10		5	9	

Covariance is a concept linking correlation and variance. Whereas variance quantifies how much the value of one particular thing varies, covariance measures how much two things vary, relative to each other.

Correlation coefficient

$$= \frac{\text{sum of } (x \times y) - (n \times (\text{mean of } x) \times (\text{mean of } y))}{\sqrt{\begin{array}{l}((\text{sum of } (x^2) - (n \times (\text{mean of } x)^2)) \\ \times (\text{sum of } (y^2) - (n \times (\text{mean of } y)^2)))\end{array}}}$$

Covariance = correlation coefficient

$\times$ (standard deviation of x) $\times$ (standard deviation of y)

$$= \frac{\text{correlation coefficient}}{n}$$

$$\times \sqrt{(\text{sum of } (x\text{-mean of } x)^2 \times \text{sum of } (y\text{-mean of } y)^2)}$$

where n is the number of pairs of data.

Example 12

What are the correlation coefficient and covariance of the following price series x and y?

	First price x	Second price y	$x \times y$	x^2	y^2	$(x\text{-ave of } x)^2$	$(y\text{-ave of } y)^2$
Day 1:	94	75	7,050	8,836	5,625	1	4
Day 2:	95	74	7,030	9,025	5,476	4	1
Day 3:	93	73	6,789	8,649	5,329	0	0
Day 4:	91	72	6,552	8,281	5,184	4	1
Day 5:	92	71	6,532	8,464	5,041	1	4
Totals:	465	365	33,953	43,255	26,655	10	10

$$\text{average of } x = \frac{465}{5} = 93 \qquad \text{average of } y = \frac{365}{5} = 73$$

$$\text{variance of } x = \frac{10}{4} = 2.5 \qquad \text{variance of } y = \frac{10}{4} = 2.5$$

standard deviation of $x = \sqrt{2.5} = 1.5811$

standard deviation of $x = \sqrt{2.5} = 1.5811$

correlation coefficient

$$= \frac{33,953 - (5 \times 93 \times 73)}{\sqrt{((43,255 - (5 \times (93)^2)) \times (26,655 - (5 \times (73)^2)))}} = 0.80$$

covariance $= 0.80 \times 1.5811 \times 1.5811 = 2.0$

0.80 is a reasonably high level of correlation, indicating that the price of x and the price of y move together to some extent (see Figure 12.3).

Probability density

The *probability density* of a series of numbers is a description of how likely any one of them is to occur. Thus the probability density

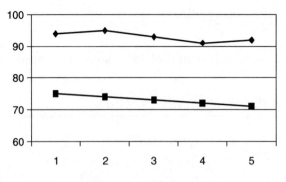

Figure 12.3 Correlation.

of the results of throwing a die is $\frac{1}{6}$ for each possible result. The probability density of the heights of 100 adult men chosen at random will be relatively high for around 170 cm to 180 cm, and very low for less than 150 cm or more than 200 cm. The shape of the probability density therefore varies with the type of results being considered.

One particular probability density which is used as an approximate description of many circumstances in life is known as the *normal* probability function.

If the probabilities are as shown in Figure 12.4, for example, a number less than -3 or more than $+3$ is extremely unlikely, while a number between say -1 and $+1$ is rather likely.

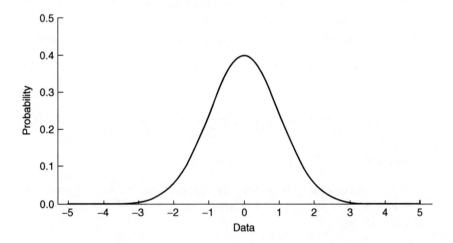

Figure 12.4 Normal probability density function.

The normal probability function is not mathematically straightforward – the equation for the graph is in fact:

Normal probability function

$$\text{probability density} = \frac{1}{\sqrt{2\pi}\,e^{\frac{x^2}{2}}}$$

This function is important here because it is widely used in VaR calculations.

Probability distribution

The *cumulative probability distribution* of a series of numbers is the probability that any one of them will be no greater than a particular number. Thus the probability distribution for throwing the die is:

probability $\frac{1}{6}$ that the number thrown will be 1
probability $\frac{2}{6}$ that the number thrown will be 1 or 2
probability $\frac{3}{6}$ that the number thrown will be 1, 2 or 3
probability $\frac{4}{6}$ that the number thrown will be 1, 2, 3 or 4
probability $\frac{5}{6}$ that the number thrown will be 1, 2, 3, 4 or 5
probability $\frac{6}{6}$ that the number thrown will be 1, 2, 3, 4, 5 or 6

The normal probability function shown in Figure 12.4 has the corresponding probability distribution shown in Figure 12.5. If the standard deviation were greater, so that the curve in Figure 12.4 was shorter and fatter, then the curve in Figure 12.5 would also be more stretched out horizontally. If the standard deviation were less, it would be compressed horizontally.

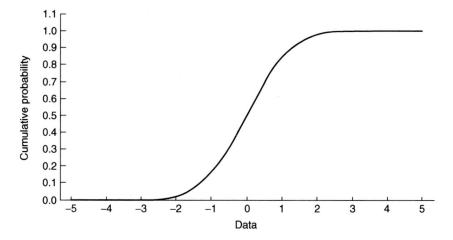

Figure 12.5 Normal cumulative probability distribution.

With this normal probability distribution, there is a probability of around 84.1% that the outcome will be less than or equal to 1 standard deviation higher than the mean; a probability of around 97.7% that the outcome will be less than or equal to 2 standard deviations higher than the mean; a probability of around 99.9% that the outcome will be less than or equal to 3 standard deviations higher than the mean, and so on.

In each of these examples, we are considering the probability of any number being in a range which goes down to minus infinity but goes up only to a certain defined level (1, 2, 3 and so on), leaving a *tail* excluded at the top. As the normal curve is symmetrical, we could equally well consider a range which goes up to plus infinity but goes down only to a certain defined level (−1, −2, −3 and so on), leaving a tail excluded at the bottom. This one-tailed measurement is what is generally used in risk calculations, because a risk manager is worried about how much loss the bank might make, rather than how much profit.

We have now reached the important point. If we assume that the probability distribution for a particular price is normal and can estimate the standard deviation, it is possible to calculate what is the probability of any particular number being less than −1, or less than −2 etc. A similar calculation can also be made based on the assumption of a probability distribution other than a normal one. In financial risk management, this translates into being able to estimate the probability of a loss being worse than a particular level.

Overview of VaR

In order to control market risk, the bank needs to be in a position to measure it. In line with EU and BIS regulations, banks have therefore increasingly developed computer models to assess market risk, with a view to deriving an overall measurement of the bank's risk – value at risk (VaR) or *earnings at risk.*

VaR is the maximum potential loss which the bank might suffer on its positions over a given time period, estimated within a given confidence level. Suppose, for example, that the bank has a VaR of USD 10 million with a time horizon of 30 days and a confidence level of 95%. This means that if the bank's positions remain unchanged, there is a 95% probability that its total losses will not exceed USD 10 million over the next 30 days – or to put it another way, a 5% probability that the total losses will exceed this amount. The total expected loss would be smaller (greater) if the time horizon were less (more) than 30 days and smaller (greater) if the confidence level were lower (higher) than 95%.

> ### VaR is:
>
> the maximum potential loss which the bank might suffer
> over a given time period
> estimated within a given confidence level.

In arriving at this summary number of USD 10 million, the bank must make certain assumptions. Firstly, there is an assumption about the probability distribution of price movements for each instrument in which the bank has a position – what is the pattern of price movement and are the price changes up and down expected to be large or small? Mathematically, this means: What is the probability distribution and what is its standard deviation? Typically, banks use an assumption that asset returns show a normal probability distribution as the basis for risk assessment, and the standard deviation used will be based on historic movements.

Secondly, the bank will take into account correlation between different instruments. Suppose, for example, that a particular dollar-based bank is long of 1 million euros and short of an equivalent amount of Swiss francs. Because there is some correlation between euros and Swiss francs, the bank is less vulnerable to market movements than if it were only long of 1 million euros without any offsetting position. In this particular case, the greater the correlation, the less risky the position. If the two positions were both long (rather than one long and one short), then the riskiness of the total position would instead increase with higher correlation, rather than decrease. In general, a portfolio of positions is less risky if it is more diversified.

Variance/covariance, Monte Carlo and historic approaches

There are 3 widely used approaches to calculating VaR, each with advantages and disadvantages.

Variance/covariance

The approach considered so far for estimating VaR is essentially the *variance/covariance* approach. This approach involves the following:

- Assume a probability distribution – generally taken to be the normal distribution.
- Assume a variance for each financial instrument and a covariance between each pair of different financial instruments – generally based on historic data.
- Because it is impractical (and gives rise to mathematical difficulties) to use variance and covariance data for each instrument in a

portfolio, only a selection of standard instruments is used. Each instrument in the actual portfolio is then expressed in terms of an equivalent number of these standard instruments. For example, a foreign exchange forward can be expressed in terms of a spot position and two loans or deposits; an interest rate-based security can be broken down to individual cashflows and expressed as an equivalent strip of zero-coupon instruments. This process is known as *mapping*, and vastly reduces the number of instruments to be considered.

- Calculate the VAR.

The variance/covariance approach has the advantage of being relatively straightforward. A matrix of variances and covariances for the standard instruments can be obtained from third parties, such as JP Morgan's *Riskmetrics*. The properties of the normal distribution are well known (a 95% confidence level, for example, implies a VaR of 1.65 standard deviations below the mean) and allow for relatively simple risk assessment. If the standard deviation is doubled, for example, the VaR is doubled as well; if the time horizon is doubled, the VaR is multiplied by the square root of 2.

A disadvantage is that the relationship between the VaR and the underlying risk variables is linear (i.e., they are directly proportional). For example, it assumes that if yields move by a certain amount, security prices will move in direct proportion. Similarly, it assumes that option values move in direct proportion to underlying prices. In practice, this is not the case, so that for an option portfolio, the variance/covariance approach is generally unsatisfactory.

Monte Carlo simulation

An alternative is to use a *Monte Carlo* simulation. This involves generating a very large number of random prices, applying these to the current portfolio of instruments and measuring the net effect:

- For each instrument or set of instruments, choose a probability distribution and pricing model.
- Assume variances and covariances.
- Generate a random set of data (changes in prices, rates, option volatilities). Although this computer-generated series of prices is random, it must still fit an assumed probability distribution; if the current price of an asset is 100, for example, a move to 50 is much less likely than a move to 99.
- Apply these data to the portfolio and calculate the resulting profit or loss.

- Repeat this process many times, to generate a large number of possible profit or loss outcomes.
- List these results in order. For a 95% confidence level, for example, exclude the worst 5% of results. The VaR will then be the worst result remaining.

A disadvantage of this technique is that it is more expensive in terms of computer time than the variance/covariance approach. It is also more complex to set up and to explain and still depends on the assumptions made about probability distributions and variances and covariances. It can, however, be much more reliable for option-related instruments.

Historic
Another possibility is to use historic price movements and apply these to the current portfolio of instruments, on the assumption that future price movements will mimic past ones, and look at the net effect, as with a Monte Carlo simulation. This approach is therefore as follows:

- Map the actual portfolio to a selection of standard instruments for which historic price data are available, either from a third party or from an in-house database.
- Estimate the change in value of the entire portfolio that would have arisen over a particular period in the past – for example, from 365 days ago until 335 days ago – by applying actual historic price changes. Then measure the change that would have arisen from 364 days ago until 334 days ago, then the change from 363 days ago until 333 days ago, and so on.
- List all these results and, for a 95% confidence level, exclude the worst 5% of results. The worst result remaining is the VaR for a 30-day time horizon.

This approach has the advantage of being a simpler technique mathematically than the variance/covariance and Monte Carlo approaches, and simple to explain in concept. No particular probability distribution (such as a normal one) needs to be assumed, as the probability distribution is implicit in the historic data used. Similarly, the variances and covariances do not need to be measured or even known, because they are also implicit in the historic data. It also does not suffer from the same linear restrictions as the variance/covariance approach.

However, this method still suffers from the drawback that the size of price movements and the relationships between price movements of different instruments (i.e. their correlations or covariances) might not be the same in the future as in the past. It also depends on the choice of historic period. Too short a period might be unrepresentative (for example, it might have been a particularly volatile or quiet period). Too long a period might include a period so long ago that variances and/or covariances have changed significantly since then.

General problems with VaR calculations

One obvious difficulty with the variance/covariance calculation lies in the assumption of a normal probability distribution. In practice, the probability distribution relating to financial price movements tends to have fatter tails than suggested by the normal curve (the left-hand and right-hand ends of the graph are fatter than shown above). This suggests a greater probability of large profits or losses.

There is also a likelihood of *negative skewness* – a greater probability of a large downward movement in prices than of a large upward movement. This is because a falling market can trigger panic stop-loss sales which accelerate prices downward.

Variances and correlations are also not constant. Those seen in the past are not necessarily a good guide to the future.

A further problem with correlation is that historic relationships sometimes break down under extreme circumstances. For example, in quiet markets, the US dollar and the Singapore dollar might be very closely correlated, so that a portfolio long of one and short of the other looks relatively safe. When the market panics, however, they might diverge significantly. The use of correlation in assessing risk must therefore be partly based on historic data and partly subjective.

In using VaR for risk management, the bank must also make a decision on the holding period and confidence level (30 days and 95% in the examples above). These parameters are clearly arbitrary and depend on the bank's ability to accept risk and the speed with which it believes it can close out a loss-making position from a management point of view. They also depend on how liquid are the markets in which the bank is working, as this affects the speed and ease with which it is possible to close a position from a practical market point of view.

Stress-testing

An alternative approach to statistical analysis such as VaR is scenario analysis – assessing risk by assuming a particular scenario and seeing what happens:

- Choose a particular outcome for all the variables (FX rates, interest rates etc.).

- Calculate what would happen to the portfolio's value under these circumstances.
- Repeat the process for different assumptions.

A sensible check on a VaR model, for example, is stress testing by applying worst-case assumptions – not necessarily historical ones – to assess how different the result is for the portfolio compared with the VaR result. This might not necessarily be a basis for regulatory reporting, or for adjusting the portfolio, but is a useful additional view of both the portfolio and the VaR model.

For example, the bank can consider what is the greatest actual movement which has occurred in the past in each instrument or type of instrument. This gives rise to several problems. Firstly, history might not repeat itself because conditions do change. Secondly, the worst that has happened in the past might in fact not be as bad as the worst that could happen in the future. Thirdly, there is the problem of correlation: depending on the nature of the portfolio, it might be highly improbable that the worst will happen simultaneously in all the bank's positions.

The advantages of stress testing are that it is good for extreme events and shows up potential weaknesses in other models. As it can be based on any assumptions, it is good for 'what if' modeling. A disadvantage of course is that it is only as good as the assumptions made – garbage in, garbage out.

BIS recommendations on VaR

The BIS recommends that a supervisory authority should allow the bank to use its own internal VaR model for calculating its capital adequacy requirements (see the next section). The VaR is taken to be the greater of either the latest VaR measurement, or the average of the last 60 days' VaR measurements multiplied by a factor (which must be at least 3) determined by the supervisory authority. This gives the capital charge for market risk. However, the recommendation is that an internal VaR model can only be used if the following conditions are met:

- There should be a qualitative check on the model's use: the bank should have a risk control unit which is independent of the dealers, and also the model's results should be integrated into the bank's day-to-day controls.
- There should be a quantitative check: a test portfolio should be run through the model to check its measurements.
- VaR using the model should be calculated at least daily.

- The holding period used should be 10 days and the confidence level should be 99% (i.e. there is only a 1% probability of the loss exceeding the VaR number over a 10-day period).
- The model should be tested against the previous year's historic data (*backtesting*) to check that the losses actually incurred by the bank did agree with the results estimated by the model. Four exceptions or less would be acceptable; between five and nine exceptions would require the multiplicative factor to be increased from 3; ten exceptions or more would require the model to be investigated before it could be used.
- VaR is measured for four separate areas of business or 'portfolios' – foreign exchange, interest rate instruments, equities and commodities – and the four figures added. The bank is allowed to take correlation (i.e. diversification) into account to reduce the measured VaR within each portfolio, but not across portfolios – i.e., it may not consider any correlation effects arising from positions in two different portfolios.

Capital adequacy requirements

In order to prevent banks from taking excessive risks (and hence to protect the banking system as a whole), the European Union (EU) and the *BIS* have established guideline limits to the risks which each bank may take. In turn, each country's regulator enforces these limits, or stronger ones if it prefers, on the banks under its control. The details of these guidelines are complex, and the following remarks are necessarily a simplification of them. The concept is that if some of the risks are realized, the bank should still have adequate capital to remain in business – hence the term *capital adequacy*. The various directives from the EU which together set out the risk measurement rules are known as the *Capital Adequacy Directives (CAD)*.

Risk asset ratio

Each loan or other transaction undertaken by the bank is measured in terms of risk according to certain rules, which currently combine measures of market risk and credit risk. The total of these risks is called its *risk-weighted assets*. These must be limited in relation to the bank's *own funds* – i.e. its available capital and reserves. The capital adequacy rules state that the bank's *risk asset ratio* – the ratio of own funds to risk-weighted assets – must always be equal to at least 8%. Each regulator may impose a higher requirement than 8% on any particular bank under its control if it so chooses.

The effect of the CAD is to limit the amount, and type, of business which the bank does. If the type of deals undertaken by a particular bank are measured as mostly having a low risk, it can do more of them than if they are measured as having a high risk.

Risk asset ratio

$$= \frac{\text{own funds (i.e. available capital and reserves)}}{\begin{array}{c}\text{risk-weighted assets (i.e. the amount of money} \\ \text{put at risk by doing business)}\end{array}}$$

Risk asset ratio must be at least 8%

Own funds

Own funds are roughly equivalent to the value of the bank's share-holders' equity in the bank plus reserves and certain other funding raised by the bank. There are three tiers within own funds:

Tier 1:   equity
reserves
retained profit
minority interests
less goodwill, other intangibles and current losses

Tier 2:   reserves from fixed asset revaluations
medium-term subordinated debt
less holdings of other banks' issues

Tier 3:   daily trading profits
short-term subordinated debt

Tier 3 capital can be used only to cover *trading book* risks (see below) and there are various other restrictions on the uses and relative sizes of the three tiers in covering different aspects of risk.

Risk-weighted assets

Trading book or general banking book?

The bank's business is split into two areas – the trading book and the rest of the *banking book*. Essentially, a transaction is in the banking book if it is a cash loan made by the bank, or a long-term investment. It is in the trading book if it involves trading in financial instruments for the purpose of making trading profits, or is a hedge against something else in the trading book – largely the type of activity undertaken by the bank's dealing rooms rather than by its lending departments.

If the bank's overheads are large in comparison with its business, the risk-weighted assets are taken as being 25% of the previous year's fixed overheads. Normally, however, this constraint is not relevant and the risk-weighted assets are the total of the following:

> *Counterparty risk* on all business
> *Currency risk* on all business
> *Large exposure risk* on all business
>
> *Position risk* on trading activities
> *Settlement risk* on trading activities

Counterparty risk

The counterparty risk for any transaction takes account of two aspects – the creditworthiness of the counterparty and the nature of the transaction. For example, a USD 1 million FRA dealt with a particular counterparty does not expose the bank to the same potential loss as a USD 1 million loan made to the same counterparty. With the FRA, if the counterparty defaults, the bank can lose only the difference between two interest rates. With a loan, the bank can lose the entire principal amount as well as the interest on it. Counterparty risk is therefore measured as:

$$\text{Risk weighting for the counterparty} \times \frac{\text{factor depending on}}{\text{the transaction}}$$

Examples of measures for some different risk weightings and transactions are:

Risk weighting for counterparty

government in 'Zone A' (mostly OECD countries) or local currency transactions with government in 'Zone B'	0%
bank in 'Zone A'	20%
mortgages	50%
corporate (for derivative transactions)	50%
corporate (other transactions)	100%

Factor for transaction type

on balance sheet (e.g. loan or bond purchase)	100% of amount
off balance sheet but not *derivatives* transaction	0% for low risk (e.g. undrawn, uncommitted, short-term credit facility)

	20% for medium/low risk (e.g. documentary credits with goods as collateral)
	50% for medium risk (e.g. documentary credits and indemnities)
	100% for full risk (e.g. bill acceptances and guarantees)
exchange-traded derivatives with daily margin requirements	0%
interest rate-related derivative transactions (such as FRA) with maturity up to 1 year	mark-to-market profit
interest rate-related derivative transactions with maturity more than 1 year	mark-to-market profit plus 0.5% of amount of deal
FX-related derivative transactions with maturity up to 1 year	mark-to-market profit plus 1.0% of amount of deal
FX-related derivative transactions with maturity more than 1 year	mark-to-market profit plus 5.0% of amount of deal
repos, buy/sell-backs and securities lending in the trading book	any amount of under-collateralization (including accrued coupon on the bond and accrued interest on the cash)

(Derivative transactions can alternatively be weighted by ignoring the mark-to-market profits but considering the original exposures and using different factors.)

Thus, for example:

- The risk for a USD 1 million loan to a corporate counterparty is:

$$\text{USD 1 million} \times 100\% \times 100\% = \text{USD 1 million}$$

- The risk for a USD 1 million 2-year FRA dealt with a Zone A bank is:

$$20\% \times ((\text{the current mark-to-market profit on the deal})$$
$$+ (0.5\% \times \text{USD 1 million}))$$

In the case of the FRA, if the deal is currently running at a loss, there is clearly no mark-to-market exposure if the counterparty defaults. The add-on of 0.5% is to allow for the possibility of the deal moving into profit before a mark-to-market calculation is next made.

In assessing the risk, banks are entitled to take account of formal netting agreements with counterparties, such as that contained in ISDA documentation, so that the amount of the deal used in this add-on can be reduced by as much as 60%.

- For a reverse repo of USD 1 million with a Zone A bank where our bank has taken extra collateral, the risk is:

    $$20\% \times \text{zero} = \text{zero}$$

- For a reverse repo where the other bank has taken the extra collateral, the risk is:

    $$20\% \times (\text{USD } 1.02 \text{ million} - \text{USD } 1 \text{ million}) = \text{USD } 4,000$$

Currency risk

This measures the net exposure to foreign currencies, as the greater of the following:

- the sum of all net long positions in each currency
- the sum of all net short positions in each currency

An amount of 2% of own funds is then deducted from this total. Banks are, however, allowed to net and/or reduce the measured exposures for closely related currencies, provided that the supervisory authority allows.

Large exposure risk

The consideration of large exposure risk requires the bank to allocate more capital to its assets if the total exposure to any one counterparty is a particularly large proportion of the total.

Position risk

Position risk, which applies only to the trading book, measures exposure to changes in interest rates and security prices. This involves the most complex calculations of the CAD. The measurement is of net positions in particular issues and net positions in closely matched interest rate positions (i.e. net positions in each time bucket). For FRAs, futures, forward purchases and swaps, the bank must consider both sides of the position. For example, a 3v4 FRA is considered as a 3-month short position and a 4-month long position or vice versa.

The risk is measured in two components. The first is *specific risk*, which considers the issuer of a security held by the bank, with the amount of risk-weighted asset being between 0% and 8% of the nominal amount of the risk, depending on the nature of the issuer. The second is *general risk* for the market position. This can be measured by using the CAD's complex and detailed rules for each type and maturity of position. Alternatively, because of the complexity of assessing such risk, which varies widely from one bank's portfolio to another's, the CAD allows for each bank to use its own internal VaR models, provided that this is approved by the supervising authority.

Settlement risk

Settlement risk is the risk that the counterparty will not settle a transaction for which the settlement date has already passed. The risk is limited to mark-to-market profit which has already been made, multiplied by a factor which increases towards 100% as the delay increases.

Future developments

The BIS has proposed that the capital adequacy rules be changed in various ways, in a new framework consisting of three pillars. The first pillar is the existing system of minimum capital requirement. However, the risk-weighting system for counterparty credit described above will be replaced by one based on external credit ratings, so that dealing with a highly rated bank counterparty will absorb less capital than dealing with a low-rated bank counterparty – the reverse of the present situation. This will adversely affect weaker banks, who will find counterparties less willing to do business with them.

The second pillar is the supervisory role of the regulator in monitoring the bank. The third pillar is market discipline, encouraging high standards of disclosure by banks on their risk management.

Corporate risk management

Analysis of risks

It is worth stating at the outset that *exposure* simply means risk. In the context of corporate financial risk, it is common to use the term exposure rather than risk, so we shall do so here. Companies generally distinguish three types of currency exposure – *transaction exposure, economic exposure* and *translation exposure* – although different types of economic exposure such as *competitive exposure* are sometimes considered separately. Not everyone uses exactly the same definitions – for example, in whether a particular risk should be categorized as transaction or economic – but the importance lies in understanding the ideas, rather than in agreeing the definitions.

Transaction exposure

The term transaction exposure is used to describe transactions which have already been entered in the company's books of account, such as imports, exports, interest and dividend payments. We would also use it to describe transactions which are confidently expected to be booked soon, and transactions which are forecast, as long as the forecast is a reasonably close one. There is a point in time – not clearly definable – when transaction exposures merge into economic exposures – see below. In general, transaction exposures are relatively easy to identify.

Example 1

A US company exporting to a German customer in euros has a transaction exposure to the EUR/USD exchange rate on the money it is due to receive for sales it has already made and invoiced. If the exchange rate falls before the money is received, the company will receive fewer dollars for the transaction.

Similarly, a French importer is at risk if sterling rises and he has invoices to pay in sterling. Interest payments due in a foreign currency are also transaction exposures.

Translation exposures

Translation exposures or *balance sheet* exposures arise from the effect of converting foreign currency assets and liabilities into the balance sheet-reporting currency. This might be because of foreign currency loans and investments, or because the company has over-seas subsidiaries.

Example 2

A UK company has a US subsidiary. If the subsidiary's balance sheet is unchanged from one year-end to the next, the UK company is unaffected. However, if the US dollar weakens over the same period, the subsidiary's net assets will fall in value as measured in sterling. Therefore when the subsidiary's value is consolidated into the parent company's sterling balance sheet, the value of the balance sheet will show a fall from the previous year. This loss does not represent any cash outflow.

Hedging translation exposures

If the parent company wishes to protect against this risk, it must consider selling dollars for a date at least as far forward as the balance sheet reporting date, or going short of dollars in some other way. This could be by taking a dollar loan, or using options.

Example 3

A European shipping company is buying some new ships and needs to finance the purchases. The company's analysis shows that its revenues are largely in euros, while its expenses are mostly in US dollars. The company believes that the nature of the ship industry is such that the future value of the ships on its balance sheet will be essentially a dollar value. In what currency should the ships be financed?

If the company is focusing entirely on the balance sheet, it should probably consider financing in dollars. Then, if the dollar weakens, the fall in the value of its assets, which might form a large part of its balance sheet, will be offset by a fall in the liability side of the balance sheet. However, the business of the company represents a continual net inflow of euros and outflow of dollars. On a cashflow basis therefore, a dollar loan would put the company at even greater risk than it already is to a strengthening of the dollar. On this basis therefore, the company should probably consider euro financing instead. The issue is essentially whether the company wishes to focus on its net asset value, or its continuing business.

Economic exposure

The term economic exposure may be used to describe any exposure which is forecast to become a transaction exposure in due course – although if the forecast can be made fairly accurately, this would often be regarded as a transaction exposure. In general, the term economic exposure describes the extent to which a company is vulnerable to currency movements in addition to its transaction and translation exposures. This can happen in a variety of ways.

The simplest example is when a forecast transaction exposure might not occur. For example, the sales budget for next year (as opposed to next week) can only be an estimate. If we forecast sales in euros of 50 million but only achieve 30 million, the difference of 20 million is a transaction exposure which we expected but which never occurred. It would therefore have been unwise to hedge the whole exposure because if we had hedged against it and the euro had weakened, we would have made a currency loss with no income to offset it.

Another example is where the currency underlying the economics of the goods or services is not the same as the currency of payment. Suppose, for example, that a Japanese company is paying for fuel in euros but that the price of the fuel in the medium term is linked to the US dollar – because that is the currency in which oil is traded internationally. The fuel purchases which have already been invoiced, but not paid, represent a euro risk – a transaction exposure; the company will suffer if the euro rises against the yen, but is indifferent to the fate of the dollar. However, future purchases represent a US dollar risk – an economic exposure; if the dollar strengthens, the euro invoices will rise in line, so that the company must buy dollars rather than euros if it wishes to hedge against the risk for these future purchases.

A type of economic exposure which is much more difficult to analyse is competitive exposure. Suppose we have an Australian company whose main competitor is a Japanese company. If the Japanese yen weakens sharply, our competitor might be able to reduce his prices and steal some of our market share. If we wished to hedge against this risk, we would need to consider selling Japanese yen. It is of course often very difficult to be at all precise about such risks.

As mentioned, the definitions of economic and transaction exposures vary, and are less important than the underlying concepts. A transaction exposure is one which is readily identifiable in the currency in which it arises. For example, if a company has made a sale of goods for USD 100 and an invoice has been issued, there is clearly a transaction exposure to USD 100 (although it could be argued that the exposure is not quite definite, since the customer might default on payment). Similarly, sales which have been made but not invoiced, sales which are about to be made, sales which are forecast etc. are all exposures which are identifiable, but with decreasing levels of certainty. Once the exposure is uncertain, or not genuinely in the currency in which the transaction is settled, it is usually called an economic exposure rather than a transaction exposure.

Consider the following further Examples of economic exposure:

Example 4

A Norwegian company makes a sales agreement for the year, with a UK customer, to sell at a fixed euro price. It agrees, however, to invoice the customer in sterling. There will be a series of transactions in sterling, with the transaction exposures arising in sterling until settlement of any invoices already issued, but economic exposures in euros for subsequent sales.

The company could sell sterling forward to cover those invoices which have already been issued. For the exposure arising from the anticipated income over the rest of the year, it sells euros forward instead. As each sterling invoice is issued, it converts the forward euro cover to sterling cover by buying back the euros forward against sterling.

Example 5

The product sold in Example 4 is oil, which is priced internationally in dollars. Suppose that the sales agreement is reviewed after 6 months, and the dollar has fallen sharply. The UK customer will be in a strong position to renegotiate the price downwards. The economic exposure therefore becomes a dollar one rather than a euro one after some months ahead.

The same company might sell sterling forward to cover invoices issued (as above), sell euros forward to cover sales beyond that (again as above), but only up to 6 months, and sell dollars forward beyond that. The dollar cover would need to be converted to euro cover after a new price fixing, and to sterling cover after invoice.

Example 6

The product sold in Example 4 is one for which the major competitor is Japanese. Suppose that the yen falls sharply so that competing products become much cheaper. Again, the UK customer might be in a position to renegotiate the price, so that there is a competitive exposure to yen some months ahead.

Again, the company could sell yen forward beyond a certain period, and maintain a rolling hedge. Alternatively, it could maintain some of its debt in yen. The difficulty of course is knowing how much to sell or borrow. Another possibility is to buy long-term out-of-the-money yen put options, so that any significant yen fall can be offset.

Example 7

The Japanese competitor in the previous example might source all his products directly from Australia, so that the competitive exposure is in fact not yen but Australian dollars.

Forward sales, debt, or long-term Australian dollar put options would similarly provide some protection.

Example 8

A UK company sells consumer products to Sweden in euros. There is a 10% devaluation of the Swedish krona. Although there is no direct competition, Swedish consumers are less willing than before to buy the goods at the same price. The UK company therefore needs to reduce the euro price to maintain sales. This is therefore an economic exposure to the Swedish krona.

Again, sales of kronor beyond a certain period, or krona debt, might be effective. Another possibility is to change the currency of invoice to kronor, in order to make the transaction exposures and economic exposures coincide better. This might not, however, be an attractive proposition. It might be preferable to live with the economic krona exposure unhedged, and take advantage of the time lags between changes in the krona and changes in the euro price which the company is able to achieve.

Example 9

A UK hi-fi manufacturer making equipment sourced entirely from UK parts and sold entirely to the UK market has a yen exposure, because a weak yen gives his Japanese competitors in the UK market an advantage.

Such effects are generally very difficult to quantify, particularly as they are likely to involve several currencies. In general, the question to be asked is: At each point in the future, given various changes in exchange rates internationally, what are the net effects in terms of my home currency? Ideally, the company needs to measure the correlation of changes in particular exchange rates with changes in profit as measured in the home currency.

Suppose, for example, that a US company sells a product to the UK in sterling but suspects that, over time, the sales price which it achieves is linked to the euro because its main competitors are in the euro-zone rather than the UK or the USA. An approach would be to compare a graph of the sterling price over time with a graph of the same price converted to euros. If the suspicion is correct, the second graph might show a more regular trend than the first. If this is so, the company should perhaps be protecting against a euro risk – with an appropriate time lag to allow for price adjustments – rather than a sterling risk.

Such a task is immensely complicated and in practice there are rarely sufficient data for a complete analysis, particularly as continual changes in economic conditions and many other external factors will distort the analysis. The company must therefore use its knowledge and experience of the economics of its own business as a starting point in this analysis.

Hedging economic exposures

To some extent, economic exposures are hedged in exactly the same way as other exposures, as outlined in the examples above. A more fundamental approach involves longer-term planning. The exposures in Examples 6 and 7, as well as the UK hi-fi manufacturer's exposure in Example 9, might be reduced best by changing the company's own sourcing to some extent. If the company in Example 7 also sources some materials from Australia, for example, this exposure is reduced. Conversely, the consumer products company in Example 8 might do well to seek to diversify his sales to euro countries as well.

Establishing a policy

It is a fact of life that doing business might give rise to currency risks – whether these are clearly apparent as in the case of transaction and translation exposures, or are more obscure, as in the case of economic exposure. These risks can be approached in two ways – they can be managed or they can be ignored. A treasurer can be criticized for ignoring a risk that his company faces, but should not be criticized for managing the risk. Often, although certainly not always, this implies taking action on the best available information regarding currency movements.

Over the years, companies involved in hedging currency exposures have increasingly realized the advantages of having at least some formal guidelines for managing these exposures. The more such a policy is written down and formally approved by the company's top management, the better.

The importance of this can be seen from both ends of the operation: firstly, no one can doubt that the currency and interest rate markets can be extremely volatile from time to time. Such movements must therefore be of vital importance to the top management of many companies. The financial markets can be complex, however, and the instruments used to protect against them sometimes more so. It is therefore an essential exercise for the company board to be forced to consider the intricacies of such matters, even if only occasionally. Being presented with a written policy document to read, understand and authorize concentrates the mind on this. There have of course been notable occasions where following a prudent formal policy might well have avoided significant embarrassment.

Secondly, the person responsible for managing the risks day-to-day is also in a far more satisfactory position if he knows precisely the guidelines within which to work. This does not mean that the guidelines need to be oppressively restrictive, as the policy might quite deliberately give considerable flexibility to the treasury department. The point is that as long as the treasurer acts within the policy, he should not feel his job is in jeopardy.

What subjects then should such a policy document specifically include?

What should be managed?

The first policy decision concerns which exposures it is possible, or desirable, to manage. Does the company decide that only transaction exposures should be managed – and if so, how far forward? – or should the policy also cover economic exposures? Should the balance sheet be protected against the effect of currency fluctuations? The exact answers to these questions must vary from company to company, according to both differing circumstances and differing attitudes. The company's preference might, for example, be not to manage balance sheet risks in the sense of taking short-term or medium-term hedges to protect the position at the next financial year-end. This is because such a hedge might, if exchange rates go the other way, result at some point in a cash loss which is offset by a non-cash balance sheet gain. This is, however, a controversial issue, and many companies maintain the opposite view – that they must protect against relatively short-term balance sheet fluctuations, albeit at a possible cost, because of shareholder concern or the perception of the banks lending to the company.

Economic exposures are something which in theory all companies should consider managing. These are often very uncertain however, so that even with the best of intentions, useful management might be difficult.

Should the company speculate?

The next important point to consider is the company's objectives. There is no single answer to the question "What should the treasurer be trying to achieve?" because the answer will vary from company to company, and depend on the nature of the business and the attitude to risk of the company's management. However, the broad distinction can be made that, unlike a bank, a company's currency management is generally directed towards protecting the company's non-financial business rather than towards trading for financial speculative profit. Specifically this will lead, at least as far as transaction exposures are concerned, to a consideration of particular exchange rate levels which need to be protected. This is considered further in 'Setting commercial target rates' below.

A key question is therefore whether a company whose business is essentially non-financial should speculate or not. The immediate gut reaction to this is "No!" However, it begs a further question: "What is speculation?"

A relatively straightforward situation arises when a company has both payables and receivables in the same foreign currency. In this case, covering the payables but not the receivables – or vice versa – is probably speculative. The safest approach is almost certainly to consider the net position.

Extending this idea, it might be safest also to consider netting two different foreign currencies where these are closely related. Suppose, for example, that a sterling-based company has euro payables and Danish krone receivables, and that it hedges the payables because it is worried that the euro might strengthen. If in fact the euro weakens against sterling instead of strengthening, then the Danish krone is also likely to weaken against sterling – because there is a closer market relationship between the euro and the krone than between either of them and sterling. The result of the one-sided hedge might therefore be to open up a risk which did not exist before to a significant extent, or at least to increase the risk rather than decrease it. Before any cover was taken, there was a net long krone/short euro exposure, which is generally not very volatile. After the cover, however, there is a net long krone/short sterling exposure, which is more volatile. The purchase of euros has therefore increased risk rather than reduced it. If we consider speculation to be anything which increases the vulnerability of the company to currency movements, then what was intended as a hedge can possibly be seen to be speculation instead. There is no perfect answer, but taking the wider view and looking at currency relationships is important.

Suggestion

Speculation is action which increases vulnerability and hedging is action which reduces it.

This idea can be extended to parallel hedging – although many companies would consider this to be unacceptable. Suppose that the company has only euro payables, and has no exposure at all to the Danish krone. Is it acceptable to hedge the short euro position by buying forward Danish kroner against sterling, instead of buying euros against sterling? The original position was short euros against sterling, and the position after taking cover is short euros against kroner. If it can be argued that the resulting position is less risky than the original position, then can the action be considered as justifiable hedging?

Another question is whether it is it acceptable to reverse foreign exchange cover which has already been taken. In one sense, this is usually increasing vulnerability to risk by reopening an exposure. If the cover has proved profitable, however, and the currency market outlook has changed, is it sensible not to take the profit?

The next suggestion is even more controversial. Despite the hazards, it is not necessarily wrong for a company to speculate. In the same way that a company might deliberately seek to make a profit through two quite different lines of business, it might also deliberately seek to make a profit through financial dealings as well as, say, manufacturing. (In saying this, we are of course deliberately ignoring any constraints imposed by national exchange controls.) If this is accepted, there is, however, an important caveat:

> It is essential that the board of the company must understand and accept clearly what the company's treasury department is doing and that – just as with manufacturing in bad times – it might make losses rather than profits.

It is also essential that the policy document circumscribes precisely the limits of the losses which may be made, the way in which profits and losses will be measured, the instruments which may be used, and the extent to which specific personnel may be involved. Problems are generally not so much when losses arise, but when losses come as a surprise to those at the top who should have been well prepared for the possibility.

Yet another example can arise even if the company believes it is carefully hedging everything. Suppose that the company imports heavily from Sweden and that it hedges all its Swedish krona payables for the next year. It can relax in the knowledge that it has avoided any speculative view on the krona for 12 months. The krona then devalues and the company's major competitor has hedged nothing. That competitor can now steal a market advantage by cutting its sales price, because its costs are lower. So was our company's forward purchase of kronor in fact good hedging or speculative?

How much cover?

Assuming that the pattern of transaction exposures can be predicted, the next question must be: Over what future period is it in fact desirable to manage exposures?

For example, if the exchange rates currently available in the market are used to calculate selling prices, exactly on the basis of a certain profit margin, then a completely risk-averse organization might wish to hedge 100% of receivables at the time those prices are fixed. This would ensure that the calculated profit margin is preserved.

However, if foreign currency prices of sales are set on another basis – for example, according to what the market will bear – the rationale for automatic hedging at the time of pricing disappears. In this case, covering exposures either before prices or sales volumes are known, or some time afterwards, does not create any new difficulties in the decision-making of setting prices and making sales. Rather, hedging beforehand might enable sales to be made with greater knowledge regarding profitability.

There is therefore no universal rule for automatically hedging a specific fixed amount of payables or receivables (all, none, or part) at the time when sales are made. Rather, assuming continuing business for the foreseeable future, the extent to which currencies are hedged at any time could reflect:

- The extent to which management is confident that the current exchange rates are the best
- The extent to which management is confident that exposures have been forecast correctly
- The risk that exchange rates will move away from an important commercial target level (see below) for the company

Within these confidence levels, exposures can be hedged from any time between the time horizon of long-term forecasts, and the time when the cashflow eventually occurs. This is not to say that any particular exposure should necessarily be hedged, but that consideration should be given to hedging it as soon as it can be identified.

This again raises the issue of economic exposure: is a dollar inflow forecast to arise in one year's time really a dollar exposure, or an economic exposure in another currency? The proportion of cover taken on any particular exposure at any time should therefore generally be flexible and should depend on both the time horizon and the view of likely currency movements. For example, a company might decide that up to the time horizon of booked exposures, it is reasonable to take cover between 0% and 100%, in the context of very strong views on currency movements, and between say 25% and 75% otherwise. Beyond this time horizon, it might seem imprudent to take more than say 75% or even 50% of cover, even with very strong currency views, in case the eventual cashflows in that currency are less than forecast.

One possible approach is to use a value-at-risk (VaR) measurement to quantify currency risks and to set a VaR limit to determine how much should be covered at any point. This is covered more in Chapter 12. One problem with applying VaR to corporate currency exposures is that a company generally has a relatively small number of exposures at any one time, compared with a bank. As VaR is a statistical approach, the risk might be rather great of the VaR measurement being misleading.

Which instruments?

There is then the question of which instruments the company should use for hedging. For economic exposures, it is often more a question of planning – perhaps diversifying the company's markets, sourcing and manufacturing base. For transaction exposures, the most common form of hedge is a forward currency deal whereby foreign currency can be sold or bought at a fixed exchange rate for delivery on a future date. There are other forms of hedge, such as foreign currency borrowings and deposits, although these provide the same effective hedge as forward sales and purchases of foreign currency, because of the link between forwards and interest rates.

An alternative is for a company to buy a currency option, whereby it pays an up-front insurance premium for a contract to cover an exposure at a particular rate. In return for the premium cost, the company has the flexibility not to use the contract if it turns out not to be advantageous. The rate used in this case can also be set at a different level from the actual market forward rate – although this affects the size of the up-front premium. Although more complex, the purchase of an option for hedging requires the same basic considerations as a forward deal – i.e. the comparison of the forward rate available, with the company's forecast rates and its own target rates.

As long as the instruments are properly understood, a company's policy document could reasonably include all available market instruments as permitted within the policy when appropriate. There should, however, be restrictions on how they are used. For example, buying an option to sell the currency of a receivable can clearly be seen as a hedge, whereas selling an option is far more likely to create risks. Care must also be taken over synthetic bank products which hybridize options. A range forward, for example (setting maximum and minimum exchange rates within which a deal will be settled), is essentially exactly the same as buying one currency option and simultaneously selling another. If the company is for any reason not happy to authorize using the underlying options, it should also not be happy to authorize dealing in such quasi-forwards – although such a product is generally quite acceptable.

Another area of fuzziness relates to foreign currency borrowings. Companies sometimes maintain significant borrowings in a foreign currency which bears a low interest rate, but in which it has no commercial interest, explicitly in order to achieve lower borrowing costs. However, the same company would often be quite opposed to the idea of making forward sales of those same currencies, because they would be speculative. The 2 actions are of course economically equivalent. If the forward sales are not authorized, why should the borrowings be?

Who is responsible?

Some more mechanical issues are just as important. Who exactly is responsible for dealing? Perhaps the treasury assistant may deal for up to a certain amount and up to a certain period ahead, the treasurer up to a greater amount and further ahead, and the finance director's agreement is necessary beyond these limits. What controls are in place to ensure that these limits are respected? Are regular meetings scheduled to review exposures, markets, strategies and targets?

The detailed answers to all these questions must vary from company to company. The importance lies in forcing everyone concerned to consider the questions in the first place, to review them regularly, and to arrive at answers which everyone understands and respects.

Forecasts, hedging decisions and targets

An important issue regarding forecasts is that in trading for speculative profit, a bank dealer is seeking to maximize currency gains on the basis of forecast currency movements. In protecting a commercial position, however, a treasurer cannot afford to be as aggressive regarding forecasts. For example, if the current US dollar/Swiss franc rate has already fallen to the absolute minimum at which he is prepared to sell 6-month dollar receivables into francs, he should probably act to take cover now – even if this is contrary to his forecast which suggests that the dollar is likely to strengthen. The forecast might, after all, be wrong. This is a question of weighing up the possible opportunity loss (if he covers the receivables now and the dollar strengthens) against the possible loss against target (if he does not cover now and the dollar weakens). The practical importance of clear corporate objectives is in laying the ground rules for deciding between such choices and hence how boldly forecasts should be followed at different times.

Setting commercial target rates

This raises the question of the exchange rate at which a company would be happy to hedge any particular exposure if possible. If a company wishes to hedge flexibly, according to its view of exposures and the currency markets, it is important to have a basis for establishing commercial target exchange rates at which the company would like to be able to hedge exposures. It is of course impossible to deal at a rate better than that which is actually available in the market – and flexible hedging implies an attempt to hedge at a better than average exchange rate over the life of the exposure, regardless of targets. In practical terms, however, always obtaining the best exchange rate is impossible, and it is valuable to have in mind a target based on acceptable levels of profitability, given the underlying commercial situation.

> It is important that such a commercial target rate should be based on commercial profitability, rather than on a budget rate unrelated to profitability calculations.

Suppose, for example, that our company is based in euros but pays for imports in Swiss francs. Is it possible to assess an exchange rate at which the company makes profitable commercial business? Perhaps, for example, if we can buy our francs at 1.70 then we will just meet our anticipated target return on our commercial business overall. This kind of consideration helps to establish commercial target rates which should be treated as very important levels by those doing the day-to-day dealing. Usually the only reason for ignoring such a target is a certain forecast by the dealer that the exchange rate will improve; however, the only certain thing about forecasts is that they can go wrong!

Setting short-term dealing targets

Within the commercial targets, it is also helpful to set short-term dealing target levels at which to take action. There is often a danger that the company has determined a level at which it would wish to deal, and which it thinks is likely to be near the best available rate – but that when the market reaches that level, it hesitates; perhaps now is not quite the perfect moment to sell or buy; perhaps it is worth waiting a little longer. Unless circumstances have changed to alter the basic forecast, it is often wiser to act on its own predetermined targets. No-one can hit tops or bottoms all the time, and from the point of view of corporate hedging it is often dangerous to try.

In setting such short-term targets for dealing, it is useful to be in a position to monitor easily progress so far in covering an exposure: How big is the whole exposure? Is it significant to the company's overall position? What percentage of the exposure has already been covered? At what average rate? If the remainder of the exposure were covered now, what would be the average rate for the whole exposure?

Answers to these questions help to define the risks being faced, and hence establish whether in fact it is appropriate to take a more, or less, cautious approach.

Range forecasts

For hedging, it is always useful to widen the scope of a forecast. If the company is looking at the US dollar/Swiss franc exchange rate in exactly 6 months' time and forecasts a single number for this, it is almost certainly going to be at least slightly wrong. It is better to ask the following questions also:

- What are the highest and lowest rates likely in 6 months' time?
- What is the maximum trading range for the rate likely to be between now and then?
- Where is the rate likely to be moving over the longer term?
- What are the risks and probabilities surrounding these forecasts?

The point here is that if the company accepts that the forecast is unlikely to be precisely correct, it must be prepared to cover an exposure at an exchange rate which is a good one in the context of its wider expectations of market movements, rather than expect to deal at the tops and bottoms of the market. If the highest rate likely in 6 months' time is only slightly higher than currently available, but the lowest is very much lower, it might be more prepared to sell now than wait. A very wide expected trading range might suggest that it could be more optimistic when targeting a hedging rate better than today's level, despite a generally adverse trend. If the longer-term trend is expected to be unfavourable, it might be more cautious regarding a favourable short-term forecast.

Example 10

Suppose that the GBP/USD rate is 1.40 now, and that it is forecast to be 1.30 in 3 months' time. Suppose also that the rate is forecast to reach both 1.45 and 1.25 during the next 3 months. Exactly how a company might respond to these forecasts could depend on its situation.

If, for example, our company has an important target to sell sterling at 1.35 or better, and has taken no cover so far, one might recommend selling much of the requirement now at 1.40. The company is unlikely to hit the top of the market (expected at 1.45), the current rate is better than the important target level, and if the company waits too long, the rate might in fact soon fall below that target.

> Consider now a different company looking at the same forecast. This time, the company has a target to sell sterling at 1.30 and has already sold some sterling forward at 1.45. In this case, the company might feel more able to wait, aiming for higher than the current rate. If in fact a higher rate is never seen, the opportunity loss is probably not as serious commercially as it would have been for the first company.

These are not formulas to be followed, but general examples to suggest the value of having a clear objective and, as suggested above, forecast ranges rather than single-point forecasts.

Forward premiums and discounts

Another forecasting issue concerns forward premiums and discounts. It might be, for example, that the discount for selling a currency forward is so great that a precise forecast becomes of less value. For example, there might be a difference of 6% between South African rand and US interest rates, so that one could sell US dollars one year forward against rand at a premium of 6%. Unless the rand is expected to weaken by more than 6% over a year, it could be better to sell dollar receivables forward against rand (or buy 12-month rand payables against dollars). Put simply, the forecasting question is: "Is the rand expected to weaken by more than 6% against the dollar over the next year?" It is important to consider forecasts in the context of forward exchange rates for the period rather than just spot exchange rates.

The same 12-month forward premium available might later fall sharply, again reflecting the interest rate differentials between the rand and the dollar. It is therefore important to forecast not only how a spot exchange rate might move, but also how the forward premium or discount will change, particularly when selling or buying forward for longer periods since the premium or discount will be correspondingly greater. This in turn means forecasting interest rate changes.

Some important elements of a written policy

Which exposures it is possible, or desirable, to manage?
What should the treasurer be trying to achieve?
How is speculation defined?
Should exposures be managed net or gross?
Is parallel hedging acceptable?

Under what circumstances can existing cover be reversed?
Over what future period is it desirable to manage exposures?
Is the amount of cover taken automatic or flexible?
Which instruments should the company use for hedging?
Who is responsible, who is permitted to deal, and to what
  extent?
What are the commercially based target exchange rates?
What is the system for monitoring exposures and existing
  cover?
What controls are in place to ensure adherence to the policy?

Currency exposure reporting

A company's reporting systems should be designed with the objective
of providing the necessary information for the management of the
company's overall currency positions. The reporting systems should
cover three areas:

1. Reporting from operational divisions to the finance department
2. Internal reporting within the finance department
3. Reporting from the finance department to operational divisions

Reporting from divisions

The reporting from the operational divisions to the finance department
must form the basis for all currency management decisions; it is
therefore crucial that accurate information is available regularly.
The reporting systems should cover all currency flows and should be
based on the timing of anticipated cashflows rather than the timing of
sales and purchases. It is important that all divisions monitor closely
their collection and disbursement periods to ensure that currency
positions based on purchases and sales are accurately reported in
the period in which the funds are expected to flow.

Under an annual budgeting procedure, all divisions should report
a detailed breakdown of cash payments by currency and by month
for the full year of the budget. Inflows and outflows of each currency,
in each month, should be reported separately.

As part of the normal monthly reporting system, divisions should
communicate the same information as in the annual budgeting procedure but based on a rolling 12-month time horizon. At the same
time, divisions should update cashflow positions within the period
by communicating changes in volume expected and also changes
to the timing of cashflows. Major changes to the previous reported

figures should be highlighted if possible so that the appropriate currency management decisions can be implemented for the changed positions.

In addition to the regular monthly reporting of exposure positions, each division should report major changes to exposures as soon as these become known.

Internal reporting within the finance department

On receipt of each division's budget submissions and monthly updates for inflows and outflows, the finance department should produce a consolidated position for each currency for the whole group. This consolidation should again be done separately for inflows and outflows and then, for those currencies with two-way flows, a net position produced.

The summary for each currency should show total positions for each month, as well as the amount of cover already taken and the actual rate dealt. Where the position remains at least partly open, the current forward rate to maturity should be used to quantify the remaining exposure. This, together with the cover taken already, can be compared with the total original exposure converted at a target or budget rate. In addition to the summary of the exposures reports, the finance department should preferably produce a cash receipts and payments report for each division, to highlight differences between projected cashflows and actual cashflows.

The finance department should maintain a register of all outstanding forward currency contracts for both sales and purchases. The register should be maintained by currency and show the date on which the contract was opened, the two currency amounts, the rate, the maturity date and a reference to the commercial position against which the contract was taken.

Reporting from finance department to divisions

In addition to reporting from the divisions to the finance department and within the finance department, there is benefit in a reporting system from the finance department back to the divisions. The finance department should be responsible for setting budget exchange rates and providing the operating divisions with a regular update to these exchange rates as the year unfolds.

Different rates might be used for each quarter, and the rates should preferably be based on the forward market rates available at the time. These rates are for planning and reporting purposes and do not represent a commitment by the finance department to provide actual transactions at these rates. Companies often use forecasts as budget rates. A forecast, however, does not necessarily represent either a rate which it is possible for the company to achieve, or a rate which would result in profitable commercial business if it did achieve it.

Evaluating the success of treasury management

Evaluation is something that comes after the event and in finance departments with few resources is often overtaken by more immediate problems. Much depends on the objective of the finance department. If the objective is to be a profit centre rather than a cost centre, then detailed evaluation is essential to justify the continued contribution of the finance department to the company.

There are two stages to evaluation. How successful are we currently on our outstanding exposures? How successful have we been in the past? The first question has already been mentioned above in 'Setting short-term dealing targets' and in 'Internal reporting within the finance department'. The second question can be answered in various ways as follows. A combination of these ways might be necessary to give a fair appraisal:

1   Compare the exchange rate achieved with the spot rate available at the time the exposure is first managed.
2   Compare the exchange rate achieved with the exchange rate at which the exposure is booked in the accounts – often the spot rate available at the time of booking, and possibly the same as in (1).
3   Compare the exchange rate achieved with the forward rate available at the time the exposure is first managed. This is equivalent to comparing against a very conservative policy of hedging 100% when the exposure is first managed. Some companies hedge when they can secure foreign exchange profits relative to this initial forward rate. Such an approach might encourage a company to place emphasis on a short-term perspective rather than manage the exposure over its whole life.
4   Compare the exchange rate achieved with the spot rate at maturity. This is equivalent to comparing against a policy of hedging nothing and might indeed encourage a company to take a very passive approach to risk management.
5   Compare the exchange rate achieved with the average forward rate available from the creation of the exposure until maturity.
6   Compare the exchange rate achieved with the highest and lowest forward rates available from the creation of the exposure until maturity. This is evaluating against the best- and worst-case

situations and highlights the impossibility of always achieving the best available rate. A progressive hedging strategy implies an averaging approach, but comparison with the highest and lowest rates provides a useful method of assessing relative success or failure.

7 Compare the exchange rate achieved with the budget rate. This is probably the most common system of evaluation but depends on the relationship of budget rates to the underlying commercial business. Many companies use forecast average rates for the accounting period as their budget rates, and many take no explicit account of the forward market in budgeting. Rarely are the budget rates related to the break-even rates necessary for profit on the sale of receivables, or minimum acceptable profit levels. Although budget rates are usually set annually, some companies adopt a quarterly or bi-annual planning period and revise budget rates if the market situation dictates.

(1) and (2) represent rates which the currency manager is not in a position to obtain – because they do not relate to the forward rates at which he can deal – and are therefore not generally satisfactory as measures of performance.

(3), (4) and (5) are useful measures of performance, in that they compare what was actually achieved with what could have been achieved in practice. (3) compares performance against a policy of automatically hedging everything, (4) against hedging nothing, and (5) against a random policy over a long time. If, on average, a company's treasury department cannot do better than each of these 3, it raises the question of whether it is worthwhile having an active treasury department at all. (3) and (4) are relatively simple to record but (5) is more complicated.

(7) can be an extremely important measure by which to take action, but should not be used alone as a measure of performance. As with (1) and (2), it does not necessarily relate to rates which are achievable in practice. If too much emphasis is placed on these, it might encourage the currency manager to suggest unrealistic budget exchange rates.

Exercises

1 In March, a US company reports that it has an outflow of EUR 1 million which will occur in May and an inflow of EUR 1 million which will occur in June. In March, to what risk is the company exposed?

2 You are a Swiss airline company. Tickets which you sell in the UK for scheduled flights all over Europe are sold in sterling. However,

your competitors in this industry are European, not UK ones. If sterling weakens or strengthens, these competitors will ensure that the price of a ticket in the UK goes up or down in sterling terms to compensate partly for the weaker or stronger pound. You have analysed that a 10% fall (or rise) in sterling against all other currencies unilaterally would result in a 7% increase (or decrease) in UK ticket prices in sterling terms, but no change in the volume of ticket sales. You have budgeted that your sales to the UK over the next 12 months will be GBP 100 million. You are worried that sterling will fall sharply, and wish to hedge against that risk. How much of what do you sell to hedge the risk?

Answers to exercises

Chapter 2

1. ACT/365 basis: $5,000,000 \times 0.067 \times \dfrac{136}{365} = 124,821.92$

    ACT/360 basis: $5,000,000 \times 0.067 \times \dfrac{136}{360} = 126,555.56$

    30/360 basis: $5,000,000 \times 0.067 \times \dfrac{133}{360} = 123,763.89$

2. Interest rate on ACT/360 basis

    $=$ interest rate on 30/360 basis

    $\times \dfrac{\text{days in period measured on 30/360 basis}}{\text{days in period measured on ACT/360 basis}}$

    $= 6.7\% \times \dfrac{133}{136} = 6.552\%$

    Interest rate on ACT/365 basis

    $=$ interest rate on ACT/360 basis $\times \dfrac{365}{360}$

    $= 6.552\% \times \dfrac{365}{360} = 6.643\%$

3. $\text{Present value} = \dfrac{\text{amount of future cashflow}}{\left(1 + \left(\text{interest rate} \times \dfrac{\text{days}}{\text{year}}\right)\right)}$

    $= \dfrac{\text{EUR } 5,327.21}{\left(1 + \left(0.042 \times \dfrac{276}{360}\right)\right)} = \text{EUR } 5,161.02$

4 $\text{Yield} = \left(\dfrac{\text{cashflow at the end}}{\text{cashflow at the start}} - 1 \right) \times \dfrac{\text{year}}{\text{days}}$

$\phantom{\text{Yield}} = \left(\dfrac{2{,}350{,}000.00}{2{,}345{,}678.91} - 1 \right) \times \dfrac{365}{7} = 0.0961 = 9.61\%$

5 $9.00\% + \left((9.15\% - 9.00\%) \times \dfrac{(193 - 183)}{(214 - 183)} \right) = 9.0484\%$

6 Equivalent rate with interest paid four times per year

$= \left(\left(1 + \left(\dfrac{\text{rate with interest paid 12}}{12} \right) \right)^{\left(\frac{12}{4} \right)} - 1 \right) \times 4$

$= \left(\left(1 + \left(\dfrac{0.0735}{12} \right) \right)^{\left(\frac{12}{4} \right)} - 1 \right) \times 4 = 0.07395 = 7.395\%$

7 6.7% annual bond basis.

8 $\text{Effective rate} = \left(1 + \left(\text{nominal rate} \times \dfrac{\text{days}}{\text{year}} \right) \right)^{\left(\frac{365}{\text{days}} \right)} - 1$

$\phantom{\text{Effective rate}} = \left(1 + \left(0.046 \times \dfrac{45}{360} \right) \right)^{\left(\frac{365}{45} \right)} - 1 = 0.0476 = 4.76\%$

9 $\left(\left(1 + \left(0.051 \times \dfrac{183}{360} \right) \right) \times \left(1 + \left(0.053 \times \dfrac{92}{360} \right) \right) - 1 \right) \times \dfrac{360}{275}$

$= 0.05213 = 5.213\%$

Chapter 4

1 $\text{GBP } 2{,}000{,}000 \times \left(1 + \left(0.045 \times \dfrac{273}{365} \right) \right) = \text{GBP } 2{,}067{,}315.07$

2 The net position is short of EUR 4 million at an average rate of 4.31%:

$-10{,}000{,}000 \times 0.0428 = -428{,}000$
$-3{,}000{,}000 \times 0.0423 = -126{,}900$
$\underline{+9{,}000{,}000 \times 0.0425 = +382{,}500}$
$-4{,}000{,}000 -172{,}400$

$\dfrac{-172{,}400}{-4{,}000{,}000} = 0.0431 = 4.31\%$

3 (a) Maturity proceeds $= \text{USD } 5,000,000 \times \left(1 + \left(0.047 \times \dfrac{181}{360}\right)\right)$

$$= \text{USD } 5,118,152.78$$

   (b) Purchase amount $= \dfrac{\text{USD } 5,118,152.78}{\left(1 + \left(0.048 \times \dfrac{129}{360}\right)\right)}$

$$= \text{USD } 5,031,609.10$$

   (c) Sale amount $= \dfrac{\text{USD } 5,118,152.78}{\left(1 + \left(0.051 \times \dfrac{122}{360}\right)\right)} = \text{USD } 5,031,196.93$

   (d) Yield over holding period $= \left(\dfrac{\text{USD } 5,031,196.93}{\text{USD } 5,031,609.10} - 1\right) \times \dfrac{360}{7}$

$$= -0.0042 = -0.42\%$$

   or:

   yield over holding period $= \left(\dfrac{\left(1 + \left(0.048 \times \dfrac{129}{360}\right)\right)}{\left(1 + \left(0.051 \times \dfrac{122}{360}\right)\right)} - 1\right) \times \dfrac{360}{7}$

$$= -0.0042 = -0.42\%$$

   This is a negative yield because the value of the investment has fallen.

   (e) To achieve 4.80%, we would need:

$$\left(\dfrac{\left(1 + \left(0.048 \times \dfrac{129}{360}\right)\right)}{\left(1 + \left(\text{sale yield} \times \dfrac{122}{360}\right)\right)} - 1\right) \times \dfrac{360}{7} = 0.048$$

   This can be rearranged to give:

$$\text{Sale yield} = \left(\dfrac{\left(1 + \left(0.048 \times \dfrac{129}{360}\right)\right)}{\left(1 + \left(0.048 \times \dfrac{7}{360}\right)\right)} - 1\right) \times \dfrac{360}{122}$$

$$= 0.04796 = 4.796\%$$

4 The maturing proceeds of the deposit, if it is not broken, would be:

$$\text{EUR } 5,000,000 \times \left(1 + \left(0.0464 \times \dfrac{92}{360}\right)\right) = \text{EUR } 5,059,288.89$$

If you repay the cash early, you would need to refinance at around 1-month LIBOR plus 5 basis points, which is 4.85%. The present value of the maturing deposit at this rate of discount is:

$$\frac{\text{EUR } 5,059,288.89}{\left(1 + \left(0.0485 \times \frac{31}{360}\right)\right)} = \text{EUR } 5,038,247.21$$

This is therefore the most that you would repay. In practice, you might take a more pessimistic view on the rate at which you could refund yourself in the market.

Chapter 5

1 $\dfrac{\text{USD } 10 \text{ million}}{\left(1 + \left(0.0435 \times \frac{24}{360}\right)\right)} = \text{USD } 9,971,083.86$

2 $\text{USD } 10 \text{ million} \times \left(1 - \left(0.0435 \times \frac{24}{360}\right)\right) = \text{USD } 9,971,000,00$

3 $\dfrac{4.97\%}{\left(1 - \left(0.0497 \times \frac{147}{360}\right)\right)} = 5.073\%$

   $5.073\% \times \dfrac{365}{360} = 5.143\%$

4 $\dfrac{4.5567\%}{\left(1 + \left(0.045567 \times \frac{83}{365}\right)\right)} = 4.51\%$

5 Purchase price $= \dfrac{\text{GBP } 10,000,000}{\left(1 + \left(0.051 \times \frac{163}{365}\right)\right)} = \text{GBP } 9,777,318.23$

   Sale price $= \dfrac{\text{GBP } 10,000,000}{\left(1 + \left(0.0515 \times \frac{156}{365}\right)\right)} = \text{GBP } 9,784,630.89$

   $\text{Yield} = \left(\dfrac{\text{GBP } 9,784,630.89}{\text{GBP } 9,777,318.23} - 1\right) \times \dfrac{365}{7} = 0.0390 = 3.90\%$

or:

   $\text{Yield} = \left(\dfrac{\left(1 + \left(0.051 \times \frac{163}{365}\right)\right)}{\left(1 + \left(0.0515 \times \frac{156}{365}\right)\right)} - 1\right) \times \dfrac{365}{7} = 0.0390 = 3.90\%$

6 Purchase price $= \text{USD } 10{,}000{,}000 \times \left(1 - \left(0.051 \times \dfrac{163}{360}\right)\right)$

$= \text{USD } 9{,}769{,}083.33$

Sale price $= \text{USD } 10{,}000{,}000 \times \left(1 - \left(0.0515 \times \dfrac{156}{360}\right)\right)$

$= \text{USD } 9{,}776{,}833.33$

Yield $= \left(\dfrac{\text{USD } 9{,}776{,}833.33}{\text{USD } 9{,}769{,}083.33} - 1\right) \times \dfrac{360}{7} = 0.0408 = 4.08\%$

or:

Yield $= \left(\dfrac{\left(1 - \left(0.0515 \times \dfrac{156}{360}\right)\right)}{\left(1 - \left(0.051 \times \dfrac{163}{360}\right)\right)} - 1\right) \times \dfrac{360}{7} = 0.0408 = 4.08\%$

7 Bond-equivalent yield

$$= \dfrac{\left(\left(\left(\dfrac{190}{366}\right)^2 + \left(2 \times \left(\dfrac{190}{366} - 0.5\right)\right)\right) \times \left(\dfrac{1}{\left(1 - \left(0.0499 \times \dfrac{190}{360}\right)\right)} - 1\right)\right)^{0.5} - \left(\dfrac{190}{366}\right)}{\left(\dfrac{190}{366} - 0.5\right)}$$

$= 0.05205 = 5.205\%$

8 Effective yield $= \left(\left(\dfrac{100}{98.08}\right)^{\left(\frac{365}{103}\right)}\right) - 1 = 0.07112 = 7.112\%$

9 Norwegian bill:

Simple yield (365-day basis)

$= \left(1.057^{\left(\frac{119}{365}\right)} - 1\right) \times \dfrac{365}{119} = 0.05594 = 5.594\%$

Simple yield (360-day basis)

$= 5.594\% \times \dfrac{360}{365} = 0.05517 = 5.517\%$

US bill:

Simple yield (360-day basis)

$$= \frac{0.055}{\left(1 - \left(0.055 \times \frac{119}{360}\right)\right)} = 0.05602 = 5.602\%$$

The US bill has the higher yield.

10 For comparison, convert each rate to the same method of quotation – for example, a yield on a 360-day basis:

UK sterling Treasury bill at 4.98% (discount rate on 365-day basis):

Yield on a 365-day basis $= \dfrac{4.98\%}{\left(1 - \left(0.0498 \times \frac{91}{365}\right)\right)} = 5.0426\%$

Yield on a 360-day basis $= 5.0426\% \times \dfrac{360}{365} = 4.97\%$

UK euro Treasury bill at 4.98% (yield on 360-day basis):

Yield on a 360-day basis $= 4.98\%$

Sterling domestic CP at 5.10% (yield on 365-day basis):

Yield on a 360-day basis $= 5.10\% \times \dfrac{360}{365} = 5.03\%$

Sterling ECP at 5.10% (yield on 365-day basis):

Yield on a 360-day basis $= 5.10\% \times \dfrac{360}{365} = 5.03\%$

US dollar Treasury bill at 4.81% (discount rate on 360-day basis):

Yield on a 360-day basis $= \dfrac{4.81\%}{\left(1 - \left(0.0481 \times \frac{91}{360}\right)\right)} = 4.87\%$

US dollar domestic CP at 4.93% (discount rate on 360-day basis):

Yield on a 360-day basis $= \dfrac{4.93\%}{\left(1 - \left(0.0493 \times \frac{91}{360}\right)\right)} = 4.99\%$

US dollar ECP at 4.93% (yield on 360-day basis):

Yield on a 360-day basis = 4.93%

Therefore in ascending order:

US dollar Treasury bill	4.87%
US dollar ECP	4.93%
UK sterling Treasury bill	4.97%
UK euro Treasury bill	4.98%
US dollar domestic CP	4.99%
Sterling domestic CP	5.03%
Sterling ECP	5.03%

Chapter 6

1 Use the bid side for 9 months and the offered side for 6 months:

$$\text{Forward-forward rate} = \left(\frac{\left(1 + \left(0.05 \times \frac{273}{360}\right)\right)}{\left(1 + \left(0.0525 \times \frac{182}{360}\right)\right)} - 1 \right) \times \frac{360}{91}$$

$$= 0.0438 = 4.38\%$$

2 This is a forward-forward calculation. Overnight on Friday is 3 days.

$$\text{Break-even rate} = \left(\frac{\left(1 + \left(0.043 \times \frac{7}{360}\right)\right)}{\left(1 + \left(0.0425 \times \frac{3}{360}\right)\right)} - 1 \right) \times \frac{360}{4}$$

$$= 0.04336 = 4.336\%$$

3 You sell the FRA at 7.30%

FRA settlement amount

$$= \text{GBP } 2,000,000 \times \frac{(0.073 - 0.0715) \times \frac{91}{365}}{\left(1 + \left(0.0715 \times \frac{91}{365}\right)\right)} = \text{GBP } 734.85$$

You receive this amount because you sold the FRA and LIBOR is fixed lower than the FRA rate.

4 (a) You need to protect the rate at which you can lend again in 3 months' time. You therefore sell an FRA.
   (b) 4.80%

(c)   Cover exactly the amount which you will need to lend again. This is the maturing amount (principal plus interest) of the 3-month loan you have already made. This is EUR 7,087,655.55:

$$\text{EUR } 7{,}000{,}000 \times \left(1 + \left(0.049 \times \frac{92}{360}\right)\right)$$
$$= \text{EUR } 7{,}087{,}655.55$$

(d)   LIBOR is fixed at 5.05%. You pay the settlement because you have sold the FRA and LIBOR is fixed higher than the FRA rate. The amount is EUR 8,688.19:

$$\text{EUR } 7{,}087{,}655.55 \times \frac{(0.048 - 0.0505) \times \dfrac{181}{360}}{\left(1 + \left(0.0505 \times \dfrac{181}{360}\right)\right)}$$
$$= -\text{EUR } 8{,}688.19$$

(e)   After 3 months, you receive the maturing amount of the 3-month loan (EUR 7,087,655.55) but pay the FRA settlement of EUR 8,688.19. You therefore receive a net EUR 7,078,967.36. You therefore lend out this amount at LIBID, which is 4.95%, to give you total proceeds at the end of 9 months of EUR 7,255,145.16:

$$\text{EUR } 7{,}078{,}967.36 \times \left(1 + \left(0.0495 \times \frac{181}{360}\right)\right)$$
$$= \text{EUR } 7{,}255{,}145.16$$

Also at the end of 9 months, you will repay EUR 7,260,108.33 as the principal and interest on the 9-month borrowing:

$$\text{EUR } 7{,}000{,}000 \times \left(1 + \left(0.049 \times \frac{273}{360}\right)\right)$$
$$= \text{EUR } 7{,}260{,}108.33$$

There is therefore a total net loss of EUR 4,963.17 (= EUR 7,255,145.16 − EUR 7,260,108.33)

5   You expect interest rates to rise. The size of a euro futures contract is EUR 1 million. You have made a loss of 11 basis points on each contract.

$$10 \times \text{EUR } 1{,}000{,}000 \times 0.0011 \times \frac{3}{12} = \text{EUR } 2{,}750$$

or $10 \times 11 \times \text{EUR } 25 = \text{EUR } 2{,}750$

6 (a) If the 3v6 period is covered separately, it is cheaper to buy
        an FRA at 5.39% than to sell June futures at 94.60 (implied
        interest rate 5.40%).
   (b) If the 6v9 period is covered separately, it is cheaper to sell
        September futures at 94.57 (implied interest rate 5.43%)
        than to buy an FRA at 5.45%.

Combining (a) and (b) in a strip, the 3v9 period can be covered
at 5.447%. This is cheaper than buying a 3v9 FRA at 5.47%:

$$\left(\left(1+\left(0.0539 \times \frac{92}{360}\right)\right) \times \left(1+\left(0.0543 \times \frac{91}{360}\right)\right) - 1\right) \times \frac{360}{183}$$

$$= 0.05447 = 5.447\%$$

The choices are therefore reduced to:

- Borrow 9-month cash at 5.45%
- Borrow 6-month cash at 5.35% and sell September futures
  at 5.43% to give a combined strip cost of 5.43%:

$$\left(\left(1+\left(0.0535 \times \frac{184}{360}\right)\right) \times \left(1+\left(0.0543 \times \frac{91}{360}\right)\right) - 1\right) \times \frac{360}{275}$$

$$= 0.0543 = 5.43\%$$

- Borrow 3-month cash at 5.20%, buy a 3v6 FRA at 5.39% and
  sell September futures at 5.43% to give a combined strip cost
  of 5.41%:

$$\left(\left(1+\left(0.0520 \times \frac{92}{360}\right)\right) \times \left(1+\left(0.0539 \times \frac{92}{360}\right)\right)\right.$$

$$\left. \times \left(1+\left(0.0543 \times \frac{91}{360}\right)\right) - 1\right) \times \frac{360}{275} = 0.0541 = 5.41\%$$

Of these, the last is the cheapest.

7 The FRA is from May to October. You therefore use a combination
   of futures contracts which overlap this period – March, June and
   September.

8 You are overborrowed. You therefore need to lend again in the
   future. You therefore need to sell an FRA at 6.51% or buy a
   futures at 93.51 (implied interest rate 6.49%). The better choice
   is to sell an FRA at 6.51%.

9 Strip together the June and September futures to give 4.30%:

$$\left(\left(1+\left(0.0439 \times \frac{92}{360}\right)\right) \times \left(1+\left(0.0416 \times \frac{91}{360}\right)\right) - 1\right) \times \frac{360}{183}$$

$$= 0.0430 = 4.30\%$$

10 Buy June futures and sell December futures for example, or sell
    a near-dated FRA and buy a longer-dated FRA

Chapter 7

1   The number of Norwegian kroner equal to 1 Singapore dollar.

2   You will deal on the right-hand side because you are buying the base currency and the market-maker is selling the base currency. You therefore want the best possible right-hand side, which is 1.4361.

3   You have bought EUR 5 million, at 0.9503.

4   For AUD/USD, one point on a deal of AUD 1 million is worth USD 100. For USD/JPY, one point on a deal of USD 1 million is worth JPY 10,000.

5   You have a loss of 6 points which is CAD 6,000 (10,000,000 × 0.0006 = 6,000).

6   You should quote 0.9502/07. You are currently long of EUR and therefore wish to sell them. You therefore want to encourage the counterparty to deal on the right-hand side of the price you are quoting. You must therefore make that side of the price more attractive to the counterparty than the current general market price.

7   You sell the customer CHF 5 million at CHF/USD 0.6338. You therefore receive USD (5,000,000 × 0.6338) = USD 3,169,000. To cover this, you buy CHF 5 million at USD/CHF 1.5783. You therefore pay USD (5,000,000 ÷ 1.5783) = USD 3,167,965.53. You therefore make a profit of USD (3,169,000.00 − 3,167,965.53) = USD 1,034.47.

8   The position is short EUR 2 million. The average rate is 0.93055. The loss is GBP 3,054.99

	EUR		USD
	−5,000,000	at 0.9320:	+4,660,000
	+2,000,000	at 0.9325:	−1,865,000
	+4,000,000	at 0.9330:	−3,732,000
	−3,000,000	at 0.9327:	+2,798,100
Position:	−2,000,000		+1,861,100

$$\text{Average rate:} \quad \frac{1,861,100}{2,000,000} = 0.93055$$

	+2,000,000	at 0.9328:	−1,865,600
	−		−4,500

$$\text{Loss:} \quad \frac{-4,500}{1.4730} = -3,054.99$$

9   $1 \div 1.0528 = 0.9498$ and $1 \div 1.0523 = 0.9503$. Therefore the rate for NOK/SEK is 0.9498/03.

10 (a) $2.3895 \div 1.5389 = 1.5527$ and $2.3905 \div 1.5384 = 1.5539$. Therefore CHF/SGD is 1.5527/39. The customer sells SGD (i.e. the market-maker sells CHF, the base currency) on the right at 1.5539.

   (b) $0.9678 \div 0.5443 = 1.7781$ and $0.9683 \div 0.5438 = 1.7806$. Therefore EUR/AUD is 1.7781/06. The customer buys EUR (i.e. the market-maker sells EUR, the base currency) on the right at 1.7806.

   (c) $0.9678 \times 1.5384 = 1.4889$ and $0.9683 \times 1.5389 = 1.4901$. Therefore EUR/CHF is 1.4889/01. The customer buys CHF (i.e. the market-maker buys EUR, the base currency) on the left at 1.4889.

   (d) $0.5438 \times 1.5384 = 0.83658$ and $0.5443 \times 1.5389 = 0.83762$. Therefore AUD/CHF is 0.83658/0.83762. $1 \div 0.83762 = 1.1939$ and $1 \div 0.83658 = 1.1953$. Therefore CHF/AUD is 1.1939/53. The customer sells CHF (i.e. the market-maker buys CHF, the base currency) on the left at 1.1939.

Chapter 8

1   (a) and (c) are true.

   (b) and (d) are the wrong way round.

   In (e) the EUR interest rate would be 5.0% if it were on a 365-day year, the same as sterling. On a 360-day year as normal, however, it is:

$$5.0\% \times \frac{360}{365} = 4.93\%.$$

   In (f) the trader would use only the T/N swap.

2   $1.7123 \times \dfrac{\left(1 + \left(0.0275 \times \dfrac{92}{360}\right)\right)}{\left(1 + \left(0.0515 \times \dfrac{92}{360}\right)\right)} = 1.7019$

3   $1.7123 \times \dfrac{\left(\left(0.0280 \times \dfrac{92}{360}\right) - \left(0.0510 \times \dfrac{92}{360}\right)\right)}{\left(1 + \left(0.0510 \times \dfrac{92}{360}\right)\right)} = -0.0099$

   $1.7123 \times \dfrac{\left(\left(0.0270 \times \dfrac{92}{360}\right) - \left(0.0520 \times \dfrac{92}{360}\right)\right)}{\left(1 + \left(0.0520 \times \dfrac{92}{360}\right)\right)} = -0.0108$

   The swap price is therefore 108/99

4   The quoting bank is selling and buying the base currency, USD. You are buying and selling USD. This is equivalent to borrowing USD and lending CHF. Currently, the USD is at a forward discount to the CHF – i.e. USD interest rates are higher than CHF interest rates. You are expecting this difference to widen – for example, USD interest rates to rise more than CHF rates or CHF rates to fall more than USD rates.

5   The yield curves cross: EUR interest rates are higher than USD rates at 3 months, but lower at 6 months.

6   With the customer, you buy and sell EUR, the base currency, on the right at +61. The settlement rates are therefore 0.6215 and 0.6276. When you cover the position, the quoting bank is also buying and selling EUR, on the right at +62. The settlement rates are therefore 0.6205 and 0.6267. Your cashflows arising from the two deals are therefore:

		Spot		3 months
Original deal:	+EUR	16,090,104.59	−EUR	15,933,715.74
Original deal:	−GBP	10,000,000.00	+GBP	10,000,000.00
Cover:	−EUR	16,116,035.46	+EUR	15,956,598.05
Cover:	+GBP	10,000,000.00	−GBP	10,000,000.00
Net cashflows:	−EUR	25,930.87	+EUR	22,882.31

You could therefore be said to have a loss of EUR (25,930.87 − 22,882.31) = EUR 3,048.56.

However, this does not take account of the time value of money (see Chapter 2). The NPV of the net cashflows is:

$$-\text{EUR } 25{,}930.87 + \frac{\text{EUR } 22{,}882.31}{\left(1 + \left(0.04 \times \dfrac{182}{360}\right)\right)} = -\text{EUR } 3{,}502.12$$

7   (a)   USD/CAD   spot: 1.5671/1.5677
                        swap: 0.0030/0.0033
                        outright: 1.5701/1.5710

       USD/SEK   spot: 10.3458/10.3468
                        swap: 0.0070/ 0.0067
                        outright: 10.3388/10.3401

       $10.3388 \div 1.5710 = 6.5810$
       $10.3401 \div 1.5701 = 6.5856$

   Therefore the CAD/SEK 6-month outright is 6.5810/56
   The customer can sell CAD at 6.5810

(b) USD/CAD   spot: 1.5671/1.5677
     USD/SEK   spot: 10.3458/10.3468

$$10.3458 \div 1.5677 = 6.5993$$
$$10.3468 \div 1.5671 = 6.6025$$

CAD/SEK   outright: 6.5810/6.5856
           spot: 6.5993/6.6025
           swap: 0.0183/0.0169

Therefore the CAD/SEK 6-month swap is 183/169
The customer can sell and buy CAD at −169 points.

8 With the customer, you sell and buy the base currency, GBP, on the left at −435 points. The settlement rates are 178.10 and 173.75. For the cover, you buy and sell GBP against USD on another bank's price on the left at −73 points. The settlement rates are 1.4260 and 1.4187. You also buy and sell USD against JPY on another bank's price on the left at −240 points. The settlement rates are 124.85 and 122.45. The cashflows are as follows:

		Spot		6 months
Original deal:	−GBP	1,000,000	+GBP	1,000,000
Original deal:	+JPY	178,100,000	−JPY	173,750,000
Cover:	+GBP	1,000,000	−GBP	1,000,000
Cover:	−USD	1,426,000	+USD	1,418,700
Cover:	+USD	1,426,000	−USD	1,426,000
Cover:	−JPY	178,036,100	+JPY	174,613,700
Net cashflows:	+JPY	63,900	+JPY	863,700
			−USD	7,300

9 173.74. There are four possibilities:

(a) spot: sell GBP against JPY
     swap: buy and sell GBP against JPY

sell GBP against JPY spot	178.05
buy and sell GBP against JPY	−4.35
effective outright rate:	173.70

(b) spot: sell GBP against USD; sell USD against JPY
     swap: buy and sell GBP against USD; buy and sell USD against JPY

sell GBP against USD spot	1.4255
buy and sell GBP against USD	−0.0073
	1.4182

sell USD against JPY spot   124.80
buy and sell USD against JPY   −2.40
                                                   ─────
                                                   122.40

effective outright rate: $1.4182 \times 122.40 =$ 173.59

(c)   spot: sell GBP against USD; sell USD against JPY
      swap: buy and sell GBP against JPY

      sell GBP against USD spot   1.4255
      sell USD against JPY spot   124.80

                        $1.4255 \times 124.80 =$ 177.90
      buy and sell GBP against JPY   −4.35
                                                    ─────
      effective outright rate: 173.55

(d)   spot: sell GBP against JPY
      swap: buy and sell GBP against USD; buy and sell USD
      against JPY

      To calculate effective cross-rate swap:
      cross-rate outright (from (b) above)   173.59
      cross-rate spot (from (c) above)   177.90
                                                     ─────
      cross-rate swap: −4.31

      sell GBP against JPY spot   178.05
      cross-rate swap: −4.31
                                                     ─────
      effective outright rate: 173.74

The last possibility (d) is the best.

10 (a) spot: 1.4253 /1.4258
         S/N: 0.00022/0.00017
                                     ─────────────────
         outright day after spot: 1.42508/1.42563

    The customer buys GBP at 1.42563

    (b) spot: 1.4253 /1.4258
         T/N: 0.00021/0.00016
                                     ─────────────────
         outright tomorrow: 1.42546/1.42601

    The customer sells USD at 1.42601

    (c) spot: 1.4253 /1.4258
         T/N: 0.00021/0.00016
         O/N: 0.00018/0.00013
                                     ─────────────────
         outright today: 1.42559/1.42619

    The customer sells GBP at 1.42559

(d) S/N: 0.00022/0.00017
     3 months: 0.0183 /0.0178
     forward-forward: 0.01813/0.01758

(e) O/N: 0.00018/0.00013
     T/N: 0.00021/0.00016
     3 months: 0.0183 /0.0178
     forward-forward: 0.01869/0.01809

11 Wednesday 29 October 2003 and Friday 28 November 2003 ('modified following' convention because 29 November is a Saturday and the next working day – Monday 1 December – is in the next month).

12 Friday 27 February 2004 (which is the last working day of February because 29 February is a Sunday) and Wednesday 31 March 2004 ('end-end' convention).

13 (a) $12 - (-11) = 23$; $18 - (-15) = 33$ The price is therefore 23/33
    (b) The quoting bank is selling and buying the base currency, which it does on the left at +23 points.
    (c) Middle spot is 1.4240. Middle 2-month swap is -13 points. Therefore middle 2-month outright would be $1.4240 - 0.0013 = 1.4227$. Therefore set the 2-month settlement rate as 1.4227 and the 5-month settlement rate as $1.4227 + 0.0023 = 1.4250$. The 2-month settlement rate could be slightly different from this, but must be a current market rate for two months forward, not the spot rate. Whatever 2-month settlement rate is chosen, the 5-month settlement rate must then be 23 points higher.

14 The swap is $-8/+18$. The outright is 1.4227/63.

15 Original transaction
    at 301.55:   buy HUF 1,000,000,000   sell USD 3,316,199.64
    Settlement rate 295.71: sell HUF 1,000,000,000   buy USD 3,381,691.52

    Profit: USD   65,491.88

Chapter 9

1 (a) and (c). In (b), the swap should be 'sell and buy' EUR, not 'buy and sell' EUR.

2 The cashflows arising from the original transaction and hedge are as follows:

	Spot		3 months	
Original deal:	+EUR	10,000,000.00	−EUR	10,000,000.00
Original deal:	−USD	9,120,000.00	+USD	9,163,000.00
Lend EUR:	−EUR	10,000,000.00	+EUR	10,075,833.33
Borrow USD:	+USD	9,120,000.00	−USD	9,235,266.67
Net cashflows:	−		+EUR	75,833.33
			−USD	72,266.67

In order to remove any risk in USD, you could, for example, buy USD 72,266.67 3 months forward outright.

3   For the hedge, you need to do one of the following:

(i)   Sell and buy euros forward-forward at −93 points (= −162+69).

or (ii)   Sell a euro FRA at 4.0% or buy euro futures at 95.96 and buy a Swiss franc FRA at 1.6% or sell Swiss franc futures at 98.39.

In (ii), buying a euro futures at 95.96 implies a rate of 4.04%. This is better than selling an FRA at 4.0%. However, selling Swiss franc futures at 98.39 implies a rate of 1.61%, which is not as good as buying an FRA at 1.6%. Therefore the strategy would be to buy euro futures and buy a Swiss franc FRA, if this combination is cheaper than the forward-forward at −93 points.
The effective rate achieved through the FRA and futures is:

Forward swap

$$= \text{2-month outright}$$

$$\times \frac{\left(\left(\substack{\text{variable currency} \\ \text{interest rate}} \times \dfrac{\text{days}}{\text{year}}\right) - \left(\substack{\text{base currency} \\ \text{interest rate}} \times \dfrac{\text{days}}{\text{year}}\right)\right)}{\left(1 + \left(\text{base currency interest rate} \times \dfrac{\text{days}}{\text{year}}\right)\right)}$$

$$= 1.5976 \times \frac{\left(\left(0.016 \times \dfrac{91}{360}\right) - \left(0.0404 \times \dfrac{91}{360}\right)\right)}{\left(1 + \left(0.0404 \times \dfrac{91}{360}\right)\right)}$$

$$= -0.0098 = -98 \text{ points}$$

This is better than the forward-forward at −93 points. The expected profit is the difference between the −90 points at which you have bought and sold euros in the original deal and the −98 points at which you effectively now sell and buy. This 8 points profit on EUR 10 million is worth CHF 8,000 (10 million × 0.0008 = 8,000). In practice, the profit is uncertain because it depends on whether the 3-month swap price at which the deal will probably be reversed in 2 months' time is in line with LIBOR at that time (because the FRA and futures contract will settle against LIBOR then) and on bid/offer spreads at that time.

4 Investing via dollars is as follows:

Sell EUR 3 million and buy dollars, value spot.
Invest the dollars at 4.5%.
Sell forward the maturing dollar deposit amount back into euros.

The swap involves selling and buying euros, at −1.1 points. If the quoting bank determines 0.9129 as the spot rate, the settlement rates are 0.9129 (spot) and 0.91279 (1 week).

The synthetic yield can be calculated using the formula as follows:

Dollar interest rate created synthetically

$$= \left(\left(1 + \left(\text{USD rate} \times \frac{\text{days}}{\text{USD year}} \right) \right) \right.$$
$$\left. \times \frac{\text{EUR/USD rate for near date}}{\text{EUR/USD rate for far date}} - 1 \right) \times \frac{\text{EUR year}}{\text{days}}$$

$$= \left(\left(1 + \left(0.045 \times \frac{7}{360} \right) \right) \times \frac{0.9129}{0.91279} - 1 \right) \times \frac{360}{7}$$

$$= 0.0512 = 5.12\%$$

Alternatively, the cashflows are as follows:

	spot	6 months
dollar deposit:	−USD 2,738,700	+USD 2,741,096.36
swap:	+USD 2,738,700	−USD 2,741,096.36
	−EUR 3,000,000	+EUR 3,002,986.84
net cashflows:	−EUR 3,000,000	+EUR 3,002,986.84

The net result is effectively a one-week deposit of EUR 3,000,000 with total proceeds of EUR 3,002,986.84 – i.e. effective interest received of EUR 2,986.84.

This interest earned is for a period of 7 days. It can be expressed as an interest rate per annum of 5.12%:

$$\frac{2,986.84}{3,000,000} \times \frac{360}{7} = 0.0512 = 5.12\%$$

5   The dealer borrows euros at 3.3%, then sells and buys euros against sterling at $+1.2$ points. If the settlement rates are 0.6250 (today) and 0.62512 (tomorrow), the effective cost is 5.68%. The settlement exchange rates could be slightly different but without a significantly different result as long as the swap points of $+1.2$ are correctly applied:

Sterling interest rate created synthetically

$$= \left(\left(1 + \left(\text{EUR rate} \times \frac{\text{days}}{\text{EUR year}} \right) \right) \right.$$

$$\left. \times \frac{\text{EUR/GBP rate for far date}}{\text{EUR/GBP rate for near date}} - 1 \right) \times \frac{\text{GBP year}}{\text{days}}$$

$$= \left(\left(1 + \left(0.033 \times \frac{3}{360} \right) \right) \times \frac{0.62512}{0.6250} - 1 \right) \times \frac{365}{3}$$

$$= 0.0568 = 5.68\%$$

An alternative approach is to consider the cashflows, based on an arbitrary amount. For example, based on EUR 1 million, these would be:

Interest on EUR 1 million borrowing

$$= 1,000,000 \times 0.033 \times \frac{3}{360} = 275$$

Principal + interest

$$= 1,000,000.00 + 275 = 1,000,275$$

	Friday		Monday	
euro borrowing:	+EUR	1,000,000	−EUR	1,000,275.00
swap:	−EUR	1,000,000	+EUR	1,000,275.00
	+GBP	625,000	−GBP	625,291.91
net cashflows:	+GBP	625,000	−GBP	625,291.91

$$\frac{291.91}{625,000} \times \frac{365}{3} = 0.0568 = 5.68\%$$

6   The FX forward-forward price is 178/168. As a price-taker, you will deal at -168 points (you sell and buy sterling). Based on a middle 2-month outright of 2.3921, this gives 2-month and 5-month settlement rates of 2.3921 and 2.3753.

Swiss franc interest rate created synthetically

$$= \left(\left(1 + \left(\text{GBP rate} \times \frac{\text{days}}{\text{GBP year}} \right) \right) \right.$$

$$\left. \times \frac{\text{GBP/CHF rate for far date}}{\text{GBP/CHF rate for near date}} - 1 \right) \times \frac{\text{CHF year}}{\text{days}}$$

$$= \left(\left(1 + \left(0.061 \times \frac{92}{365} \right) \right) \times \frac{2.3753}{2.3921} - 1 \right) \times \frac{360}{92}$$

$$= 0.03226 = 3.226\%$$

Chapter 10

1 The cashflows arising from the original transaction are as follows:

	2 months	6 months
Original deal:	−EUR 5,000,000	+EUR 5,000,000
	+CHF 7,975,000	−CHF 7,925,000

The net present value of the euro cashflows is:

$$- \frac{\text{EUR } 5{,}000{,}000}{\left(1 + \left(0.041 \times \frac{61}{360} \right) \right)} + \frac{\text{EUR } 5{,}000{,}000}{\left(1 + \left(0.043 \times \frac{183}{360} \right) \right)}$$

$$= -\text{EUR } 72{,}457$$

The net present value of the Swiss franc cashflows is:

$$+ \frac{\text{CHF } 7{,}975{,}000}{\left(1 + \left(0.022 \times \frac{61}{360} \right) \right)} - \frac{\text{CHF } 7{,}925{,}000}{\left(1 + \left(0.024 \times \frac{183}{360} \right) \right)}$$

$$= +\text{CHF } 115{,}901$$

An appropriate hedge could therefore be to buy EUR 72,457 spot against sterling and to sell CHF 115,901 spot against sterling.

Chapter 13

1 There is no risk to the EUR/USD spot rate; if the EUR strengthens or weakens, the two exposures will offset each other. There is, however, an exposure to interest rates. This can be seen either as the cost of funding the EUR 1 million shortfall from May to June, or as the risk that the forward-forward exchange rate from May to June will change. To hedge the risk, the company could buy and sell EUR 2v3 forward-forward.

2   Suppose that the current GBP/CHF exchange rate is 2.0000 for both spot and forward and that you have sold all your budgeted income forward at 2.0000, for expected proceeds of:

100 million × 2.0000 = CHF 200 million.

If sterling in fact strengthens by 10% to GBP/CHF 2.2000, your sales receipts would fall in sterling terms from GBP 100 million to GBP 93 million, because of the fall in ticket prices in sterling terms. After such a change, you would need to buy back GBP 7 million at a rate of 2.2000. The cost of this would be:

7 million × 2.2000 = CHF 15.4 million

This would result in total net receipts from the hedge of:

CHF 200 million − CHF 15.4 million = CHF 184.6 million

Similarly, if sterling had in fact fallen as you expected, you would have ended up with net proceeds of correspondingly more than CHF 200 million. By selling all the expected sterling, you have overhedged, because the true exposure is not entirely a sterling one.

Because the sterling amount changes 7% with a 10% move in sterling, the exposure is in fact only around 30% a sterling exposure and 70% something else (perhaps a euro exposure, depending on what you consider to be the dominant forces in your particular market). Suppose therefore that you had only sold GBP 30 million forward, for proceeds of:

30 million × 2.0000 = CHF 60 million

After a 10% strengthening in sterling, your expected total sales receipts would fall to GBP 93 million, so that it would be necessary to sell a further GBP 63 million, at the new rate of 2.2000. The additional proceeds would therefore be:

63 million × 2.2000 = CHF 138.6 million

The total proceeds would therefore be:

CHF 60 million + CHF 138.6 million = CHF 198.6 million

– much closer to your expectation.

A summary of money market day/year conventions

Country	Day/year basis for domestic instruments	Day/year basis for international ("Euromarket") instruments
Euro-zone (the single 'domestic' currency for the European Monetary Union countries), Denmark, Switzerland,	ACT/360	ACT/360
Australia, Canada, Japan, New Zealand	ACT/365	ACT/360
Hong Kong, Singapore, South Africa, Taiwan	ACT/365	ACT/365
Norway		
(T-bills)	ACT/365[1]	
(other money market)	ACT/360	ACT/360
Sweden		
(T-bills)	30/360	
(other money market)	ACT/360	ACT/360

(*continued overleaf*)

(*continued*)

Country	Day/year basis for domestic instruments	Day/year basis for international ("Euromarket") instruments
UK		
(BAs and sterling T-bills)	ACT/365[2]	
(other money market)	ACT/365	ACT/365
US		
(BAs, T-bills and domestic CP)	ACT/360[2]	
(other money market)	ACT/360	ACT/360

Notes

1 Quoted as an effective (annual equivalent) yield rather than a simple rate.

2 Quoted as a discount rate rather than as a true yield.

A summary of calculation procedures

Throughout, 'days' means the number of days in the period, including the first date but not the last date; in the money markets, this generally means the number of actual calendar days in the normal way. 'Year' means the number of days in a conventional year, which in the money markets is generally 360 or 365.

Essential financial arithmetic

Day/year conventions

Interest rate on ACT/360 basis = interest rate on ACT/365 basis $\times \dfrac{360}{365}$

Interest rate on ACT/365 basis = interest rate on ACT/360 basis $\times \dfrac{365}{360}$

Interest rate on ACT/360 basis = interest rate on 30/360 basis

$\qquad \times \dfrac{\text{days in period measured on 30/360 basis}}{\text{days in period measured on ACT/360 basis}}$

Interest rate on 30/360 basis = interest rate on ACT/360 basis

$\qquad \times \dfrac{\text{days in period measured on ACT/360 basis}}{\text{days in period measured on 30/360 basis}}$

Present value and yield

$$\text{Present value} = \dfrac{\text{amount of future cashflow}}{\left(1 + \left(\text{interest rate} \times \dfrac{\text{days}}{\text{year}}\right)\right)}$$

$$\text{Yield} = \left(\frac{\text{cashflow at the end}}{\text{cashflow at the start}} - 1 \right) \times \frac{\text{year}}{\text{days}}$$

Creating a strip

The simple interest rate for a period up to one year

$$= \left(\begin{array}{l} \left(1 + \left(\text{first interest rate} \times \dfrac{\text{days in first period}}{\text{year}}\right)\right) \\[2mm] \times \left(1 + \left(\text{second interest rate} \times \dfrac{\text{days in second period}}{\text{year}}\right)\right) \\[2mm] \times \ldots\ldots\ldots \\[2mm] \times \left(1 + \left(\text{last interest rate} \times \dfrac{\text{days in last period}}{\text{year}}\right)\right) - 1 \end{array} \right) \times \frac{\text{year}}{\text{total days}}$$

Straight-line interpolation

Interpolated rate = the first rate

$$+ \left(\begin{array}{c} \text{(the second rate} \\ - \text{ the first rate)} \end{array} \times \frac{\begin{array}{c}\text{(days between the first date} \\ \text{and the required date)}\end{array}}{\begin{array}{c}\text{(days between the first date} \\ \text{and the second date)}\end{array}} \right)$$

Equivalent interest rates

Equivalent rate with interest paid M times per year

$$= \left(\left(1 + \left(\frac{\text{rate with interest paid } N \text{ times per year}}{N}\right)\right)^{\left(\frac{N}{M}\right)} - 1 \right) \times M$$

$$\text{Effective rate} = \left(1 + \left(\text{nominal rate quoted} \times \frac{\text{days}}{\text{year}}\right)\right)^{\left(\frac{365}{\text{days}}\right)} - 1$$

Deposits and coupon-bearing instruments

Fixed deposits

$$\text{Interest earned} = \text{principal amount} \times \text{interest rate} \times \frac{\text{days}}{\text{year}}$$

Maturity proceeds = principal amount

$$+ \left(\text{principal amount} \times \text{interest rate} \times \frac{\text{days}}{\text{year}}\right)$$

or:

$$\text{Maturity proceeds} = \text{principal amount} \times \left(1 + \left(\text{interest rate} \times \frac{\text{days}}{\text{year}}\right)\right)$$

Certificate of deposit

Maturity proceeds

$$= \text{face value} \times \left(1 + \left(\text{coupon rate} \times \frac{\text{days from issue to maturity}}{\text{year}}\right)\right)$$

$$\text{Amount paid} = \frac{\text{face value} \times \left(1 + \left(\text{coupon rate} \times \dfrac{\text{days from issue to maturity}}{\text{year}}\right)\right)}{\left(1 + \left(\text{yield} \times \dfrac{\text{days from settlement to maturity}}{\text{year}}\right)\right)}$$

Yield over holding period

$$= \left(\frac{\left(1 + \left(\text{purchase yield} \times \dfrac{\text{days from purchase to maturity}}{\text{year}}\right)\right)}{\left(1 + \left(\text{sale yield} \times \dfrac{\text{days from sale to maturity}}{\text{year}}\right)\right)} - 1\right) \times \frac{\text{year}}{\text{days held}}$$

To calculate the total amount repayable when a fixed deposit is broken

1 Calculate the principal plus interest due on the normal maturity date
2 Calculate the present value of this, using the bank's funding rate

To value a CD with more than one coupon payment outstanding

1 Calculate each future cashflow
2 Discount the final cashflow back to the previous coupon date, using the current yield as the rate of discount
3 Add the coupon on that date and repeat the process until the nearest outstanding coupon
4 Add that coupon and discount back to the settlement date

Discount Instruments

Maturity proceeds = face value

Discount instruments quoted on a yield

$$\text{Amount paid} = \frac{\text{face value}}{\left(1 + \left(\text{yield} \times \dfrac{\text{days from settlement to maturity}}{\text{year}}\right)\right)}$$

(the following formula is the same as for a CD)

Yield over holding period

$$= \left(\left(\frac{\left(1 + \left(\text{purchase yield} \times \dfrac{\text{days from purchase to maturity}}{\text{year}}\right)\right)}{\left(1 + \left(\text{sale yield} \times \dfrac{\text{days from sale to maturity}}{\text{year}}\right)\right)}\right) - 1\right) \times \frac{\text{year}}{\text{days held}}$$

Discount instruments quoted on a discount rate

Amount paid = face value

$$\times \left(1 - \left(\text{discount rate} \times \frac{\text{days from settlement to maturity}}{\text{year}}\right)\right)$$

$$\text{Yield} = \frac{\text{discount rate}}{\left(1 - \left(\text{discount rate} \times \dfrac{\text{days to maturity}}{\text{year}}\right)\right)}$$

$$\text{Discount rate} = \frac{\text{yield}}{\left(1 + \left(\text{yield} \times \dfrac{\text{days to maturity}}{\text{year}}\right)\right)}$$

Yield over holding period

$$= \left(\left(\frac{\left(1 - \left(\text{discount rate on sale} \times \dfrac{\text{days from sale to maturity}}{\text{year}}\right)\right)}{\left(1 - \left(\text{discount rate on purchase} \times \dfrac{\text{days from purchase to maturity}}{\text{year}}\right)\right)}\right) - 1\right) \times \frac{\text{year}}{\text{days held}}$$

Bond-equivalent yield for US Treasury bill

If there are 182 days or less to maturity:

$$\text{Bond-equivalent yield} = \left(\frac{\text{discount rate}}{\left(1 - \left(\text{discount rate} \times \dfrac{\text{days}}{360}\right)\right)}\right) \times \frac{365}{360}$$

If there are more than 182 days to maturity:

Bond-equivalent yield

$$= \frac{\left(\left(\left(\frac{\text{days}}{365} \right)^2 + \left(2 \times \left(\frac{\text{days}}{365} - 0.5 \right) \right) \right) \times \left(\frac{1}{\left(1 - \left(\text{discount rate} \times \frac{\text{days}}{360} \right) \right)} - 1 \right) \right)^{0.5} - \left(\frac{\text{days}}{365} \right)}{\left(\frac{\text{days}}{365} - 0.5 \right)}$$

If 29 February falls in the 12-month period starting on the purchase date, replace 365 by 366 in both formulas.

Norwegian Treasury bill

$$\text{Amount paid} = \frac{\text{face value}}{\left((1 + \text{effective yield})^{\left(\frac{\text{days to maturity}}{365} \right)} \right)}$$

$$\text{Effective yield} = \left(\left(\frac{\text{face value}}{\text{amount paid}} \right)^{\left(\frac{365}{\text{days to maturity}} \right)} \right) - 1$$

Simple yield on 365-day basis

$$= \left((1 + \text{effective yield})^{\left(\frac{\text{days to maturity}}{365} \right)} - 1 \right) \times \frac{365}{\text{days to maturity}}$$

Forward interest rates, FRAs and futures

For periods up to one year:

Forward-forward rate

$$= \left(\frac{\left(1 + \left(\begin{array}{c} \text{interest rate for} \\ \text{longer period} \end{array} \times \frac{\text{days in longer period}}{\text{year}} \right) \right)}{\left(1 + \left(\begin{array}{c} \text{interest rate for} \\ \text{shorter period} \end{array} \times \frac{\text{days in shorter period}}{\text{year}} \right) \right)} - 1 \right)$$

$$\times \frac{\text{year}}{\text{days difference}}$$

Theoretical FRA rate

$$= \left(\frac{\left(1 + \left(\begin{array}{c}\text{LIBOR for} \\ \text{longer period}\end{array} \times \frac{\text{days in longer period}}{\text{year}}\right)\right)}{\left(1 + \left(\begin{array}{c}\text{LIBOR for} \\ \text{shorter period}\end{array} \times \frac{\text{days in shorter period}}{\text{year}}\right)\right)} - 1 \right)$$

$$\times \frac{\text{year}}{\text{days difference}}$$

FRA settlement amount = notional principal amount

$$\times \frac{(\text{FRA rate} - \text{LIBOR}) \times \dfrac{\text{days in FRA period}}{\text{year}}}{\left(1 + \left(\text{LIBOR} \times \dfrac{\text{days in FRA period}}{\text{year}}\right)\right)}$$

For periods longer than a year but less than 2 years:

FRA settlement amount = notional principal amount

$$\times \left(\frac{(\text{FRA rate} - \text{LIBOR}) \times \dfrac{\text{days of FRA period in first year}}{\text{year}}}{\left(1 + \left(\text{LIBOR} \times \dfrac{\text{days of FRA period in first year}}{\text{year}}\right)\right)} \right.$$

$$\left. + \frac{(\text{FRA rate} - \text{LIBOR}) \times \dfrac{\text{days of FRA period in second year}}{\text{year}}}{\left(1 + \left(\text{LIBOR} \times \dfrac{\text{days of FRA period in first year}}{\text{year}}\right)\right) \times \left(1 + \left(\text{LIBOR} \times \dfrac{\text{days of FRA period in second year}}{\text{year}}\right)\right)} \right)$$

Short-term interest rate futures

Price = 100 − (implied forward-forward interest rate × 100)

Profit on a long position in a 3-month contract

$$= \text{contract amount} \times \frac{(\text{sale price} - \text{purchase price})}{100} \times \frac{3}{12}$$

Value basis = theoretical futures price − actual futures price

Basis = implied cash price − actual futures price

Spot foreign exchange

To calculate an exchange rate by combining two others

From two rates with the same base currency or the same variable currency:

Divide opposite sides of the exchange rates

From two rates where the base currency in one is the same as the variable currency in the other:

Multiply the same sides of the exchange rates

Given two exchange rates A/B and A/C, they can be combined as follows:

$B/C = A/C \div A/B$

Given two exchange rates B/A and C/A, they can be combined as follows:

$B/C = B/A \div C/A$

Given two exchange rates B/A and A/C, they can be combined as follows:

$B/C = B/A \times A/C$ and

$C/B = 1 \div (B/A \times A/C)$

When dividing, use opposite sides. When multiplying, use the same sides.

Forward outrights and swaps

Theoretical outright and swap:

Forward outright = spot

$$\times \frac{\left(1 + \left(\text{variable currency interest rate} \times \dfrac{\text{days}}{\text{variable year}}\right)\right)}{\left(1 + \left(\text{base currency interest rate} \times \dfrac{\text{days}}{\text{base year}}\right)\right)}$$

Forward swap

$$= \text{spot} \times \frac{\left(\left(\text{variable currency interest rate} \times \dfrac{\text{days}}{\text{variable year}}\right) - \left(\text{base currency interest rate} \times \dfrac{\text{days}}{\text{base year}}\right)\right)}{\left(1 + \left(\text{base currency interest rate} \times \dfrac{\text{days}}{\text{base year}}\right)\right)}$$

Approximation:

Forward swap $\approx$ spot $\times$ interest rate differential $\times \dfrac{\text{days}}{\text{year}}$

Combining swaps and spot:

Forward outright = spot + forward swap

- The currency with higher interest rates (= the currency at a discount) is worth less in the future. If this is the base currency, the points are negative.
- The currency with lower interest rates (= the currency at a premium) is worth more in the future. If this is the base currency, the points are positive.
- The bank quoting the price <u>always</u> 'sells and buys' the base currency on the left and 'buys and sells' the base currency on the right.
- If the swap price appears larger on the right than the left, it is positive.
- If the swap price appears larger on the left than the right, it is negative.
  <u>For outright forwards later than spot:</u>
- The left swap price is added to (or subtracted from) the left spot price.
- The right swap price is added to (or subtracted from) the right spot price.
  <u>For outright deals earlier than spot:</u>
- Calculate as if the swap price were reversed.

Forward-forwards:

First, insert '−' signs where necessary. Then:

<u>After spot:</u>

Left side = (left side of far-date swap)

     − (right side of near-date swap)

Right side = (right side of far-date swap)

     − (left side of near-date swap)

<u>From before spot until after spot:</u>

Left side = (left side of far-date swap)

     + (left side of T/N or T/N <u>and</u> O/N)

Right side = (right side of far-date swap)

     + (right side of T/N or T/N <u>and</u> O/N)

In general

- Of the two prices available, the customer gets the worse one. Thus if the swap price is 3/2 and the customer knows that the points are *in his favour* (the outright will be better than the spot), the price will be 2. If he knows that the points are *against him* (the outright will be worse than the spot), the price will be 3.

- The bid–offer spread of the resulting price is the sum of the separate bid–offer spreads.

Cross-rates

Cross-rate forward outright:

The same calculation as for a spot cross-rate, but using outrights rather than spot rates

Cross-rate forward swap:

1 Calculate the spot cross-rate as usual
2 Calculate the two individual forward outrights as above
3 From (2) calculate the forward outright cross-rate
4 Subtract (1) from (3) to give the cross-rate swap

Time option

A time option price is the best for the bank/worst for the customer over the time option period

Theoretical long-dated forwards

Forward outright

$$= \text{spot} \times \left(\left(\frac{(1 + \text{variable interest rate})}{(1 + \text{base interest rate})} \right)^{\text{number of years}} \right)$$

Forward swap

$$= \text{spot} \times \left(\left(\frac{(1 + \text{variable interest rate})}{(1 + \text{base interest rate})} \right)^{\text{number of years}} - 1 \right)$$

SAFE settlement amounts (as an amount of the variable currency)

FXA:

Settlement amount $=$ first amount

$$\times \left(\frac{\begin{array}{c} (\text{outright exchange rate} - \text{settlement spot rate}) \\ + (\text{swap price dealt} - \text{settlement swap price}) \end{array}}{\left(1 + \left(\text{variable currency LIBOR} \times \dfrac{\text{days in swap period}}{\text{variable year}} \right) \right)} \right)$$

$- \text{second amount} \times (\text{outright exchange rate}$
$\qquad\qquad\qquad - \text{spot price used for settlement})$

ERA:

Settlement amount = base currency amount

$$\times \frac{(\text{swap price dealt} - \text{settlement swap price})}{\left(1 + \left(\text{variable currency LIBOR} \times \dfrac{\text{days in swap period}}{\text{variable year}}\right)\right)}$$

The settlement amount is paid by the seller to the buyer of the FXA or the ERA (or vice versa if it is a negative amount), where the buyer is the party which 'buys and sells' the base currency.

Covered interest arbitrage, creating synthetic FRAs and hedging forward-forwards

Covered interest arbitrage

Variable currency interest rate created synthetically

$$= \left(\frac{\left(1 + \left(\text{base currency rate} \times \dfrac{\text{days}}{\text{base year}}\right)\right)}{\times \dfrac{\text{exchange rate for far date}}{\text{exchange rate for near date}}} - 1\right) \times \frac{\text{variable year}}{\text{days}}$$

Base currency interest rate created synthetically

$$= \left(\frac{\left(1 + \left(\text{variable currency rate} \times \dfrac{\text{days}}{\text{variable year}}\right)\right)}{\times \dfrac{\text{exchange rate for near date}}{\text{exchange rate for far date}}} - 1\right) \times \frac{\text{base year}}{\text{days}}$$

Creating synthetic FRAs and hedging forward-forwards

Variable currency FRA rate created synthetically

$$= \left(\frac{\left(1 + \left(\text{base currency FRA rate} \times \dfrac{\text{days}}{\text{base year}}\right)\right)}{\times \dfrac{\text{exchange rate for far date}}{\text{exchange rate for near date}}} - 1\right) \times \frac{\text{variable year}}{\text{days}}$$

Base currency FRA rate created synthetically

$$= \left(\frac{\left(1 + \left(\text{variable currency FRA rate} \times \dfrac{\text{days}}{\text{variable year}}\right)\right)}{\times \dfrac{\text{exchange rate for near date}}{\text{exchange rate for far date}}} - 1\right) \times \frac{\text{base year}}{\text{days}}$$

Forward-forward swap rate created synthetically

$$= \text{outright to near date} \times \frac{\left(\left(\begin{array}{c}\text{variable} \\ \text{currency FRA}\end{array} \times \dfrac{\text{days}}{\text{variable year}}\right) - \left(\text{base currency FRA} \times \dfrac{\text{days}}{\text{base year}}\right)\right)}{\left(1 + \left(\begin{array}{c}\text{base currency} \\ \text{FRA}\end{array} \times \dfrac{\text{days}}{\text{base year}}\right)\right)}$$

Appendix C

SWIFT currency codes

Country	Currency	Code
Abu Dhabi	UAE dirham	AED
Afghanistan	Afghani	AFA
Ajman	UAE dirham	AED
Albania	Lek	ALL
Algeria	Dinar	DZD
Andorra	Euro	EUR
Angola	Kwanza	AON
Anguilla	E Caribbean dollar	XCD
Antigua	E Caribbean dollar	XCD
Argentina	Peso	ARS
Armenia	Dram	AMD
Aruba	Florin/guilder	AWG
Australia	Dollar	AUD
Austria	Euro	EUR
Azerbaijan	Manat	AZM
Azores	Euro	EUR
Bahamas	Dollar	BSD
Bahrain	Dinar	BHD
Bangladesh	Taka	BDT
Barbados	Dollar	BBD
Belarus	Rouble	BYR
Belgium	Euro	EUR
Belize	Dollar	BZD
Benin	CFA franc	XOF
Bermuda	Dollar	BMD
Bhutan	Ngultrum	BTN
Bolivia	Boliviano	BOB

Country	Currency	Code
Bosnia & Herzegovina	Mark	BAM
Botswana	Pula	BWP
Brazil	Real	BRL
Brunei	Dollar	BND
Bulgaria	Lev	BGL
Burkina Faso	CFA franc	XOF
Burundi	Franc	BIF
Cambodia	Riel	KHR
Cameroon	CFA franc	XAF
Canada	Dollar	CAD
Canary Islands	Euro	EUR
Cape Verde	Escudo	CVE
Cayman Islands	Dollar	KYD
Central African Republic	CFA franc	XAF
Chad	CFA franc	XAF
Channel Islands	UK pound sterling	GBP
Chile	Peso	CLP
China	Renmimbi yuan	CNY
Christmas Island	Australian dollar	AUD
Cocos Islands	Australian dollar	AUD
Colombia	Peso	COP
Comoros	Franc	KMF
Congo	CFA franc	XAF
Congo Democratic Republic	Franc	CDF
Cook Islands	New Zealand dollar	NZD
Costa Rica	Colon	CRC
Croatia	Kuna	HRK
Cuba	Peso	CUP
Cyprus	Pound	CYP
Czech Republic	Koruna	CZK
Denmark	Krone	DKK
Djibouti	Franc	DJF
Dominica	E Caribbean dollar	XCD
Dominican Republic	Peso	DOP
Dubai	UAE dirham	AED
East Timor	US dollar	USD
Ecuador	US dollar	USD
Egypt	Pound	EGP
El Salvador	Colon	SVC

Country	Currency	Code
Equatorial Guinea	CFA franc	XAF
Eritrea	Nafka	ERN
Estonia	Kroon	EEK
Ethiopia	Birr	ETB
European Monetary Union	Euro	EUR
Falkland Islands	Pound	FKP
Faroe Islands	Danish krone	DKK
Fiji	Dollar	FJD
Finland	Euro	EUR
France	Euro	EUR
French Pacific Islands	CFP franc	XPF
Fujairah	UAE dirham	AED
Gabon	CFA franc	XAF
Gambia	Dalasi	GMD
Georgia	Lari	GEL
Germany	Euro	EUR
Ghana	Cedi	GHC
Gibraltar	Pound	GIP
Great Britain	Pound	GBP
Greece	Euro	EUR
Greenland	Danish krone	DKK
Grenada	E Caribbean dollar	XCD
Guadeloupe	Euro	EUR
Guam	US dollar	USD
Guatemala	Quetzal	GTQ
Guernsey	UK pound sterling	GBP
Guinea	Franc	GNF
Guinea-Bissau	CFA franc	XOF
Guyana	Dollar	GYD
Haiti	Gourde	HTG
Heard & McDonald Islands	Australian dollar	AUD
Honduras	Lempira	HNL
Hong Kong	Dollar	HKD
Hungary	Forint	HUF
Iceland	Krona	ISK
India	Rupee	INR
Indonesia	Rupiah	IDR
Iran	Rial	IRR
Iraq	Dinar	IQD

Country	Currency	Code
Irish Republic	Euro	EUR
Isle of Man	UK pound sterling	GBP
Israel	Shekel	ILS
Italy	Euro	EUR
Ivory Coast	CFA franc	XOF
Jamaica	Dollar	JMD
Japan	Yen	JPY
Jersey	UK pound sterling	GBP
Jordan	Dinar	JOD
Kazakhstan	Tenge	KZT
Kenya	Shilling	KES
Kiribati	Australian dollar	AUD
Korea (North)	Won	KPW
Korea (South)	Won	KRW
Kuwait	Dinar	KWD
Kyrgizstan	Som	KGS
Laos	Kip	LAK
Latvia	Lat	LVL
Lebanon	Pound	LBP
Lesotho	Loti	LSL
Liberia	Dollar	LRD
Libya	Dinar	LYD
Liechtenstein	Swiss franc	CHF
Lithuania	Litas	LTL
Luxembourg	Euro	EUR
Macao	Pataca	MOP
Macedonia	Denar	MKD
Madagascar	Franc	MGF
Madeira	Euro	EUR
Malawi	Kwacha	MWK
Malaysia	Ringgit	MYR
Maldives	Rufiyaa	MVR
Mali	CFA franc	XOF
Malta	Lira	MTL
Marshall Islands	US dollar	USD
Martinique	Euro	EUR
Mauritania	Ouguiya	MRO
Mauritius	Rupee	MUR

Country	Currency	Code
Mayotte	Euro	EUR
Mexico	Peso	MXN
Micronesia	US dollar	USD
Moldova	Leu	MDL
Monaco	Euro	EUR
Mongolia	Tugrik	MNT
Montserrat	E Caribbean dollar	XCD
Morocco	Dirham	MAD
Mozambique	Metical	MZM
Myanmar	Kyat	MMK
Namibia	Dollar	NAD
Nauru Isles	Australian dollar	AUD
Nepal	Rupee	NPR
Netherlands	Euro	EUR
Netherlands Antilles	Guilder	ANG
New Caledonia	CFP franc	XPF
New Zealand	Dollar	NZD
Nicaragua	Cordoba	NIO
Niger	CFA franc	XOF
Nigeria	Naira	NGN
Niue	New Zealand dollar	NZD
Norfolk Island	Australian dollar	AUD
Northern Mariana Islands	US dollar	USD
Norway	Krone	NOK
Oman	Riyal	OMR
Pakistan	Rupee	PKR
Panama	Balboa	PAB
Papua New Guinea	Kina	PGK
Paraguay	Guarani	PYG
Peru	Nuevo sol	PEN
Philippines	Peso	PHP
Pitcairn	New Zealand dollar	NZD
Poland	Zloty	PLN
Portugal	Euro	EUR
Puerto Rico	US dollar	USD
Qatar	Riyal	QAR
Ras Al Khaimah	UAE dirham	AED
Reunion Island	Euro	EUR

Country	Currency	Code
Romania	Leu	ROL
Russia	Rouble	RUB
Rwanda	Franc	RWF
San Marino	Euro	EUR
Sao Tome	Dobra	STD
Saudi Arabia	Riyal	SAR
Senegal	CFA franc	XOF
Seychelles	Rupee	SCR
Sharjah	UAE dirham	AED
Sierra Leone	Leone	SLL
Singapore	Dollar	SGD
Slovakia	Koruna	SKK
Slovenia	Tolar	SIT
Solomon Islands	Dollar	SBD
Somalia	Shilling	SOS
South Africa	Rand	ZAR
Spain	Euro	EUR
Sri Lanka	Rupee	LKR
St Christopher	E Caribbean dollar	XCD
St Helena	Pound	SHP
St Kitts & Nevis	E Caribbean dollar	XCD
St Lucia	E Caribbean dollar	XCD
St Pierre et Miquelon	Euro	EUR
St Vincent	E Caribbean dollar	XCD
Sudan	Dinar	SDD
Surinam	Guilder	SRG
Svalbard & Jan Mayen Isles	Norwegian krone	NOK
Swaziland	Lilangeni	SZL
Sweden	Krona	SEK
Switzerland	Franc	CHF
Syria	Pound	SYP
Taiwan	Dollar	TWD
Tajikistan	Somoni	TJS
Tanzania	Shilling	TZS
Thailand	Baht	THB
Togo	CFA franc	XOF
Tokelau	New Zealand dollar	NZD
Tonga	Pa' anga	TOP
Trinidad & Tobago	Dollar	TTD
Tunisia	Dinar	TND

Country	Currency	Code
Turkey	Lira	TRL
Turkmenistan	Manat	TMM
Turks & Caicos Islands	US dollar	USD
Tuvalu	Australian dollar	AUD
Uganda	Shilling	UGX
Ukraine	Hryvnia	UAH
Um Al Quwain	UAE dirham	AED
United Arab Emirates	Dirham	AED
United Kingdom	Pound sterling	GBP
Uruguay	Peso	UYU
USA	Dollar	USD
Uzbekistan	Sum	UZS
Vanuatu	Vatu	VUV
Venezuela	Bolivar	VEB
Vietnam	Dong	VND
Virgin Islands	Dollar	USD
Wallis & Fortuna Islands	CFP franc	XPF
Western Sahara	Moroccan dirham	MAD
Western Samoa	Tala	WST
Yemen	Riyal	YER
Yugoslavia	Dinar	YUM
Zambia	Kwacha	ZMK
Zimbabwe	Dollar	ZWD

Glossary

30/360

(Or 360/360). A day/year count convention assuming 30 days in each calendar month and a 'year' of 360 days; adjusted in America for certain periods ending on 31st day of the month.

360/360

Same as **30/360**.

Acceptor

The person who accepts liability for a **bill of exchange**.

Accrued coupon

The proportion of the next **coupon** payment on a **security** earned so far, from the last coupon date until settlement date.

ACT/360

A day/year count convention taking the number of calendar days in a period and a 'year' of 360 days.

ACT/365

(Or ACT/365 fixed). A day/year count convention taking the number of calendar days in a period and a 'year' of 365 days.

Adjustable peg

Management of a currency at a fixed exchange rate against another currency or basket of currencies, with *ad hoc* adjustments to that fixed rate. *See* **Crawling peg**.

A/P

See **Around par**.

Appreciation

An increase in the market value of a currency in terms of other currencies. *See* **Depreciation**, **Revaluation**.

Arbitrage

The simultaneous operation in two different but related markets in order to take advantage of a discrepancy between them which will lock in a profit. The arbitrage operation itself usually tends to cause the different markets to converge. *See* **Covered interest arbitrage**.

Around par

(Or A/P). A foreign exchange swap price is around par if the left side is negative and the right side is positive.

Ask

See **Offer**.

BA

See **Bankers' acceptance**.

Back office

The operational department of the bank.

Backtesting

Testing a model, such as a **VaR** model, against historic data.

Balance sheet exposure

See **Translation exposure**.

Bankers' acceptance

Or BA. *See* **Bill of exchange**.

Banking book

For the purposes of **capital adequacy**, that part of a bank's business which broadly involves its lending department and long-term investments.

Base currency

Exchange rates are quoted in terms of the number of units of one currency (the **variable** or counter currency) which corresponds to one unit of the other currency (the base currency)

Basis

The difference between the **futures** price which would be implied by the current cash interest rate, and the actual futures price.

Basis points

In interest rate quotations, 0.01%.

Basis risk

The risk that the prices of two instruments will not move exactly in line – for example, the value of an FRA and the value of a **futures** contract being used to hedge the FRA.

Basket

A basket of currencies is a group of currencies, each weighted differently, against which another currency is measured or managed.

Bear spread

A **spread** position taken with the expectation of a fall in value in the **underlying**.

Bearer security

A security where ownership for the purpose of paying **coupons** and principal is determined by whoever is physically in possession of the security. In order to maintain anonymity, there is no central record of ownership. *See* **Registered security**.

Bid

In general, the price at which the dealer quoting a price is prepared to buy or borrow. The bid price of a foreign exchange quotation is the rate at which the dealer will buy the **base** currency and sell the **variable** currency. The bid rate in a deposit quotation is the interest rate at which the dealer will borrow the currency involved. The bid rate in a **repo** is the interest rate at which the dealer will borrow the **collateral** and lend the cash. *See* **Offer**.

Big figure

In a foreign exchange quotation, the exchange rate omitting the last two decimal places. For example, when USD/CHF is 1.7510/20, the big figure is 1.75. *See* **Points**.

Bilateral netting

Obligation netting between two parties.

Bill of exchange

A short-term zero-coupon debt issued by a company to finance commercial trading. If it is guaranteed by a bank, it becomes a **banker's acceptance**.

BIS

Bank for International Settlements, the central banks' forum in Basle.

Bond basis

An interest rate is quoted on a bond basis if it is on an **ACT/365**, **30/360** or ACT/ACT basis. *See* **Money-market basis**.

Broken date

(Or odd date). A maturity date other than the standard ones normally quoted.

Bull spread

A **spread** position taken with the expectation of a rise in value in the **underlying**.

Buy/sell-back

Opposite of **sell/buy-back**.

Cable

The exchange rate for sterling against the US dollar.

CAD

See **Capital adequacy directives**.

Calendar spread

The simultaneous purchase (or sale) of an **FRA** or **futures** contract for one date and the sale (or purchase) of an FRA or futures contract for a different date. *See* **Spread**.

Capital adequacy

The concept that if some of a bank's risks are realized, the bank should still have adequate capital to remain in business.

Capital adequacy directives

(Or CAD). The various directives from the **EU** which together set out the **capital adequacy** rules.

Capital market

Long-term market (generally longer than one year) for financial instruments. *See* **Money market**.

Cash

See **Cash market**.

Cash market

The market for trading an **underlying** financial instrument, where the whole value of the instrument will potentially be settled on the normal delivery date – as opposed to **contracts for differences, futures** etc. (where the cash amount to be settled is not intended to be the full value of the underlying) or **forwards** (where delivery is for a later date than normal). *See* **Derivative**.

CD

See **Certificate of deposit**.

Certificate of deposit

(Or CD). A security, generally coupon-bearing, issued by a bank to borrow money.

Charting

See **Technical analysis**.

Cherry picking

Insistence by a defaulting organization on consummating profitable deals with a particular counterparty, while defaulting on unprofitable ones.

Chicago Mercantile Exchange

(Or CME). A **futures** exchange in Chicago.

Choice

A choice price is one with a zero **spread** – i.e. the **bid** and **offer** are the same.

Classic repo

(Or **repo** or US-style repo). Repo is short for 'sale and repurchase agreement' – a simultaneous **spot** sale and **forward** purchase of something, equivalent to borrowing money against a loan of **collateral**. A **reverse** repo is the opposite. The terminology is usually applied from the perspective of the repo dealer. For example, when a central bank does repos, it is lending cash (the repo dealer is borrowing cash from the central bank).

Clean deposit

Same as **fixed deposit**.

Clean price

The price of a **security** excluding **accrued coupon**.

Close-out netting

See **Netting**.

CLS

See **Continuous linked settlement**.

CME

See **Chicago Mercantile Exchange**.

Collateral

(Or **security**). Something of value, often of good creditworthiness such as a government bond, given temporarily to a counterparty to enhance a party's creditworthiness. In a **repo**, the collateral is actually sold temporarily by one party to the other rather than merely lodged with it.

Commercial paper

A short-term security issued by a company or bank, generally with a zero **coupon**.

Competitive exposure

Economic exposure which arises specifically because of a competitor.

Compound interest

When some interest on an investment is paid before maturity and the investor can reinvest it to earn interest on interest, the interest is said to be compounded. Compounding often assumes that the **reinvestment rate** is the same as the original rate. *See* **Simple interest**.

Continuous linked settlement

(Or CLS). A real-time **PvP** clearing system for settlement of FX transactions, where a payment from Bank A to Bank B is made only if, and at the same time as, the corresponding payment from Bank B to Bank A is made.

Contract date

The date on which a transaction is negotiated. *See* **Value date**.

Contract for differences

A transaction such as an **FRA**, **NDF** or **SAFE** where only the net difference between two amounts is settled, and the principal amount involved is not transferred.

Convertible currency

A currency that may be freely exchanged for other currencies.

Correlation coefficient

A measure of the extent to which two things do, or do not, move together.

Counter currency

See **Variable currency**

Counterparty risk

The risk that a counterparty might default on a contract by failing to pay amounts due or failing to fulfill the delivery conditions of the contract.

Coupon

The interest payment(s) made by the issuer of a security to the holders, based on the coupon rate and **face value**.

Covariance

A measure of the extent to which two things do, or do not, move together.

Cover

To cover an **exposure** is to deal in such a way as to remove the risk – either reversing the position, or **hedging** it by dealing in an instrument with a similar but opposite risk profile.

Covered interest arbitrage

Creating a loan/deposit in one currency by combining a loan/deposit in another currency with a forward foreign exchange **swap**.

CP

See **Commercial paper**.

Crawling peg

Management of a currency at a fixed exchange rate against another currency or basket of currencies, with a regular pre-determined adjustment to that fixed rate. *See* **Adjustable peg**.

Credit risk

The risk that a counterparty defaults on a transaction or that the issuer of a security defaults on coupon or interest payments.

Cross

See **Cross-rate**.

Cross-rate

Generally an exchange rate between two currencies, neither of which is the US dollar.

Cumulative probability distribution

The probability that any one of a series of numbers will be no greater than a particular number.

Daylight limit

The maximum size of a position which a dealer is allowed to take during the day.

Delivery versus payment

(Or DvP). A method for the settlement of a securities transaction, whereby a payment from Bank A to Bank B is made only if, and at the same time as, the corresponding security is delivered from Bank B to Bank A.

Deposit

An investment of cash in return for interest.

Depreciation

A decrease in the market value of a currency in terms of other currencies. *See* **Appreciation, Devaluation**.

Derivative

Strictly, any financial instrument whose value is derived from another, such as a **forward** foreign exchange outright, a **futures** contract, an **FRA** etc. Forward deals to be settled in full are not always called derivatives, however.

Devaluation

An official one-off decrease in the value of a currency in terms of other currencies. *See* **Revaluation**, **Depreciation**.

Direct

An exchange rate quotation against the US dollar in which the dollar is the **variable** currency and the other currency is the **base** currency.

Dirty floating

A **floating-rate regime** with some government intervention.

Dirty price

The price of a **security** including **accrued coupon**.

Discount

The amount by which a currency is cheaper, in terms of another currency, for future delivery than for spot, is the forward discount (in general, a reflection of interest rate differentials between two curren- cies). If an exchange rate is 'at a discount' (without specifying to which of the two currencies this refers), this means in London (but generally not elsewhere) that the **variable** currency is at a discount. *See* **Premium**.

To discount a future cashflow means to calculate its **present value**. The interest rate used is known as the rate of discount. This is not the same as a **discount rate**.

Discount instrument

An instrument which pays no **coupon** and is therefore always worth less than its **face value** unless interest rates are negative.

Discount rate

The method of market quotation for certain securities (US and UK treasury bills, for example), expressing the return on the security as a proportion of the face value of the security received at maturity – as opposed to a **yield** which expresses the return as a proportion of the original investment. *See also* **Discount**.

Drawee

The person to whom a **bill of exchange** is addressed, and who owes the money.

Drawer

The originator of a **bill of exchange**.

Dual rate

A system of two or more exchange rates for a currency, each used for a different type of transaction.

DvP

See **Delivery versus payment**.

Economic exposure

A company's exposure to currency movements other than **transaction exposure** and **translation exposure**.

ECU

See **European currency unit**.

Effective date

The start date of the forward period to which an **FRA** relates.

Effective exchange rate

An index of a currency's value against a basket of other currencies, weighted by trade importance to the country.

Effective rate

(Or annual equivalent rate). An effective interest rate is the rate which, earned as simple interest over 1 year, gives the same return as interest paid more frequently than once per year and then compounded. *See* **Nominal rate**.

Eligible bill

A **bankers' acceptance** which the Bank of England is willing to purchase because it has been accepted by an eligible bank.

EMS

See **European monetary system**.

EMU

See **European monetary union**.

End-end

A foreign exchange swap or money-market deal commencing on the last working day of a month and lasting for a whole number of months, maturing on the last working day of the corresponding month.

Equivalent rate

The rate of interest which would be equivalent to the **nominal rate** quoted, after compounding at a different frequency of interest payment.

ERA

See **Exchange rate agreement**.

ERM

See **Exchange rate mechanism**.

EU

European Union.

EURIBOR

The reference offered interest rate for the euro at 11:00 a.m. European time published for the purpose of providing a benchmark to fix an interest payment such as on an **FRA** settlement.

Euro

The name for the single currency of the European monetary union.

Eurocurrency

A currency owned by a non-resident of the country in which the currency is legal tender.

Euromarket

The international market in which **Eurocurrencies** are traded.

European currency unit

(Or ECU). The former basket of EU currencies which was replaced by the **euro**.

European monetary system

A former grouping of EU currencies.

European monetary union

The formation of a single currency, the euro, for a group of EU countries.

Exchange controls

Regulations restricting the free convertibility of a currency into other currencies.

Exchange rate agreement

(Or ERA). A **contract for differences** based on the movement in a **forward-forward** foreign exchange swap price. It does not take account of the effect of **spot** rate changes as an **FXA** does. *See* **SAFE**.

Exchange rate mechanism

That part of the **European monetary system** which controlled the exchange rates of its member currencies.

Exchange-traded

Instruments such as **futures** which are traded on a recognized exchange, as opposed to **forward** deals which are **OTC**.

Exposure

Risk.

Face value

(Or nominal value). The principal amount of a security, generally repaid ('redeemed') all at maturity, but sometimes repaid in stages, on which the **coupon** amounts are calculated.

FEER

See **Fundamental equilibrium exchange rate**.

Figure

When the last two digits in a foreign exchange price are zero. For example, a price of 1.7895/00 would be "One seventy-eight ninety-five, figure".

Fixed deposit

(Or time deposit or term deposit or clean deposit). A non-**negotiable deposit** for a specific **term**.

Fixed-rate regime

Management of a currency at a fixed exchange rate against another currency or basket of currencies.

Flat yield curve

A **yield curve** where rates are similar for all maturities.

Floating rate CD

(Or FRCD). **CD** on which the rate of interest payable is refixed in line with market conditions at regular intervals (usually 6 months).

Floating rate

In interest rates, an instrument paying a floating rate is one where the rate of interest is refixed in line with market conditions at regular intervals such as every 3 or 6 months. *See also* **Floating-rate regime**.

Floating-rate note

A security where the coupon is refixed at regular intervals according to an index such as **LIBOR**.

Floating-rate regime

Allowing a currency to find its own free-market level against other currencies, with no government intervention.

Forward

In general, a deal for value later than the normal value date for that particular commodity or instrument. In the foreign exchange market, a forward price is the price quoted for the purchase or sale of one currency against another where the value date is at least one month after the **spot** date. *See* **Short date**.

Forward exchange agreement

(Or FXA). A **contract for differences** designed to create exactly the same economic result as a foreign exchange cash **forward-forward** deal. *See* **ERA, SAFE**.

Forward-forward

An FX **swap**, loan or other interest-rate agreement starting on one **forward** date and ending on another.

Forward rate agreement

(Or FRA). A **contract for differences** based on a **forward-forward** interest rate.

FRA

See **Forward rate agreement**.

FRCD

See **Floating rate CD**.

FRN

See **Floating rate note**.

Front office

The trading department of the bank.

Fundamental Equilibrium Exchange Rate

(Or FEER). The exchange rate necessary to achieve a sustainable balance in the country's external current account. *See* **Purchasing power parity**.

Fundamental analysis

(Or judgemental analysis). An approach to forecasting based on external factors such as economics, government policy and political events. *See* **Technical analysis**.

Funds

The USD/CAD exchange rate for value on the next business day (standard practice for USD/CAD, in preference to **spot**).

Fungible

Able to be combined indistinguishably with an existing position in the same instrument.

Future value

The amount of money achieved in the future, including interest, by investing a given amount of money now. *See* **Time value of money**, **Present value**.

Futures contract

A deal to buy or sell some financial instrument or commodity for value on a future date. Unlike a **forward** deal, futures contracts are traded only on an exchange (rather than **OTC**), have standardized contract sizes and value dates, and are often only **contracts for differences** rather than deliverable.

FX

Foreign exchange.

FXA

See **Forward exchange agreement**.

Gap analysis

Analysis of the difference in exposures to interest rates in different periods.

General risk

In measuring **position risk** for **capital adequacy** purposes, the risk arising from the market position held by the bank. *See* **Specific risk**.

GMRA

Global Master Repo Agreement, a master agreement for repos and buy/sell-backs.

Hedge

Protect against the risks arising from potential market movements in exchange rates, interest rates or other variables. *See* **Cover**, **Arbitrage**, **Speculation**.

Herstatt risk

Same as **settlement risk** in FX.

Historic rate rollover

A **forward swap** in FX where the settlement exchange rate for the near date is based on a historic **off-market** rate rather than the current market rate. This is prohibited by many regulators.

Historic VaR

A method of calculating **VaR** by applying historic price movements to the current portfolio of instruments. *See* **Monte Carlo simulation**, **Variance/covariance**.

Hit

To hit a **bid** is to deal on the bid price quoted by someone.

IFEMA

International Foreign Exchange Master Agreement, a master agreement for foreign exchange spot and forward deals.

IMM

See **International Monetary Market**.

Indirect

An exchange rate quotation against the US dollar in which the dollar is the **base** currency and the other currency is the **variable** currency.

Initial margin

See **Margin**.

Interbank

An interbank transaction is one between two banks, as opposed to one between a bank and an end-user.

International Monetary Market

The financial sector of the **Chicago Mercantile Exchange**.

Interpolation

The process of estimating a price or rate for value on a particular date by comparing the prices actually quoted for value dates either side.

Intervention

Purchases or sales of currencies in the market by central banks in an attempt to reduce exchange rate fluctuations or to maintain the value of a currency within a particular band, or at a particular level. Similarly, central bank operations in the money markets to maintain interest rates at a certain level.

Inverted yield curve

See **Negative yield curve**.

ISDA master agreement

International Swaps and Derivatives Association master agreement for **FRA**s, swaps, options and other transactions.

Judgemental analysis

See **Fundamental analysis**.

Large exposure risk

The requirement to allocate more capital for **capital adequacy** purposes if the total exposure to any one counterparty is a particularly large proportion of the bank's total.

Legacy currency

(Or national currency unit). One of the former national currencies which became a unit of the euro.

Legal risk

The risk that the bank's business is affected by changes in laws and regulations, or by existing laws and regulations which it had not properly taken into account.

LIBID

See **LIBOR**.

LIBOR

London inter-bank offered rate, the rate at which banks are willing to lend to other banks of top creditworthiness. The term is used both generally to mean the interest rate at any time, and specifically to mean the reference rate at 11:00 a.m., published by the British Bankers' Association, for the purpose of providing a benchmark to fix an interest payment such as on an **FRA** settlement. LIBID is similarly London inter-bank bid rate. LIMEAN is the average between LIBID and LIBOR.

LIFFE

London International Financial Futures and Options Exchange.

Lift

To lift an **offer** is to deal on the offered price quoted by someone.

LIMEAN

See **LIBOR**.

Liquid

A liquid market is one where it is easy to find buyers and sellers at good prices. A liquid investment is one which can easily be turned into cash because there is a liquid market in that instrument.

Liquidity

See **Liquid**.

Liquidity risk

The risk of being unable to find a **liquid** market for a particular instrument.

Locals

Private traders on a **futures** exchange dealing for their own account.

Long

A long position is a surplus of purchases over sales of a given currency or asset, or a situation which naturally gives rise to an organization benefiting from a strengthening of that currency or asset. To a money market dealer, however, a long position is a surplus of borrowings taken in over money lent out, (which gives rise to a benefit if that currency weakens rather than strengthens). *See* **Short**.

Managed floating

Same as **dirty floating**.

Mapping

In the **variance/covariance** approach to **VaR**, the process of representing a position in terms of other standardized instruments.

Margin call

A call by one party in a transaction for **variation margin** to be transferred by the other.

Margin transfer

The transfer of a **margin call**.

Margin

Initial margin is **collateral** placed by one party with a counterparty at the time of a deal, against the possibility that the market price will move against the first party, thereby leaving the counterparty with a credit risk.

Variation margin is a payment made, or extra collateral transferred, subsequently from one party to the other because the market price has moved. Variation margin payment is either in effect a settlement of profit/loss (for example, in the case of a **futures** contract) or the reduction of credit exposure (for example, in the case of a **repo**).

In a loan, margin is the extra interest above a benchmark (e.g. a margin of 0.5% over **LIBOR**) required by a lender to compensate for the **credit risk** of that particular borrower.

Market risk

The risk that the value of a position falls due to changes in market rates or prices.

Mark-to-market

The process of revaluing a position at current market rates.

Mean

Average.

Mine

"I buy the **base currency**." For example, if someone who has asked for and received a price says "5 mine!" he means "I buy 5 million units of the base currency". *See* **Yours**.

Model risk

The risk that the computer model used to price and value an instrument is wrong.

Modified duration

A factor measuring the sensitivity of a position to changes in interest rates.

Modified following

The convention that if a value date in the future falls on a non-business day, the value date will be moved to the next following business day, unless this moves the value date to the next month, in which case the value date is moved back to the last previous business day.

Money market

Short-term market (generally up to 1 year) for financial instruments. *See* **Capital market**.

Money-market basis

An interest rate quoted on an **ACT/360** basis is said to be on a money-market basis. *See* **Bond basis**.

Monte Carlo simulation

A method of calculating **VaR** by generating a very large number of random prices, applying these to the current portfolio of instruments and measuring the net effect. *See* **Historic VaR**, **Variance/co-variance**.

Multilateral netting

Obligation netting between more than two parties.

My risk

If someone who has asked for a price says "my risk", he is acknowledging that the price may change before he has accepted it.

National currency unit

See **Legacy currency**.

NDF

See **Non-deliverable forward**.

Negative skewness

A greater probability of a large downward movement than of a large upward movement.

Negative yield curve

(Or inverted yield curve). A downward-sloping **yield curve**. *See* **Positive yield curve**.

Negotiable

A security which can be bought and sold in a **secondary market** is negotiable.

Net present value

(Or NPV). The net present value of a series of cashflows is the sum of the present values of each cashflow (some or all of which may be negative).

Netting

Obligation netting is the payment, in the normal course of business, of one net amount from one party to another instead of a gross payment in each direction.

Close-out netting allows, in the event of a default, the non-defaulting party to terminate all outstanding transactions and settle them with a single net payment or receipt.

Nominal amount

Same as **face value** of a security.

Nominal rate

A rate of interest as quoted, rather than the **effective** rate to which it is **equivalent**.

Non-deliverable forward

A forward outright where the two parties settle only the change in value between the forward rate dealt and the spot rate 2 working days before maturity, based on a notional principal amount.

Normal probability function

A particular **probability density**, with the formula

$$\frac{1}{\sqrt{2\pi}\, e^{\frac{x^2}{2}}}$$

Normal yield curve

(Or positive yield curve). An upward-sloping **yield curve**. *See* **Negative yield curve**.

Notional

Contracts for differences require a notional principal amount on which settlement can be calculated.

NPV

See **Net present value**.

O/N

See **Overnight**.

Obligation netting

See **Netting**.

Odd date

See **Broken date**.

Off

If a market maker says "Off!" he means "The price that I last quoted is no longer valid".

Off-balance sheet

An instrument where the principal amount is either not transferred, or is transferred simultaneously in both directions.

Offer

(Or ask). In general, the price at which the dealer quoting a price is prepared to sell or lend. The offered price of a foreign exchange quotation is the rate at which the dealer will sell the **base** currency and buy the **variable** currency. The offered rate in a deposit quotation is the interest rate at which the dealer will lend the currency involved. The offered rate in a **repo** is the interest rate at which the dealer will lend the **collateral** and borrow the cash. *See* **Bid**.

Off-market

A rate which is not the current market rate.

Open outcry

Trading face-to-face on a physical exchange.

Operational risk

The risk of losses due to failures in the bank's operations generally.

Option forward

See **Time option**.

OTC

See **Over the counter**.

Outright

An outright is the sale or purchase of one foreign currency against another for value on any date other than spot. *See* **Spot, Swap, Forward, Short date**.

Over the counter

(Or OTC). An OTC transaction is one dealt privately between any two parties, with all details agreed between them, as opposed to one dealt on an exchange – for example, a **forward** deal as opposed to a **futures** contract. *See* **Exchange-traded**.

Overborrowed

A position in which a dealer's liabilities (borrowings taken in) are of longer maturity than the assets (loans out). *See* **Overlent**.

Overlent

A position in which a dealer's assets (loans out) are of longer maturity than the liabilities (borrowings taken in). *See* **Overborrowed**.

Overnight

(Or O/N or today/tomorrow). A deal from today until the next working day ('tomorrow').

Overnight limit

The maximum size of a position which a dealer is allowed to take overnight.

Own funds

A bank's available capital and reserves for the purposes of **capital adequacy** rules.

Par

In foreign exchange, when the **outright** and **spot** exchange rates are equal, the **forward swap** is zero or par.

When the price of a **security** is equal to the face value, usually expressed as 100, it is said to be trading at par.

Par value

See **Parity**.

Parity

The exchange rate for a currency against another currency or basket of currencies, considered by the government as its official fixed rate, central rate or target rate.

Payee

The person to whom something is payable (for example, a **bill of exchange**).

Payment versus payment

(Or PvP). Method for the settlement of a FX transaction, whereby a payment from Bank A to Bank B is made only if, and at the same time as, the corresponding payment is made from Bank B to Bank A.

Pips

See **Points**.

Points

(Or pips). The last two decimal places in an exchange rate. For example, when USD/CHF is 1.7510/1.7520, the points are 10/20. *See* **Big figure**.

Position risk

Same as market risk, used particularly in **capital adequacy** calculations.

Positive yield curve

See **Normal yield curve**.

PPP

See **Purchasing power parity**.

Premium

The amount by which a currency is more expensive, in terms of another currency, for future delivery than for spot, is the forward premium (in general, a reflection of interest rate differentials between two currencies). If an exchange rate is 'at a premium' (without specifying to which of the two currencies this refers), this means in London (but generally not elsewhere) that the **variable** currency is at a premium. *See* **Discount**.

Present value

The amount of money which needs to be invested now to achieve a given amount in the future when interest is added. Hence, the value of future cashflow. *See* **Time value of money**, **Future value**.

Primary market

The primary market for a security refers to its original issue. *See* **Secondary market**.

Probability density

A description of how likely any one of a series of numbers is to occur.

Probability distribution

See **Cumulative probability distribution**.

Produce

To produce dollars (for example, via covered interest arbitrage) generally means effectively to borrow dollars.

Promissory note

A written promise to pay.

Public order member

A member of a **futures** exchange able to enter into transactions on behalf of customers.

Purchasing power parity

The idea that a currency's exchange rate must move, in the long term, to adjust for inflation differentials against other countries. *See* **Fundamental equilibrium exchange rate**.

PvP

See **Payment versus payment**.

Real effective exchange rate

An **effective exchange rate** adjusted for inflation differentials between countries.

Reciprocal rate

An exchange rate quoted in such a way that the **base currency** and **variable currency** are reversed.

Redeem

A security is said to be redeemed when the principal is repaid.

Registered security

A security where ownership for the purpose of paying **coupons** and principal is determined by whoever is recorded centrally as the owner. There might or might not also be a physical piece of paper evidencing ownership. *See* **Bearer security**.

Replacement risk

The risk of losing an unrealized profit because the counterparty defaults.

Repo

(Or RP). Usually refers in particular to **classic repo**. Also used as a general term to include classic repos, **buy/sell-backs** and securities lending.

Repurchase agreement

See **Repo**.

Reputational risk

The risk of damage to a bank's reputation.

Revaluation

An official one-off increase in the value of a currency in terms of other currencies. *See* **Devaluation**.

Reverse repo

(Or reverse). The opposite of a **repo**.

Reverse

See **Reverse repo**.

Risk asset ratio

The ratio of a bank's **own funds** to its **risk-weighted assets**.

Riskmetrics

A **variance/covariance** model for **VaR**, made available by JP Morgan.

Risk-weighted assets

The money which a bank has put at risk for the purposes of **capital adequacy** rules.

Rollover

See **Tom-next**. Also refers to renewal of a loan.

RP

See **Repo.**

S/N

See **Spot-next**.

S/W

See **spot-a-week**.

SAFE

See **Synthetic agreement for forward exchange.**

SDR

See **Special drawing right**.

Secondary market

The market for buying and selling a security after it has been issued. *See* **Primary market**.

Secured

Collateralized.

Security

A financial asset sold initially for cash by a borrowing organization (the issuer). The security is often **negotiable** and usually has a maturity date when it is **redeemed**.

Same as **collateral**.

Sell/buy-back

Simultaneous **spot** sale and **forward** purchase of something, with the **forward** price calculated to achieve an effect equivalent to a **classic repo**.

Serial months

Additional **futures** delivery months added to the regular cycle, so that the three nearest possible months are always available.

Settlement risk

The risk that the counterparty does not deliver its side of the deal after we have irrevocably paid or delivered our side.

Short date

A deal for value on a date other than **spot** but less than one month after spot.

Short

A short position is a surplus of sales over purchases of a given currency or asset, or a situation which naturally gives rise to an organization benefiting from a weakening of that currency or asset. To a money market dealer, however, a short position is a surplus of money lent out over borrowings taken in (which gives rise to a benefit if that currency strengthens rather than weakens). *See* **Long**.

Simple interest

When interest on an investment is paid all at maturity or not reinvested to earn interest-on-interest, the interest is said to be simple. *See* **Compound interest**.

Special drawing right

(Or SDR). The artificial basket currency of the IMF.

Specific risk

In measuring **position risk** for **capital adequacy** purposes, the risk arising from the issuer of a particular security held by the bank. *See* **General risk**.

Speculation

A deal undertaken because the dealer expects prices to move in his favor, as opposed to a **hedge** or **arbitrage**.

Spot

A deal to be settled on the customary value date for that particular market. In the foreign exchange market, this is for value in 2 working days' time.

Spot-a-week

(Or S/W). A transaction from **spot** until a week later.

Spot-next

(Or S/N). A transaction from **spot** until the next working day.

Spread

The difference between the **bid** and **offer** prices in a quotation.

A strategy in which a particular instrument is purchased and a similar instrument is sold, such as a **futures** spread, in which one futures contract is purchased and another is sold.

Square

A position in which sales exactly match purchases, or in which assets exactly match liabilities. *See* **Long**, **Short**.

Standard deviation

A measure of how spread out a series of numbers is around its **mean**.

STIR futures

Short-term interest rate **futures** contract.

Stop-loss

A price or rate which, if touched in the market, will trigger the closing of a position in order to avoid any further loss. *See* **take profit**.

STP

See **Straight-through processing**.

Straight-through processing

(Or STP). The computerization of operational tasks in such a way that each process feeds automatically to the next.

Strip

A strip of **FRA**s is a series of FRAs covering consecutive periods, which together create the effect of a longer-term instrument (for example,

4 consecutive 3-month FRAs have an effect similar to a 1 year FRA).
A strip of **futures** is similar.

Swap

A foreign exchange swap is the purchase of one currency against
another for delivery on one date, with a simultaneous sale to reverse
the transaction on another value date.

SWIFT

Society for Worldwide Interbank Financial Transfers, the system for
international payments between banks.

Synthetic agreement for forward exchange

(or SAFE). A generic term for **ERA**s and **FXA**s.

System risk

The risk of losses due to failures in the bank's computer systems.

Systemic risk

The risk of failure in the entire payment clearing system or banking
system of which the bank is a part.

T/N

See **Tom-next**.

Tail

The **exposure** to interest rates over a **forward-forward** period arising
from a mismatched position (such as a 2-month borrowing against a
3-month loan).
   A **forward** foreign exchange dealer's exposure to **spot** movements.

The extreme left- and right-hand ends of a **probability distribution**.

Take-profit

A price or rate which, if touched in the market, will trigger the closing
of a position in order to ensure that an existing profit is captured.
See **Stop-loss**.

Technical analysis

(Or charting). An approach to forecasting which considers only past
price movements. *See* **Fundamental forecasting**.

Tenor

The tenor of a security is the length of time until its maturity.

Term

The time between the beginning and end of a deal or investment.

Term deposit

Same as **fixed deposit**.

Tick

The minimum allowed price movement on a **futures** contract.

Tick value

The value of a one **tick** price change on one **futures** contract.

Time deposit

Same as **fixed deposit**.

Time option

(Or option forward). A **forward** currency deal in which the **value date** is set to be within a period rather than on a particular day. The customer sets the exact date 2 working days before settlement.

Time value of money

The concept that a future cashflow can be valued as the amount of money which it is necessary to invest now in order to achieve that cashflow in the future. *See* **Present value**, **Future value**.

Today–tomorrow

See **Overnight**.

Tom-next

(Or T/N or rollover). A transaction from the next working day ('tomorrow') until the working day after ('next' day – i.e. **spot** in the foreign exchange market.)

Trading book

For the purposes of **capital adequacy**, that part of a bank's business which broadly involves its trading department.

Transaction exposure

The risk to currency movements arising from a definite, or closely forecast, transaction.

Translation exposure

(Or balance sheet exposure). The risk to currency movements arising from an asset or liability on the balance sheet which is denominated in a foreign currency.

Treasury bill

A short-term security issued by a government, generally with a zero **coupon**.

True yield

The yield which is equivalent to the quoted **discount rate** (for a US or UK treasury bill, for example).

Two-way

A two-way price includes both **bid** and **offer** sides of the price.

Under reference

If a market-maker or his broker says that a price he has quoted is "under reference", he means that the price must be reconfirmed before a counterparty can deal on it.

Underlying

The underlying of a **futures** contract is the commodity or financial instrument on which the contract depends.

US-style repo

Same as **classic repo**.

Value at risk

(Or VaR). The maximum potential loss which an organization might suffer on its positions over a given time period, estimated within a given confidence level.

Value basis

The theoretical **futures** price, less the actual futures price.

Value date

(Or settlement date or maturity date). The date on which a deal is to be consummated.

VaR

See **Value-at-risk**.

Variable currency

(Or counter currency). Exchange rates are quoted in terms of the number of units of one currency (the variable or counter currency) which corresponds to 1 unit of the other currency (the **base currency**).

Variance

The square of the **standard deviation** of a series of numbers.

Variance/covariance

A method of calculating **VaR** which applies assumed **variances** and **covariances** to a **probability distribution** which is generally taken as **normal**. *See* **Historic VaR**, **Monte Carlo simulation**.

Variation margin

See **Margin**.

Yard

One American billion – i.e. 1,000,000,000.

Yield

The interest rate which can be earned on an investment, currently quoted by the market or implied by the current market price for the investment – as opposed to the **coupon** paid by an issuer on a security, which is based on the coupon rate and the face value.

Yield curve

A graph showing the current interest rate for each maturity.

Yours

"I sell the **base currency**". For example, if someone who has asked for and received a price says "5 yours!", he means "I sell 5 million units of the base currency". *See* **Mine**.

Zero-coupon

A zero-coupon security is one that does not pay a **coupon**. Its price is correspondingly less to compensate for this.

Index

Lightning Source UK Ltd.
Milton Keynes UK
UKOW04n0350080814

236581UK00006B/71/P